The Economic Order
and Religion

THE
Economic Order
and Religion

FRANK H. KNIGHT

Professor of the Social Sciences
University of Chicago

AND

THORNTON W. MERRIAM

Director of U.S.O. Training,
National Council of the Y.M.C.A.
Formerly Chairman of the Board of Religion,
Northwestern University

HARPER & BROTHERS PUBLISHERS

NEW YORK AND LONDON

Contents

Part I

LIBERALISM AND CHRISTIANITY
by Frank H. Knight

Part II

ECONOMIC IDEALS OF LIBERAL CHRISTIANITY
by Thornton W. Merriam

v

Contents

Part III

DISCUSSION AND CRITICAL COMMENTS
by the Authors

Editor's Preface

In this highly fragmented culture of ours books are needed to integrate fields of interest ordinarily considered separately, to state their common problems and to deal with their differences in the light of other criteria than the separate functions and local loyalties of the special interests in themselves. This book was originated with that purpose in mind. Other books in the group are *Politics and Public Service* by Leonard D. White and T. V. Smith, *Architecture and Modern Life* by Baker Brownell and Frank Lloyd Wright, *Organized Labor and Production* by Morris L. Cooke and Philip Murray, *Agriculture in Modern Life* by O. E. Baker, Ralph Borsodi and M. L. Wilson, *The Small Community* by Arthur E. Morgan, *New Schools for a New Culture* by Charles M. MacConnell, Ernest O. Melby and C. O. Arndt.

Specifically this book deals with the practical dualism of our modern morals. With the traditional Christian ethic at one pole and the variegated, often contradictory assemblage of practices and precepts of our secular life at the other, it has never been co-ordinated or made intelligible from within.

The authors: Frank H. Knight is perhaps the best-known writer in the field of ethics in relation to modern economic policy. He is Professor of the Social Sciences and also Professor of Philosophy at the University of Chicago. Formerly he was Professor of Economics at the University of Chicago. He is the author of *Risk, Uncertainty and Profit,* the Hart Schaffner & Marx Prize Essay later reprinted by the London School of Economics. He also is the author of *The Ethics of Competition and Other Essays,* collaborator in *The Philos-*

vii

ophy of American Democracy and author of numerous papers in economic theory and social ethics.

Thornton W. Merriam is Director of U.S.O. Training of the National Council of the Y.M.C.A. He was formerly Chairman of the Board of Religion at Northwestern University. He was also Executive Director of the National Council on Religion in Higher Education, and a member of the faculty of the School of Applied Social Sciences in Western Reserve University. In 1918-1919, he was a member of the Signal Corps of the A.E.F. He is a member of the Board of Education of the Northern Baptist Convention; also a member of the board of the Religion and Labor Foundation. His interests and experience have been focused in religious practice and policy.

BAKER BROWNELL, Supervising Editor

April 10, 1944

The Economic Order
and Religion

CHAPTER ONE

Introduction

By the Authors

THIS book is mainly two essays, the first by Knight, the second by Merriam. A brief critical study by each author of the main essay of the other makes up the third part of the book. Only this Introduction is a joint product of both of us.

In discussing with each other the problems underlying the book the authors attempted more to achieve clarity with respect to the issues and their own positions than to debate them. The main essays are independent works each written without explicit reference to the position of the other. Only in the critical studies in Part III is an attempt made to point out the specific differences between them and to explore their grounds. To understand problems that are indubitably real and serious, not to wrangle over them, is our main purpose.

It remains for this Introduction to indicate the common grounds of our respective positions as well as their general differences. Men who have grown up in the same cultural environment may be expected to agree on general values—truth, beauty, goodness, freedom, authority—and to disagree only on their concrete interpretation and application. It is difficult to state briefly and sharply any proposition in the field of religion, ethics and social policy on which there is real opposition, since these disagreements are usually matters of interpretive detail.

The issue between us is focused mainly in the relation between religion, or Christianity, and liberalism. For Knight

Christianity and liberalism are opposed in important respects; for Merriam they are basically harmonious. While both authors consider themselves liberal, Merriam does and Knight does not claim the designation "Christian." Because modern liberalism, including the main ethical ideals of our civilization, is commonly thought of as essentially Christian, the burden of proof rests on Knight. His essay therefore comes first in the book.

This formal issue has three components: The final grounds of difference may be (1) in the authors' actual intellectual positions, or in divergent interpretations (2) of Christianity or (3) of liberalism. We shall consider these three possibilities and begin with the second.

We agree in recognizing Christianity as an historical concept in which religion and ethics are both involved. We agree also that both the religion and the ethics, and the relationship between them, have been variously interpreted by individuals and by groups, at different times in the nineteen centuries or so of Christian history, and also by different groups and individuals at the same historical epoch, all calling themselves Christians. Both of us are liberals, in this field, first of all in recognizing the "right" of such individuals and groups to their opinion that they are Christians. We both repudiate any supposed authoritative definition of Christianity as a religion or as an ethical doctrine or system. In discussing such claims to authority, however, some distinction must be made between certain historical documents, or "Scriptures," and the claim of human beings, individually or organized as churches, to give an authoritative interpretation of, or to supplement or repeal, the documents themselves, and so expressly to change their meaning. We agree that it is a matter for historical scholarship and linguistic and philosophical analysis and criticism to determine what the documents say or mean. On this point the only authority is the intrinsic appeal of facts and evidence to competent and impartially truth-seeking minds.

With respect to the authority of the documents themselves, there is less agreement between us. In connection with the question of the objective justification of any person or group to call himself or itself "Christian," Knight is more inclined to insist on the scriptural character of Christianity, throughout its history, and to hold that a religious or ethical position which is not reasonably derived from, or at least harmonized with, the content of the New Testament in some defensible interpretation should not be called Christian. Merriam, on the other hand, is more inclined to view Christianity as a movement, in the literal sense of something which moves, grows and changes. He would not deny the legitimacy of the use of the designation "Christian" by people who consider their position as belonging to this movement, even if they explicitly say that a substantial part of the beliefs actually taught in the New Testament must now be rejected outright, in the light of the growth of knowledge and changes in the accepted ultimate premises of theology, religious philosophy and ethics. Knight thinks that if this view is accepted in an extreme form, it becomes impossible to assert any conflict or opposition between Christianity and any other religious, philosophical or ethical position, if the continuity is actually affirmed by any considerable number of people whose judgment is entitled to respect. The question is whether such a position is intellectually tenable. The bounds of what beliefs or doctrines are reasonably to be called Christian is therefore the first issue between the two authors. This is implied by the orientation of their respective essays under the general title of this book as a whole. It is to some extent a technical or even a verbal matter, in contrast with the positive content of the views presented on the problem of social betterment.

Knight's greater emphasis on the history of the Christian movement as a whole is central to the issue. If he is to make out a case for the opposition between the doctrinal teachings of Christianity and any particular modern position on ethical or social problems, it must obviously rest on historical grounds, and Scripture is only one factor in historical Christianity. It becomes incumbent upon Knight, as an opponent of the view that modern liberalism is properly to be called Christian, to show in historical terms that there is a fundamental antithesis between them. He must show that throughout its history down to the present, through all its divergent interpretations, Christianity has carried, and still carries, a core of meaning so opposed to the fundamentals of liberalism that confusion of thought must result from any attempt to use this historical name to designate ideas that are radically different. He asserts that restriction of Christianity to consonance with its Scriptures is more formal than substantial. This follows from the vast range of possible interpretation which it actually receives at the hands of believers and of scholars and thinkers whose integrity and competence are not to be called in question. It will also be clear that, in addition to the different emphases upon the historical content of Christianity, the authors will present considerably divergent views of the history itself.

Two further questions cannot be ignored: One centers in the nature and role of churches, or "the church," the other in the problem of theology. It may be asked whether distinctively religious practices or observances on the one hand, and theistic doctrine or belief on the other, can be separated from moral and social endeavors. The three have been closely associated as aspects of religion, in the meaning which it has worn throughout the history of Christianity, and which it still presents. Neither the problem of the religious functions of the church nor the issues of theology are explicitly discussed in this book. There is no great difference in our positions with respect to either problem, considered independently and on its merits. We agree that churches, as they exist, are institutions to be accounted for in historical terms, and that their "rightful" character is that of free associations for the cultivation by their members of the reli-

gious and ethical life, in any reasonable interpretation the
membership may agree upon. We ask to what extent institutionalized religious life can be given less of a theological,
or a ritualistically religious, and more of an ethical as well
as an esthetic and intellectual content. With respect to theology, theism or deism, we are agreed that belief in God is a
matter of metaphysical position on the one hand, and the
meaning of terms on the other, and that the issue remains
of the same character if the conception of God is restricted
to a "personal" deity.

The inspiration of any particular doctrine or tradition, or
the supernatural character or origin of any particular Scripture, or institution, or of its author or founder, would be
approached in the same way. Such matters could not be discussed without a long, technical argument of a character very
different from that of this book.

On the narrower issue, as to the relations between the
distinctively religious doctrines and practices of churches
and their ethical position and activities, however, the reader
will see that the positions of the two authors present a considerable difference. Knight is inclined to hold that the connection between these three aspects of religion, and of Christianity in particular, is close and probably indissoluble, that
the choice lies between religion and rational secular ethics.
Merriam is inclined to view Christianity and its institutional embodiment in essentially ethical terms, to the neglect
of ritualistic and theological aspects, or to reinterpret these
in ethical and social terms.

Liberalism, and the propriety of using the name as a designation for any particular position, is only partly parallel
to Christianity. We may speak, however, of limits to the
"right" of the adherent of any position to call it liberalism, in view of the prestige which has come to be attached to
the name, in our culture milieu. Liberalism is also a historical movement, the meaning and bounds of which have

changed in time. Since its beginning they have been subject to disagreement, and to discussion and debate. The differences, vis-à-vis Christianity, are of course great, partly because of the vastly greater intellectual and cultural changes in the course of the longer history of the latter. Liberalism furthermore has never given rise to any closely organized movement of the nature of a church, whether "catholic" in its claims or frankly sectarian. Liberalism has never claimed any authority except that of reason, and only in a sense too vague to be considered seriously would it be said to have any definite historical origin, any original founder or later authoritative prophets or apostles, or any authoritative scripture.

In recent decades, roughly the present century, the term has developed a radically new meaning. This has given rise to a divergence and opposition between two schools of thought, which shows a strong resemblance to sectarianism. With reference to the proper or legitimate use of the word, it is possible in this case to set up a criterion, within certain limits, or at least to formulate the issue, by appealing to the intrinsic meaning of the term itself, as a linguistic relative of "liberty," as well as to the historically original meaning.

Liberalism is a name for an intellectual position, and to a large extent an ethical and political movement, which grew up in the late eighteenth and nineteenth centuries, primarily in the English-speaking world (and in France, but with considerable difference in content and history). The word originally referred to individual freedom from the control of government, law and tradition in all fields of action, including religion, social relations and economic life. This freedom was early associated with political liberty in the sense of free or democratic government, through representative institutions. Political functionaries are responsible to public opinion, formed by free discussion, and popular control is made effective by having these functionaries chosen ("elected") by the vote of more or less the whole responsible adult population.

Though there has been no important change in liberal attitudes toward religious or social freedom, or toward democratic political institutions, there has occurred in respect to economic life an important bifurcation between individual liberty and governmental control as they impinge on economic interests and activities. The later nineteenth and the twentieth centuries have seen the development of a school of thought which has insisted on using the name of liberalism, but which advocates to a large extent a reversal of the original liberal attitude toward governmental regulation of economic activities and relationships. As against leaving these to the control of the free or competitive market, operating through the pricing of goods and services, in consumption and production, various degrees and forms of political control are proposed. The more extreme proponents of this new liberalism, or "neo-liberalism," advocate a large measure of collectivism—replacement of exchange transactions by direct administration of economic affairs by political agencies. The argument of the neo-liberals is that political action is capable of securing a much larger degree of "real" liberty or freedom to the individual. Thus its claim to the designation of liberalism is logically unquestionable, since it does not go back on or abandon liberty as a moral principle or ideal. The issue is reduced to a twofold question of the meaning of freedom and the facts as to the effective way to realize it.

In this latter field, there is "in principle" no issue between the two authors of the present book. Both accept the ideal of maximum liberty for individuals as the main criterion of the rightness of political institutions and policies. A reading of the two main essays, however, will reveal that there is a substantial issue on the question of fact as to the extent to which maximum liberty is to be achieved through governmental action, or at least through what may be called "positive" in contrast with negative action. By negative economic action we mean maintaining the freedom of the market by policing against violence and fraud, and preserving other conditions necessary for effective competitive markets. There are issues also as to the form of positive action to be taken. In addition, there is probably some difference of view between the two authors with respect to the ultimate meaning of liberty as well as the mere amount of liberty which may be expected to result from different lines of policy.

The reader may well sense a greater disposition on the part of Knight to take the concept of liberty or freedom in a more literal meaning, which may be regarded as more negative, and in the essay of Merriam a disposition to read into the term more of the content of welfare or well-being. In the one meaning, liberty is individual freedom of action, including free co-operation; in the other it is being in a position to get or to have what one wants, or even what one ought to want and to have. Emphasis on these different conceptions is bound up with the question of the degree to which the state should rely upon the knowledge and competence of individuals to promote their own well-being, in contrast with being coercively paternalistic. Such differences are a matter of degree and of detail. Certainly, the authors are in agreement that the state should promote both freedom and well-being within the widest feasible limits; and it would be futile to attempt to state in terms of a formula how far either of these two values should be sacrificed to the other in cases where they conflict and some choice has to be made.

Both authors admit that "liberal" and "liberalism" may be properly conceived in terms broad enough to include even a wider range of social-philosophical position and social attitude than those which divide us or our essays. The issue on which we meet in opposition is primarily the merits of different policies for realizing the liberal ideal. Secondarily, we do not see eye to eye on the meaning of religion and its role in social ethics. Further discussion of both questions must be left to the main essays and the authors' reviews. Our interest centers primarily in the first question. It is relatively an incidental matter whether it is desirable to call either form of liberalism Christian or religious, in the general meaning which the latter term bears when we refer to Christianity, or Judaism, as a religion. Yet this secondary issue is important because of its bearing on clarity of understanding, which is requisite to the solution of social and ethical problems in a free society.

Part I

LIBERALISM AND CHRISTIANITY

Frank H. Knight

CHAPTER TWO

Religion and Morality in Social Life

READERS of Goethe's *Faust* will recall that the hero, seized with a sudden zeal for translating the New Testament, began with the Gospel of John, and after due deliberation rendered the first sentence "In the beginning was the deed." This expression might serve as a text for a comparative discussion of the approaches of religion and of modern secular thought to the problems of life and society. These approaches are alike in seeking to understand present conditions in terms of their past. This is particularly required for an understanding of religion itself; for, to the extent that any religion is established, i.e., not momentarily fresh from the lips of the Prophet, it explicitly finds its authority in the past.

But modern thought also employs other methods, notably that of science, while it differs radically from the religious view of history itself, as held in our own Judeo-Christian tradition. Religious thought craved a literal "beginning" (Genesis 1:1 is another example) but the modern view finds the religious mind amazingly "easy to satisfy" in this respect. In addition, modern thought views human history as a brief moment in an indefinitely long course of development, the broad sweep of which shows "progress" from lower to higher, to be continued indefinitely in the future. But in the religious tradition the beginning was an ideal state and the course of history has been marked by fall and retrogression, destined to end in a final cataclysm.

We shall begin our discussion with a brief survey of the role of religion in social life. For this purpose, it is convenient to view the evolution of modern civilized society in terms of three or four great historical stages since man ceased to be brute and became human. The sound objections of historians and anthropologists to the idea of stages do not seem to invalidate the use which will be made of it here. Our scheme is a refinement of the well-known formula of Sir Henry S. Maine, describing legal history as a progression "from status to contract." At the first stage, of primitive or tribal society, social relations and the pattern of life as a whole were chiefly a matter of custom. Even the earliest human society of which we can have any knowledge was very different from the social life of animals, where there is elaborate organization, as among the colonial insects. On one hand, custom is very different from instinct, the principle of order in insect society. The behavior patterns are perpetuated by social inheritance, in contrast with biological. They are acquired by the individual in early life through unconscious imitation of the behavior of the older generation, not built into his physical make-up. But custom is equally mechanical, conservative and opposed to individual freedom.

On the other hand, it is certain that human society was never constructed and regulated entirely on the principle of custom. The human being is by nature an individual, partly socialized, but also anti-social in comparision with the ant or termite. His learning or acculturation is never merely automatic, and his conformity to established usage is never entirely voluntary; human beings have conflicting interests and claim and recognize "rights," as insects apparently do not. Primitive society embodies various forms of compulsion, or "sanctions" to enforce the customary law. In addition to the psychological compulsion of custom itself, and of public opinion, which is the primitive meaning of morality, we must consider politics and religion as mechanisms for enforcing conformity. In primitive society, politics and religion are not clearly differentiated; in fact, all activity tends to be stereotyped and reduced to a ritual, carried on with an eye to the approval of the group and of supernatural powers.

The essential point for our purpose is that the function of religion in primitive society is to enforce conformity to tribal custom as it is, and not to improve or change its content. This is well brought out and emphasized by the late Professor B. Malinowski, a leading authority on primitive social life. He tells us that:

> The spirits are in general conceived of as guardians of tradition. They will be satisfied when people follow custom, scrupulously carry out magic and observe taboos, conform to rules of family life, kinship, and of tribal organization. The two stock answers always given to the question why custom is observed and tradition followed are: "It has been ordained as of old," or else, "The spirits would be angry if we did not follow custom." If you press further as to who it is that has "ordained of old," references will be made immediately to a specific myth; or you will perhaps be told, "Our ancestors in olden days always did that. They live now as spirits in the other world. They like us to behave as they did. They become angry and make things bad if we do not obey custom."[1]

It is noteworthy that while belief in an afterlife of some sort is present, the punishment which is feared occurs in this world, and that it typically affects the community as a whole.

The great advance which first created a relatively high civilization was marked on the side of political structure by the establishment of large kingdoms or empires, expanded from agricultural villages or city-states. Government was highly authoritarian and despotic. The center of gravity in the social order shifted to a degree from religion to politics, or, as we may say, from church to state. We are thinking in particular of the ancient history of the Near East, but this pattern of change seems to hold quite generally where new civilizations have arisen. It would appear that only under despotic government, with the real power in the hands of a political tyranny, and with religion in a supporting role, has any people been able to establish a combination of ordered

[1] *Foundations of Faith and Morals,* pp. 25-26.

unity and adaptability on a scale sufficient for a high civilization in the various aspects of technology, art and literature,
and intellectual life. Participation in the higher culture
achieved was of course restricted to a small élite, and while
the masses were doubtless better off materially than under
barbarism, they had little freedom and by our standards were
exploited.

In an abstract sense, the function of religion was the same
in imperial civilization as under barbarism; it sanctioned
the established order of things. But with the great change in
the nature of the established order, religion itself underwent
profound changes. With society symbolized by, and virtually
embodied in, a monarch, who posed on one hand as the
agent of divine powers and on the other as the father of his
people, religion tended to become more personal and more
monotheistic, or at least came to view one deity as supreme
over others. (The most advanced religions still recognize
different orders of supernatural beings.) For related reasons,
religion also tended to become universal, rather than tribal
or local, in its claims, and at the same time more spiritual
in content. It is an important fact that the "great" religions
of today trace their origins to despotic civilization. Indeed,
we can hardly imagine a fundamentally new religion coming
into existence in liberal democratic society, apart from its
transformation into an authoritarian form.

Our main concern is with Judaism, particularly in the
age of the Great Prophets, as the historical source of most of
the Christian religious-ethical tradition. The "Israelites"
of this time (now divided between two kingdoms) had taken
over an old city-state civilization and the monarchial political
order of surrounding peoples. But they had also inherited a
theocratic ideal, based on the tradition of a Covenant between
the tribe or people and the supreme, more or less uniquely
real, deity, Yahweh. Yahweh had given his chosen people,
through Moses (an Egyptian name) a code of law which, as
it has come down to us, embodies an exceptionally pure,

humane and spiritual standard of morals and internal social relations—for the times and surrounding conditions. But Hebrew religious history is perhaps most distinguished by the role which prophets were allowed to play, in relation both to the monarchy and to the priestly religion. The perpetual theme of the prophets was insistence on the "restoration" of the ideals of righteousness and brotherhood, characteristic of a desert tribe, against the "corruptions" of urban life and regal politics. The essential fact is that, through terrible adversity and suffering, some remnant of Jews not only remained faithful to Yahweh and the Covenant but became more and more devoted, and also progressively raised the moral and spiritual tone of their divinely revealed law. In later times we find a tendency to reinterpret religious thought and the Covenant in the direction of individualization, i.e., in terms of a happy future life for the individual as a reward for righteousness, in place of the prosperity of the people Israel.

Christianity, destined to become a new religion, but for alien peoples of the West, after rejection by the Jews themselves, came into being as the culmination of a new prophetic movement.

This arose under imperial-despotic conditions in an aggravated form, resulting from subjugation of Palestine by Rome. The movement began with the mysterious character called John the Baptizer, and was based on the obscure and varied expectation of a divine kingdom, with or without a "Messiah," which had become current in Judaism. As to the intentions of Jesus of Nazareth, who took up the work of John, we can now have no definite knowledge. He certainly did not intend to start a new religion, or even a sect within Judaism. The historically problematic records which have come down to us (saturated with miracle stories, often of a very naive type) show the most intense faith in the God of the fathers and the Covenant, the latter in a more or less individualized interpretation.

The central feature of Jesus' religious teaching was this conviction of the imminence of the establishment, apparently on earth, in Palestine and among the Jews, of the "Kingdom of God." The only problem of importance for the individual was his salvation for this Kingdom, which was to depend on "repentance" and "righteousness." To what extent and on what terms the Kingdom might include non-Jews is a question upon which different texts in the Gospels give divergent indications. It certainly was to be established by supernatural intervention, and was to be supernatural in character, involving "a new Heaven and a new earth." It is clear that life in the Kingdom would involve none of the mundane material or social problems of actual human life in this world. Even sex life and the family would not exist (Mt. 22:30; Mk. 12:25; Lk. 20:35). The people of the Kingdom would enjoy all material blessings, in a "spiritual" life of absolute faith and trust in God and universal love. The recorded preaching of Jesus is not based, in general, on a direct appeal to the rewards of righteousness (but this statement will require qualification later—in Chapter Three).

Christianity was of course founded (as a reform movement within Judaism) by the followers of Jesus, after he had (like John) run afoul of the authorities and been executed—in his case for claiming to be "the king of the Jews." (This is the real meaning of the Semitic word "Messiah" literally "anointed," translated into Greek as "Xristos.") The new movement was founded on the belief that Jesus had risen from the dead and that this proved him to have been the expected Messiah, and also confirmed his view that the Kingdom was to be established for the righteous faithful by an act of God. The first Christians believed in an immediate second coming (Parousia) of Jesus to found the Kingdom. When the Gospel (good news) made little headway among the Jews in Jerusalem and rather aroused opposition, the Apostles began to preach it in wider circles. However, the movement would probably have died out if it had not been for the activities of a miraculously converted new Apostle, Paul, who energetically espoused the idea of spreading it among the Gentiles and effectively did so without requiring adherence to Judaism or conformity with the more ritualistic part of Jewish law.

In connection with the establishment of Christianity as a religion distinct from Judaism we must note that, unlike Jesus and the original Apostles, Paul was something of a scholar; he knew Greek, and was familiar with contemporary religious developments. This means familiarity in particular with the "mystery religions." Regarding these, it is possible here to say only that the expression covers a half-dozen or so cults similar in general description to Christianity, including semi-ascetic moral ideals which had grown up in Greece and the Near East in the centuries between Alexander's conquests and the beginning of our era. All of them offered individual salvation for immortal blessedness through acceptance of a cult hero, and initiation into the brotherhood of followers. The original preaching of Christianity presented it as essentially a mystery religion, a way to miraculous salvation. It is true that Jesus is rarely referred to in the New Testament as "Saviour" (Greek, "*Soter*"); but he must have been presented to the non-Jewish world as *Soter*, for this idea was familiar, while the title "Christ" would have meaning only to Jews or converts or sympathizers. The New Testament Confessions and the early Christian creeds contain no direct reference to the moral life.

When the Parousia failed to arrive and this expectation faded out, the meaning of the Christian gospel underwent changes, making its syncretic character as a blend of Judaism and mystery cult even more pronounced. The divine Kingdom was gradually transferred to the afterlife, the Greek idea of the immortality of the soul replacing the Jewish one of the physical resurrection of the body. The conception of the future life was elaborated into heaven, with its counterpart hell (ruled over by the devil), with the addition of the interesting idea of purgatory. Fully as important was the development of "the Church," highly organized and called "Catholic," though never really unified; it became the "New Israel," replacing the Jewish people as the heir to the Covenant. The Jewish Scriptures were the sacred book of the Christians—with the addition of later writings now generally referred to as Apocrypha. From the second century to the fourth, various writings supposed to have been Apostolic were gradually added as a New Testament.

The story of the fifteen centuries or so of Christianity, from its triumph and establishment as a state religion to the beginning of the present culture-epoch in the eighteenth century, is essential to an understanding of present-day Christianity. But the main facts are known as a matter of general history and only a few high points can be mentioned here. Its acceptance as an incident of the successful struggle of Constantine for the imperial throne, specifically the symbol of the cross and the motto, "IHSV" on the banner of conquering armies, is an interesting example of the irony of history. With the decline of the Roman Empire and of classical civilization in the West, the Roman Church, under a hierarchical and more and more autocratic organization, fell heir to political power in western Europe, and this led to important changes in its polity and doctrine. It became a theocracy somewhat on Old Testament lines, existing alongside a various and shifting political complex of empire and feudalism, and of new monarchical states as these gradually evolved out of feudal Europe. The history was profoundly affected by the introduction of monasticism, and then by the rise of Islam and the long struggle with this kindred religious and political system.

The fact of most direct concern to us here was the development of the medieval dualistic ethics involving two different sets of principles, the counsels of perfection and precepts for guidance. The Church frankly held that the literal teachings of the Gospels, notably the Sermon on the Mount, were applicable only in a sinless world, as in the Garden of Eden or the New Jerusalem of the future. This pattern of life was supposed to be approximated in the convent. The precepts for guidance were also supposed to reflect Christian principles as far as practicable; in fact they embodied a code of utilitarian expediency based on the customary morality, which assumed a society organized on the principle of status. Economic life was to be regulated much as in primitive society with fair prices and no lending at interest (between Christians). Trade was frowned upon, and individual effort to get ahead condemned as sinful—except through ecclesiastical channels. Social virtue consisted of obedience to established authority, meaning finally to the Church. An interesting feature of the system was the notion of "supererogatory" merit, accumulated by martyrs and saints and made available to those in need of it on suitable terms; in this connection, the doctrine of purgatory flourished and found useful application.

At the apogee of its power, in the twelfth and thirteenth centuries, the Western Church was a political and military system. In every department of life it played the political game according to the usual rules, i.e., "reasons of state"—in this case, of church—i.e., that the end, the power of the church, justifies any means. It resorted without compunction to force, deceit or treachery when there was a reasonable prospect that it could maintain or increase its power by so doing. Apart from being the power behind thrones, it had its own law and judicial system, with a wide jurisdiction over temporal affairs. It also owned a large part of the wealth of western Europe (largely through monastic and other establishments under its control) and collected taxes far in excess (in many regions) of those paid to the secular power.

The late Middle Ages and early modern times (as history is usually divided, around the end of the fifteenth century) represent a period of transition. The term "Renascence" is largely a misnomer, even with respect to the cultural awakening, and is not applicable at all to the great political and social changes. These were North-European, and the primary phenomenon was the development of national dynastic states. In the field of religion, the "Reformation" is also a misnomer. It fairly describes the original intention of Luther; but he soon found that if his movement was to escape extermination as a heresy, he had to get political power back of it. Consequently, he adopted the principle of *cuius regio, eius religio*; this means two things, the control of the state over religion and that of the prince over the state. The religious result was the establishment of a number of "little Catholicisms," primarily along state lines and under state control. In substance this applies to the Church in countries which remained officially Catholic (France and even Spain) as well as to England and other countries which accepted Protestantism. Under compulsion all the states had to tolerate more or less religious dissent.

The important social-moral change, in the light of later history, was a movement toward individual liberty, in spite of the fact that the new political-ecclesiastical absolutism was in many respects retrogressive in this regard. Social and economic status (serfdom) gradually disappeared beginning in the late Middle Ages, especially in England, which became the home of the modern development. More decisive at this time was the fragmentation of ecclesiastical authority, and especially the intellectual liberation of the mind. This was both cause and effect of the development of science, particularly the revelations of the telescope and microscope. But the intellectual awakening began with travel, geographical discovery and culture contact, with the introduction of modern Arabian mathematics and such inventions as the compass, gunpowder and paper and printing. The modern interest in facts and the new conception of the nature and function of reasoning, together with the interest in the practical application of knowledge, had no close parallel in antiquity, to say nothing of the Middle Ages.

From the standpoint of the broad sweep of historical change, northern Europe in the early medieval Dark Age may be viewed as practically a barbarian society. The change to modern conditions may be viewed in terms of two great revolutions, on the pattern already suggested. The first consisted of the late medieval and Renascence developments, already sketched, especially the growth of dynastic states. The second change was far more revolutionary, and led to the historically unique conditions of modern culture. It was marked on the political side by the development of democracy under representative institutions. The dramatic political events were the two English revolutions of the seventeenth century and the American and especially the French in the late eighteenth. The expressions, "Age of Reason," and "Enlightenment" refer especially to conditions in France, and to French influence; but France, which led the Continent, largely followed England. In that country, the striking changes of this period were in the field of technology and have come to be referred to as the Industrial Revolution. The result was the establishment in western Europe of political and economic individualism and the consummation of religious and intellectual liberation. The dynamic drive came largely from the side of economics and technology, the interest in religion having become secondary. A crucial role was played by new "frontiers." Vast fields for individual activity were or had been opened up by the new science and technology and by the addition to European civilization of large areas relatively unpeopled and suitable for exploitation, especially in the New World. The new political freedom had the two inseparable aspects of free or representative government and a minimizing of the functions of the state. Individual liberty, or *"laisser faire,"* gradually became the ideal in all fields—religion, culture and social life, as well as economics.

In all these revolutions, "the Church" or the new Churches, remained fundamentally reactionary. Religion opposed tooth and nail every phase of what we now view as progress, particularly the intellectual advance. In the second great movement of change, the position of religion differed from that of the Renascence era chiefly in that rationalism had largely destroyed its power for obstruction. In general, it still sanctioned whatever was established, also conquest and enslavement. As soon as any issue in politics or economics became openly controversial, Christianity was used as an argument on both sides with equal assurance. And as soon as any change was definitely accomplished, the result became the state of affairs called for by the original Gospel, and a product of its teachings.

The modern economic order of free enterprise and market competition has been Christian to those who favored and unchristian to those who opposed it (at least those Christians) from its inception to the days of social planning. Democracy as a political system, once established, became the only Christian form of government, just as absolute monarchy was the only Christian form in pre-revolutionary France and England, and as feudalism had been a little while before. In our United States, slavery (justified by the theory of racial inferiority) was finally abolished by war in the third quarter of the century. On this issue the churches divided neatly along the boundary between the area in which the institution had already been abolished (or where the settlers had come from such territory) and that where it had not, and they were at least as fervid in their support in the South as in their rather laggard opposition in the North. Even biological evolution, which in the late nineteenth century caused a furor of religious opposition equal to that which greeted the heliocentric astronomy in the sixteenth and seventeenth, has now largely taken its place as a pillar of the Christian world-view.

In the heyday of liberalism, in the nineteenth century, the conviction became general that "science"—no longer "reason" in the Greek or medieval meaning, but knowledge directed by rational and humanitarian ends—would ultimately realize something like a kingdom of heaven upon earth. The conception of progress, originated by the Enlightenment, was both strengthened and reinterpreted in consequence of the new science of geology and its offspring, the Darwinian theory of evolution through natural selection. This inclined many leading minds toward a belief in the inevitability of progress, and even to the view that social action is pernicious. But the scientific interest shifted from biology to new sciences of culture, which strengthened the movement for popular education, and the environmentalists won out over the proponents of heredity. In the meantime, the various phases of the intellectual movement produced the romantic idealism of Hegel, the "positive" politics of August Comte and its diametric opposite, the individualistic ethics of Herbert Spencer, as well as the inverted dialectic of Marx and Engels and also modern "liberal Protestantism" and Reformed Judaism. In the latter part of the century, particularly in America, universal free education came to be viewed as virtually a panacea for all the ills of life in the liberal social order.

These ills, whatever their substantial reality, became increasingly challenging. They gave rise to various social movements and political parties, some advocating violent revolution. Popular agitators stirred up and organized the underprivileged classes, to demand more and more positive action by the state on their behalf, and the processes of democratic politics, made it relatively easy for them to get it. As Western civilization moved into and out of World War I and then into depression, to be followed by World War II, liberalism in the meaning of the Enlightenment and the nineteenth century seemed to be going into eclipse. In the light of this view of our social-ethical problem and its setting, we turn to consider the two great systems of ethical ideals, the religious and the liberalistic, which dominate modern thought.

CHAPTER THREE

Christianity and Ethics

IT IS not the intent in this essay to attack Christianity (or Judaism) as a religion or as an ethical system, or to criticize the role of the churches in present-day society. The troubles of our modern world, and specifically the present "crisis of civilization," are not to be attributed in any important degree to excessive devotion to nominally Christian ideals. (For brevity the word "Christian" may be used instead of "Jewish Christian," and the role of other religions in our culture ignored.) Organized religion is undoubtedly one of the forces which stand for the good in modern life, and it emphasizes some moral values which tend to be neglected. On the whole, it is also a force which makes for social stability and unity—the functional role of religion in general. The religious differences in the Western world of today, i.e., within Christianity and Judaism, are not a serious threat to peace and order. But Christian ethical teaching has limitations, as well as various meanings, especially from the standpoint of social problems, and these it will be the task of the present chapter briefly to explore. Ultimately, as this chapter and those to follow will make clear, our criticism is not directed against Christian ethics specifically but against the broader principle of "moralism," the idea that goodness alone, in any meaning, will solve our social problems.

From the standpoint of modern thought Christianity may be viewed as consisting of two main parts, a religion and a system of ethical doctrine. Any religion also contains two elements, a body of belief and a set of practices. With religious ritual and church organization we are not concerned, and religious belief will be considered only in relation to ethical ideals and conduct, and primarily in the field of social organization. We may assume, for example, that the Biblical cosmology is not a part of the religion of the modern Christian, and that Biblical history is to be studied and read in the light of available knowledge from all sources, and of modern standards of credibility. It should also be said at the outset that this discussion is addressed only to those who wish to order their beliefs on the basis of facts and reasoning, not to those for whom all questions in this field have been answered, long before their birth, by deference to some individual or organization, or doctrine or tradition, which claims supernatural authority. Hence, for practical purposes we are discussing modern "liberal" Christianity. Most of those who will read seriously an objective discussion of religion in relation to moral problems doubtless hold this position in effect, regardless of religious affiliations or the creeds of churches to which they belong and which they nominally accept.

The vagueness and diversity of the religious belief which goes under the name of Christianity are rooted in its history as a religion. The content of modern Christianity can be neither dissociated from antecedent religious history nor in any simple way integrated into that history. Liberal Christianity is an outgrowth of Protestantism, which means a plurality of sects divergent in all degrees and innumerable ways among themselves and from their parent, Roman Catholicism; and the last, as it now exists, in non-Catholic countries, is essentially a sect. Our difficulties are aggravated by the fact that religious reformism, in the Middle Ages and down to the present, has typically claimed the form and mission of a "restoration" of original Christianity. This situation constantly forces us into history, and even back to beginnings. Christianity was an outgrowth of Judaism, also a product of a long evolution. Like its parent, it is a scriptural religion. This fact makes change itself difficult and productive of confusion and also makes the history doubly hard to interpret. The New Testament is the only source for the earliest history of Christianity and must also be regarded as in some sense an authority for any position which can properly be called Christian today. But the susceptibility of the documents to widely varying interpretation is shown by the interpretations actually met with, not merely in different sects and between individual members of every sect, but at the hands of the most competent and unprejudiced scholars.

With respect specifically to the ethical teaching, which is our main concern, the same vagueness and ambiguity prevail but the historical background is different. As pointed out in Chapter Two, Christianity exemplifies the general rule that religion sanctions the established morality of custom and law; but at different times and places in the course of its history, different types of social order and ideals have actually prevailed. The social and ethical teaching of present-day Christianity is diverse, ambiguous and self-contradictory because in our culture the prevalent beliefs about what is right have this character. The reason for this in turn is historical. What is "established" among us, as in any society, consists of a mass of principles which have grown up, more than they have been deliberately thought out; and the process has been one of superposing new doctrines and beliefs upon old, without either repealing and rejecting the old or working out a rational integration and reconciliation. This applies particularly to the new and distinctive modern social ethic of individual liberty and equality, as the recognized basis of order in our society and culture, in relation to survivals of the status principle from preceding societies.

The roots of the ambiguity of Christian ethical teaching, which makes it possible for any group or individual to hold on Christian grounds and principles nearly any social or ethical position, are to be found in the original theological basis of Christianity as a religion. This was of a character which made concrete content, or intelligibly definite principles, particularly of social ethics, a matter of no consequence, or at least a field which did not present any real problem. The core of the message or Gospel, or the teachings of Jesus and Paul, was the imminence of the Kingdom of God, to be established on earth by supernatural intervention with such a transformation of the conditions of life that the ordinary problems of living, material and social, would no longer exist. The only problem which confronted the individual was that of achieving "salvation" for the new Kingdom. The concrete nature of the Kingdom itself or of the alternative— for what or from what the individual was to be saved—is a historical and speculative problem which it would be out of place to go into here. The essential fact is that salvation was to be achieved through faith, an attitude of will, not by rational thought or action; rather it explicitly opposed critical reflection in favor of leaving everything to the divine will. The early professions and creeds hardly refer to the moral life or even to religious practice or ritual; as in the mystery religions of the time, other than Christianity, salvation was a matter of belief, of accepting the divine nature and saving mission of the cult hero, in this case Jesus, and joining the brotherhood of those saved by this act.

On the other hand, the records make it clear that the Christian was expected and in fact required to live a moral life in accord with extremely high and austere standards; indeed, the standards set were impossible to maintain without destroying the material and social basis of life. The nature of this content and its rational justification are, however, intelligible in terms of Jewish history, the teachings of Jesus and the theological beliefs of the early Christians; and these in turn can to some extent be explained, from a modern point of view, in terms of historical conditions of the Alexandrian-Roman age, and social psychology. In the first place, the imminence of the establishment of the new Kingdom meant that the highly spiritual standards did not need to be maintained; the Christian was relieved of all responsibility for the future, beyond a very short interval. The teaching is often descriptively referred to as "interim ethics." It was logical for those among the first Christians who had any property to sell it for money and distribute the proceeds among the group, and for the group to live it up, as described in the fourth chapter of Acts. It was even ethically justifiable to sell the property to others outside the group, since if they resisted conversion they would be damned in any case.

The relation of the moral or spiritual life to salvation presents a more difficult problem. It may be regarded as a sign or proof of conversion, the "fruit of the spirit," as in the teaching of Paul—the view later taken up by Calvin and the Puritans. Or it may be viewed as in some way instrumental to the end of salvation, an imposed condition additional to that of belief or faith. The problem of the relation between human action and the omnipotent divine will is one for which Christian thought has never proposed any satisfactory or intelligible solution. The strain on the principles of the interim ethic was also reduced by the fact that the early converts were mostly from lowly social strata and had never had much responsibility for the future of society or even their own future. The original ethical code, as presented for example in the Sermon on the Mount, is less fantastically impossible if it is thought of as relating only to small communities or brotherhoods of people with a minimum of economic or political responsibility; and it is still less strained if it relates only or chiefly to their spiritual life, completely separated from such responsibilities.

As to the ethical content of the "Christian life," Christian scholars seem to be in fair agreement that its substance was taken over from Judaism. It was based primarily on the Jewish law (Torah—literally, "teaching") as currently interpreted, particularly by the advanced rabbis of the main teaching group, the Pharisees, who conducted the synagogues. This had already been spiritualized to a point where strict conformity was incompatible with the requirements of everyday life for the mass of the people; it was possible only for a limited élite among the Jews themselves, not for the despised Am-ha Aretz, the "people of the land." This spiritualization is carried even further in the teaching of Jesus, so that close conformity to the law itself should not stand in the way of the spirit, or "love." Paul was considerably more realistic, with respect to work and the requirements of everyday life in the existing situation, as the expression of religious love. Quasi-ascetic ideals were in harmony with the spirit of the times in the Near Eastern world; they were characteristic of the mystery religions and the contemporary secular philosophies, Stoicism, Platonism and later Neo-Platonism. This note was accentuated, especially in the field of sex relations, through the peculiar personality of the Apostle Paul, which by modern standards bordered on morbidity.

The point at the moment is that the moral life in the concrete sense was supposed not to present any serious intellectual problems but to be a matter of right will. Most of what now has to be included in moral conduct, particularly from the standpoint of social ethics, did not matter, or was taken care of by standards supposed to be accepted and known, and by activities which would follow spontaneously if the Christian had the right "spirit," if the "heart" was right. Practically speaking, the keynote for mundane living was passive acceptance of material and social conditions as one found them and obedience to established authority, plus humaneness in personal relations. Economics and politics were a matter of indifference in comparison with "spiritual values," and even an obstacle to the spiritual life. The question as to how far Christian belief and teaching of today, as presented in the preaching and writing of orthodox (Catholic or Protestant) or liberal Christians, has departed from these ideas would simply carry us back to the ambiguity of modern ethical ideals and the meaning of liberal Christianity. Certainly the good will still receives primary emphasis, in preaching and religious discussion of social problems, as against intelligence, critical judgment and the rational use of means or power.

The question immediately raised is the meaning of good will. If Christians agree on anything, they agree in defining the good will as the will of God, and the good life as life in conformity with the divine will. This theological basis of ethics is so much insisted upon by spokesmen for Christianity that it must be considered in any discussion of the Christian view of life. The effort to interpret the idea of God in such a way as to make it acceptable to the modern intelligence, and at the same time not obviously superfluous, is perhaps the outstanding feature of current thought in both theology and metaphysics in the Western world. (One thinks of such vitalistic philosophies as that of Whitehead and his school.) It is not necessary here to go into the question of the existence of God, which in fact is the philosophical (ontological) problem of the nature of reality. We need only consider the interpretation of God's nature as "love" (cf. I John 4:8,16) and go on to examine the inference that the whole duty of man is to love God and one's fellows—the First or Great Commandment of the Synoptic Gospels, both parts of which are copied from the Torah.

The general idea that the duty of man consists in doing the will of God can be practically useful as a guide to action only if God in some way makes his will generally known to men. Communication with God may be direct, through prayer or visions, or indirect, through other individuals as priests or prophets. Both direct and indirect forms of communication have always been recognized in historical Christianity, and most religious liberals of today give them some valid meaning. One who tries to approach the problem without prepossessions encounters such difficulties as the following: (a) There seems to be hopeless disagreement as to what God wills, even among the reports and records most widely accepted as authentic. For reasons involved in the universal relationship between religion and morality, these differences relate more to specifically religious questions than to morals. (b) The modern student usually finds other explanations of the real source of what is reported much more plausible than the theory of actual communication with God. (c) As to recorded prophecy, to which Christianity as a scriptural religion gives precedent authority over any alleged direct personal message, it seems inconsistent with an ethically high conception of God to think that if He wished to say something to some individual, He would not do it directly, and in an unequivocal manner. He would hardly send his message through some other person, especially an unknown person in the distant past, throwing both its original authenticity and the channels of later transmission open to doubt. (The classical expression of this point is credited to Rousseau.) (d) Perhaps the most conclusive objection, logically, is that the concrete prophecies or revelations which are accepted as verbally authentic, specifically in Christianity, give rise to differences of opinion as to their meaning in any concrete case, differences similar in scope to those found among opinions formed independently, on the merits of the questions. Agreement in interpretation seems to depend on authority backed up by force, though force now takes in the main the form of indoctrination in unresisting infancy.

It must surely seem to the objective inquirer that both the content of revelation and its interpretation are to be accounted for by a process which is the inverse of the religious view. That is, the content is arrived at in ways that can partly be explained and in part are individual and mysterious, and is imputed to a supernatural source for reasons which are also largely explicable in terms of well-known characteristics of human nature and social process and which do not imply the validity either of the imputation or of the opinion itself. In this view, the Christian who thinks he believes that certain things are right because they are ordered or sanctioned by the divine will, as revealed in the Bible (or by his church), actually believes these things to be divinely ordered because on other grounds he believes them to be right and good, and because he believes on other grounds that the teachings of his religion ordain what is good. As it clearly works out in practice, historical Christianity, like other religions, confirms or sanctions moral beliefs already held; explanation of their origin and content is a task for social psychology and culture history.

This confirming and strengthening has its good and its bad side. On the one hand it may work against moral skepticism and cynicism, disposing men to take morality seriously. It may also work to preserve unity of belief and harmony of interests, but only in so far as these already prevail. This effect is a consequence of resisting change and so making it slow and gradual. On the other hand, mere resistance to change obstructs progress, and a force which sanctions what is already established also intensifies existing differences and makes for intolerance. This is bad intrinsically, as well as because it incites to strife. Intolerance seems to be inherent in any religion which claims universality, in contrast with tribal or local cults. The distinctive religious mode of belief explicitly demands acceptance without critical inquiry. Thus the virtue of open-mindedness develops only with the weakening of religion. But this weakening makes for skepticism and cynicism. When people come to think that what they have been taught to regard as the necessary and only reason for believing in moral values is untenable, and that their spiritual leaders are deluded or deceiving, they often incline to repudiate the moral values along with their religious basis.

The Christian view holds that universal love is the will of God for man and hence the duty of man. This logically excludes intolerance, but in so doing it raises equally serious difficulties for theistic ethics. Completely undiscriminating love is clearly without significance for action, and it is doubtful whether it is defensible as right, or is possible, or even intellectually conceivable. Human love is certainly discriminating and selective. For man, or God, to love equally and in the same way everything which exists or will exist seems to be practically identical with loving nothing. Thus the religious attitude in the moral life runs into a dilemma. When men take religion seriously, they incline either toward intolerance and fanaticism or toward a purely mystical, contemplative love of God. In this attitude, one may either love in a similar mystical fashion the whole world of nature and man, as the works of the loving God, or he may hate or despise the actual world, presumably as expressing an evil or negative principle, refuse responsibility and withdraw into the life of the spirit. The loving attitude is doubtless abstractly preferable to that of hating, but there is no visible difference for conduct; both eliminate selective choice and responsible action and destroy the moral life.

Needless to say, Christians have not generally adopted this undiscriminating attitude. The simplest compromise, and one commonly adopted by the devoutly religious, is to love selectively those who conspicuously need it and to pursue a life of "doing good" in the form of simple humane acts, comforting the disconsolate and relieving suffering. Within limits, this type of conduct raises no difference of opinion— regardless of religion or irreligion—and presents no problems. Beyond these limits, which are quite narrow, the modern mind gives a higher rating to trained and competent service, medical, legal and social, effected through division of labor and motivated in the same complex way as other vocations conscientiously followed. Personal affection and abstract mercy are beautiful and excellent motives, but they are notoriously unreliable as guides to action. It is worth noting that in organized society even the most distinctive ministrations of religion come to be provided for in the professional way.

In the New Testament we are explicitly taught, in words

attributed to Jesus (in the Sermon on the Mount), that God's love is undiscriminating, since he sends the sunshine and rain on the good and the evil alike. But what we actually learn about God by studying the processes of nature does not seem to harmonize either with the literal meaning of the love Gospel or with the more general teaching of the New Testament itself. We cannot believe that as rainfall is distributed geographically and temporally it is an expression of love for man, impartial or otherwise. The effects of nature's operations on man depend in part upon his conduct, but not at all on his will attitudes or intentions, good or bad. However, in the Gospel teaching itself, taken as a whole, God is depicted as dispensing goods to the good and evils to the evil. On the face of the record, although there is much ambiguity, Christianity is very much a religion of reward and punishment. If the Christian has sufficient· love and faith, "all these things will be added unto" him—referring explicitly to food and raiment. In fact, he is explicitly promised a hundredfold repayment in this life for anything he gives up for the sake of his religion, besides eternal life in the world to come (Mt. 19:29-30; Mk. 10:29-30, Lk. 22:29-30). (On the other hand, again, we are repeatedly told, in words attributed to Jesus, that God loves the sinner more than the righteous man; cf. the parables of the Lost Sheep or the Ninety and Nine, of the Prodigal Son, etc.)

Since the faith enjoined in the Sermon on the Mount is impossible to a modern adult mind, the liberal Christian of today has a different interpretation or rationalization of the spirit of Christian morality. This consists in the view we have called moralism, which goes back to primitive retributive thinking, i.e., that men know what is good and that the evil in the world is due to wrong choices and would disappear if all of men's acts flowed from good will. The concrete working principle of original Christian social morality is not so much love as obedience; established custom, law and authority are to be accepted as the will of God. And from the beginning, the humanly natural conclusion has been drawn that if this is not done voluntarily it should be enforced by the most effective procedure. The specific content goes back through Jewish law to custom, established authority and primitive sentiments of tribal brotherhood. The will-of-God motif is derived from the Old Testament, but with increased emphasis upon the spirit of righteousness and the twofold love, in contrast with law. Subject to the important reservation just indicated, the logical principle of the Christian ethic could be summed up in the dictum of Augustine, *Ama et fac quod vis* (Love and do what you will), applied universally. It is virtually the position of modern "philosophical" anarchist communism.

Historical Christianity was also influenced by the Platonic doctrine that goodness consists in making the "passions" subservient to the guidance of "reason"—or in modern terms "conscience,"—i.e., the intuitive knowledge of what is right which all men are assumed to possess by nature. The modern student, of course, knows that such intuitive knowledge is chiefly derived from the cultural inheritance and differs from one cultural situation to another; or, where it is arrived at individually there is little agreement among individuals. Consequently, the natural result of hypostatizing or overexalting such reason is intolerance and war or insurrection.

In any case, the immediate appeal of religion is to custom and authority, and the concrete meaning of right conduct is held not to present any intellectual problem. From the standpoint of ethics in relation to social action, and in terms of modern ideals, the important historical fact is the acceptance of a social order based upon status, including slavery, and upon authority exercised by prescriptive right, whether political or religious. The primary duty is conformity to custom, meaning obedience to superiors by the masses, together with humane conduct for all. This is characteristic also for such secular political theory as there was, prior to the

Enlightenment. It also means that standards are tribal or national. The change effected by Christianity as a world religion was replacement of a political by an ecclesiastical definition of the particular society—and the elevation of conquest and incorporation of other societies from a right to a moral and religious duty.

It is in connection with private conduct and personal relations that we find what appeals to us as good in Jewish-Christian religious morality. This phase of the teaching merits brief consideration here because no clear line separates these branches of ethics from the problems of organized social life, with which we are concerned.

Any list of specific teachings generally associated with Christianity which might be selected as commendable by modern standards will to some extent express a personal point of view. Yet there are many items about which there will be general agreement among men of good will today in our culture, broadly conceived. Christianity has stood for peace and harmony, within any country and toward foreigners and foreign countries when they are not at war or regarded as enemies. In modern times it has given up religious propaganda based on overt force in favor of a more enlightened missionary program. As a basis for peace and harmony in face-to-face association, it has stood for friendliness and sympathy, if not literal love, expressed in action as kindliness and aid to persons in distress. The beautiful expression, "If I be lifted up, I will draw all men unto me," might be interpreted as a figurative statement of the faith that differences will disappear without conflict or rancor through the inherent appeal of truth, or the beauty of ideals. (It can hardly be interpreted as reaching agreement through rational discussion.)

Christianity has certainly taught moral self-discipline, and in spite of its doctrine of reward and punishment on a cosmic scale it has stood on the whole for the positive moral value of pain and suffering: "Whom the Lord loveth he chasteneth." The need for this emphasis is indubitable; human nature proverbially appears finer in adversity than in prosperity. Even the much-castigated doctrine of "original sin" is thus entitled to a certain amount of respect; for a realizing sense of his own limitations, in opposition to vanity and pride, is a trait of man which particularly needs cultivation.

In a general way also, Christianity has stood for the moral and spiritual values which are within reach of all and are most fully social and communal, in contrast with external and material conditions, which are naturally competitive in character and subject to influences and vicissitudes beyond human control. As a religion of personal salvation, it has perhaps tended indirectly to exalt the individual in this present world; this would make it abstractly akin to liberalism, but the claim that modern individualism derives from Christianity is historically indefensible. How far these positions or ideas are historically distinctive of Christianity is a problem for historical scholarship. Most or all of them are admitted by Christian writers to have close if not exact parallels in the records and teachings of other religions—not merely in Judaism, of which Christianity is an outgrowth, but also in Islam and the religions of India and China—and secular moralists. It is a still more difficult problem for the historian how far they are really due to religion, rather than the product of any high civilization, and specifically, in our own case, of economic mutualism, and of sport, or even of war and the natural human reaction to its horrors.

In one field only can Jesus and the apostolic founders of Christianity be said to have definitely gone beyond the contemporary liberal-Pharisaic interpretation of Judaism. That is the field of family life and sex relations. In these matters the general advance of culture and sentiment had created a serious dilemma for the Jews. The Patriarchs had of course been polygamous, and at the time of Jesus (and long after)

Jewish law still sanctioned polygamy and some magnates practiced it, or kept concubines. But the standards of the Greek and Roman moralists had come to condemn it, and the note of asceticism and "purity" was stressed in contemporary religion and philosophy. Moral progress had placed Judaism consciously on the defensive. This type of difficulty is especially serious for such a theocratic society, in which the law is textually sacred and there is no regular provision for legislative change. It was especially serious in this case because the age of prophecy was regarded as definitely closed. On the other hand, contemporary paganism was rather complacent about prostitution, and even sexual perversions, which had long been abhorrent to the Jews. These facts, together with the personal peculiarities of the Apostle Paul, account for the leaning toward sexual asceticism in early Christian ethical doctrine.

In other fields of human interest and activity the quasi-ascetic and charitable ideals of Christian teaching are not new. They derive from first-century Judaism and go back to the great Hebrew prophets, whose ideals were those of primitive nomadic simplicity; the condemnation of luxury and oppression even implied limits to inequality. Apart from their distinctive theological basis and rationalization, they are in fact little different from the morality of custom and authority and of brotherhood which is the characteristic ideal of tribal society in general, whatever the practice. In so far as Christianity represents a real change or advance, it is in the effort to extend these ideals beyond the tribe over the world. But this ideal clearly presupposed conversion of the world to Christianity and its incorporation in the "New Israel." This raises the problem of religious and political organization, which will be considered presently.

In the field of "culture" we find one of the main limitations of Christian ethics, in relation to the individual life and primary association. Our next chapter, on the ideals of liberal ethics, will deal with this subject from the positive standpoint. Here, it is needful only to observe in general terms that most of what we think of as belonging to the higher life of the mind and spirit is ignored or repudiated in the New Testament and in historical Christian teaching. Only the spiritual life, in the religious sense, is of value; the esthetic and intellectual life, science in all its branches and philosophic thought, find no place or are negatively regarded, along with business and politics (as aspirations of the common man). In the few references to beauty—in "raiment," associated with food—it is explicitly included in the field of interests about which men are not to be concerned because the Lord will provide for His own and add all such things unto them. It is true that in later times the Church as an institution made abundant use of esthetic adornment as an instrument for religious or ecclesiastical teaching, and for the enhancement of its own power and glory and that of its officials; but states and political rulers have typically done the same, while business institutions and wealthy individuals have differed only in degree.

With respect to the Christian attitude toward science and philosophy, it should suffice to mention medieval scholasticism and persecution, and for more recent times, the names of Galileo and Darwin. The religious ideal of the intellectual life is the conditioning of children in infancy to the unquestioning acceptance of dogma, myth and authority, and of the sinfulness of all criticism or questioning. To the extent that medieval man came to prefer knowledge and understanding to primitive tradition, or light and beauty to gloom and dreariness, or to encourage the active use of the mind on moral and social or scientific problems, European history was on the way out of its distinctively Christian phase. Reason, like beauty, crept in through its use to expound and defend the faith, and the authorities found to their consternation that it could not be confined within that sphere.

However, we must again be reminded of the social nature and function of religion, which is to sanction whatever is established, in belief and attitude as well as social structure and relations and the patterns of behavior. Christianity has long since accepted the Copernican astronomy and is well on the way to universal acceptance of biological evolution. Since the Enlightenment, or even the seventeenth century (particularly in England), the more enlightened Christians have accepted the general ideal of scientific progress through objective inquiry. They now commonly hold that there can be no conflict between religion, properly interpreted, and acceptance of the truths established by science, at present including even the sciences of man and society.

It is in connection with the problems of organized social life that we encounter the most serious weaknesses of Christian ethics. Somewhat as in the case of the preceding topic —the attitude toward the higher cultural values—the main content to be considered here is negative. It covers what is not found in historical Christian ethics—the problems it leaves unsolved, ignores or even repudiates as unreal. Accordingly, again, the bulk of the treatment will be left for later chapters, to be dealt with from the positive point of view. But there is an important difference, in historical Christianity, between the attitude toward cultural values and the attitude toward the economic and political organization of society.

On the face of the Gospel record of the teaching of Jesus, any interest in anything outside the spiritual life of love toward men and love and faith toward God is simply condemned outright. This view rests on the "Apocalyptic hope," and might seem to exclude even interim ethics, since life cannot be kept going even from day to day, at any level of civilization, under an attitude of complete indifference to economic and political considerations. However, in the only explicit reference in the Gospels to political conditions—

Jesus' answer to the question about giving tribute to Caesar —it is implied that indifference should be interpreted as accepting things as they are, and conforming and obeying. In the necessities of the situation, this was the only course which could possibly be followed prior to the miraculous establishment of the new Kingdom; the alternative would amount to suicide. With the founding of the Christian movement, after the Resurrection, this interpretation was inevitably relaxed to approve the performance of the necessary economic functions—at least after a short experiment (already mentioned) with communistic living out of the capital of those members of the group who had some possessions.

With reference to the political order, the early Christians soon came into conflict with the imperial power in the matter of the required gesture of sacrifice to the emperor, who was formally deified in accord with Oriental practice. The rule of "giving to Caesar that which is Caesar's" was found not to solve the problem, since there was a difference of opinion as to what belonged to Caesar. In the matter of anything that looked like worshiping strange gods, the Jewish conscience had been adamant, and the Christians naturally took the same line. The passive-resistance policy was followed—with the consequence of terrible martyrdom —as long as the Church and its members were helpless. As soon as Christianity became the official religion of the empire, and its adherents had organized power on their side, they turned this against other cults and imposed conformity or martyrdom even on divergent Christian sects and individual heretics.

We have noted that with the decline of the empire the Church set itself up as a political dictatorship, as far as possible and convenient, and this history need not again be recapitulated. The church also took over the esthetic and intellectual life, such as there was, and made both subservient to its own interests, in addition to prescribing the regulation of economic life. Much the same policies were followed by the little Catholicisms of the Reformation, to the extent that they were in a position to do so, down to the advent of modern "liberal Christianity," or substantial religious individualism.

It is true that in its own internal affairs the medieval church rather approved the pursuit of power, and of wealth as the perquisite of power, provided it was done through the church and as an agent of the church. This limited approval of individual ambition seems to have been in part a consequence of the imposition of celibacy upon the clergy and the monastic orders. Celibacy was in harmony with the early concepts of asceticism but was adopted more as a means of securing undivided loyalty and devotion. In any case, it did not prevent church offices and emoluments tending to become hereditary in families through nepotism. On occasion, the church has undoubtedly stood up for the elementary rights of the individual, and for the principles of primitive morality—against a state or political order opposing or limiting its own authority. But the church itself, claiming unlimited power in this world and the next (in "faith and morals," which sets no real limit) has typically endeavored to make good this claim, directly or on behalf of a state supporting and supported by it. It has also arrogantly insisted on the utmost deference to its human agents and to all symbols of its majesty and power. The church also interpreted the duties of its own authorities, or those of the state acting under its direction, as including the suppression of heresy. The means, justified by the end, included torture and execution by burning alive—in order to avoid the shedding of blood.

On the economic side, the pomp and lavish display which usually go with power and prestige have been as conspicuous in the church as in any secular organization. As the late Dean Shailer Mathews, D.D., was candid enough to observe, the church's denunciation of wealth has been matched only by its zeal to obtain it. The explicit teaching of the founder of Christianity, according to the sacred record, was that God is a spirit and should be worshiped in the spirit and prayed to in secret. According to Paul and the author of Acts, God dwells "in temples not made with hands," and is to be worshiped accordingly, without gifts, of which he has no need. But Henry Adams estimated that the expenditure on the construction and support of Christian "temples" in northern France in the centuries when the church was at the height of its power would strain the resources of the modern (prewar) French nation. Moreover, what is true of the church is also largely true in substance of its officials as individuals, and indeed of Christians generally. While eschewing legal title to property in their own names, churchmen have demanded as a matter of right a secure income affording a standard of living well above that of the typical laymen with whom they have to associate and at whose expense they live. There are exceptions, of course, as there are in politics and business; and we should add that what is said as to the quest of power applies to radical social reformers of non-religious and even anti-religious schools, notably the Marxists. The Christian admiration of poverty, weakness and submissiveness is a pose, not to say a hypocritical pretense, conscious or unconscious. It is usually enjoined upon others but not practiced by those who preach it, and the latter would despise anyone who took them seriously. With negligible exceptions religious people clearly admire competence and the active and courageous exercise of power and quest of power. As much as anyone they enjoy a good fight and typically describe the struggle of life as a fight. The Marxists are more candid in this regard.

The point for our argument has already been mentioned. Acceptance of the theory that universal love will solve all social problems inevitably leads in practice to the application of antithetical principles, to the solution of all problems by force and specifically to the use of force to maintain a fixed class or status system in economic and social life. Social life can be neither ruled by nor purified of interests other than "love"; rather, love itself requires some basis in concrete interests, which always involve conflict. Hence, the ideal is not merely opposed to civilization and progress but is an impossible one, to be approximated only in very small homogeneous groups content with hard conditions for a little while in the hope of a hereafter of eternal bliss as compensation. In relation to civilized life, several compromises with necessity are logically possible, and these are exemplified in the history of Christianity. The closest approach to pure spirituality is found in the life of the solitary desert saint or anchorite. Next in order is the convent, a small group living under a strict rule. In practice, the sexes must be separated, not merely for ascetic reasons but because family interests make conflicts inevitable. (Separate organizations are not strictly necessary, as was shown later by the Shaker communities.) In practice, also, the rule has to be administered by authority, ruling by some form of compulsion, and political bickering was rampant in the actual monasteries.

Continuing social life is patently impossible under either of these systems. The complete and viable social order which conflicts least with a spiritual life is a theocracy organized on caste or status lines, with ordinary activities reduced to a customary routine. While this might conceivably be accepted by all, for religious reasons, it also in fact requires authoritarian rule by coercion. Traditionalism, pure or religious, may be combined with authority in various ways and proportions, again as illustrated by Jewish history and by medieval class society, based on slavery or serfdom, which accepted Old Testament ideals as sacred. Medievalism is the true embodiment of Christian social ideals.

A high civilization could hardly be maintained long under such a system, to say nothing of progress, and it cannot approach universality. It will be sectarian, and the human interest in betterment, material and spiritual—the latter always resting upon the former—will hardly remain long in abeyance, as it ethically should not. Development of a new civilization, under some different political order, was to be expected and must be pronounced morally good and right. In fact the change led to a vast growth of tolerance, humane feeling and good will, associated with material and cultural progress. The modern aversion to suffering, even to cruelty, is a historical product of the irreligious age of the Enlightenment. Regard for the rights and feelings of others, and any real cosmopolitanism, go with the respect for oneself and others inculcated by liberalism, and not with any form of religiosity. (An attenuated and humanized Puritanism might be a partial exception.)

An analysis of power relations would need to distinguish, first, between power over other persons and power over non-human things, i.e., the material environment and the instrumentalities of individual and social life. In a general way, and to the limited extent that the two forms of power are separable (since either form inevitably confers the other), power over persons is the problem of politics, power over things, that of economic organization. With respect to the former, the original position of Christianity, in the teaching of Jesus, was dualistic. Christian community life should exclude all power relations, conforming to the ideal of anarchism. But the doctrine took for granted an established law and political power system outside the Christian fellowship, with reference to which the injunction was not only non-resistance but unquestioning, and presumably loving, obedience. On the behavior of those in authority, parents, masters or rulers, we find little in the Gospels or the New Testament. When the church came to include persons in positions of authority and power, it was doubtless assumed that their power would be exercised in accord with law and custom, and as humanely as possible without detriment to religion. But in a completely Christian society, or world, power would logically be expected to disappear entirely, as in the theories of nineteenth-century anarchists and in the ultimate classless society of the Marxian Communists.

Economic power can be rationally discussed only in terms of an analysis of which practically no trace is to be found in Christian teaching, at any date in history, or in any reformist thought. The fallacies which today vitiate popular thinking and religious and moralistic discussion of economic problems will be considered in a later chapter. The little that historical Christian teaching has to say about economic life relates to "wealth" and is superficial and indefensible. The constantly reiterated injunction to "give" to anyone in need, is so worded as to apply to wealth or capital, not merely to income. This is logically defensible from the standpoint of interim ethics, if the interim is assumed to be extremely short and the community has a substantial accumulation of provisions to start with. As we have noted, it was logical in the first Christian groups for those who had property to sell it and distribute the proceeds. It is hardly needful to observe that such indiscriminate giving both demoralizes the recipient and if kept up would quickly take society back to barbarism—or would lead to its own elimination, leaving a society ruled by some radically opposed ideal. The same statement, of course, applies to political non-resistance. The Christian negation of power is an impossible position, and hardly meaningful even as an ideal to be approximated or worked toward, under the conditions of human life on the earth.

As a natural consequence of adherence to ideals which are morally indefensible as well as impossible, the outstanding fact in the history of the Christian world, from the beginning until now, is a glaring discrepancy between Christian preaching and Christian practice. But the failure of Christians (or other idealists) to live up to their professed ideals, or really to believe in them, does not mean at all that they are bad people, or that the motives which they extol are bad motives. If men did not set limits to conformity with any simple ideal principles, however high in themselves, civilized life could not be maintained, to say nothing of progress. Insistence upon the spiritual life as the only good or value has laid Christianity open to the Communist accusation of functioning as the opiate of the people. (Opiates have their value; but like other good things, they must be used with discretion and moderation!) The idea that Christian social ideals are sound but impracticable is a fallacy, if not a subterfuge; a patently impracticable theory of conduct is a wrong theory, and if it has any practical effect, tends to create a cynical disregard of all moral obligation.

A genuinely ethical life involves social responsibility and cannot be lived without frequently passing judgment on other persons and directly exercising power over them. It is not enough to lift up the abstract ideal of having high ideals, assuming that everyone knows what they are or should be and what they mean in terms of conduct. In our modern world where, in contrast with the hopeless situation of the first Christians, the common man is a full-fledged participant in political life, in economic organization and in culture as a whole, the idea of solving the problems of social life by loving God and man and being indifferent to the problems, judging not and taking no thought, is shirking, and reprehensible rather than virtuous. The ethical man must seek and intelligently use power, in business and politics and other social relations. He must not evade even the ugly tasks of the policeman and the soldier. Neither love nor the Golden Rule shed any significant light upon the problems of organized social relations. Differences usually involve a conflict of rights as well as desires. The maxim of doing as one would be done by gives no indication as to how the matter ought to be adjudicated. It is meaningless unless each "puts himself in the other's place," and "place" is usually the matter really at issue. Love cannot replace justice, in practice or as an ideal. Personal benevolence always conflicts with other principles of equal validity and importance in personal relations, to say nothing of the requirements of social order and progress. For each party merely to defer to the other is as futile and unreasonable as for each to insist on the other yielding to him, and reduces to the ludicrous. The love-gospel, condemning all self-assertion as sin, not merely lacks definite content; it would destroy all values, the good as well as the bad in human character. It is a false approach to ethical problems. Sentiment cannot take the place of reason and judgment.

CHAPTER FOUR

Liberal Ethics

WHEN any critical comment is made upon the ethical teachings of religion, it usually refers to the "impracticability" of the Christian ideals. These are generally accepted, verbally, as finally true and valid, even when it is frankly the intention of the speaker to dismiss them, in favor of more mundane standards, as too pure and lofty for serious pursuit in a literal interpretation. The criticism is in harmony with the historical and official position of Christianity itself, which has not demanded literal conformity with its ideals because of the presence of sin in the world. The purpose of this chapter is to inquire into the nature of the ideals really accepted and admired by serious-minded people in our society, and which they think men ought to strive to realize and promote, if they do not claim to do so themselves.

Confusion regarding ideals is one of the most serious sources of difficulty in the modern social problem. This confusion is due in large part to a fact previously mentioned, the development of a new and fundamentally changed conception of the meaning of the good life, individual and social (associated with new knowledge of possibilities), and a failure to integrate the new insights with ideals which have survived in our tradition from earlier times. The position taken here is that there has been true progress in the development of ideals, and that this cause of discrepancy between aspiration and achievement is far more important than changes in the conditions of life making it more difficult to realize the same ideals. It is not contended here that the older ideals have lost their value, but merely that modern civilization has developed new views which demand equal consideration, and has not worked out a synthesis of the new and the old. The moral problem is one of right balance between conflicting values, valid goods, not one of choosing the good instead of the bad or choosing "either" one "or" another of opposed standards or norms. Our criticism is finally directed against the practice of diagnosing the social crisis, or the ills of the world, in any moralistic terms; but the Jewish-Christian religious tradition is held largely responsible for the tendency to attribute social ills to the lack of ethical ideals, or to the acceptance of corrupt or wrong ideals. In contrast with this view, we shall contend that intellectual error and inadequacy are more important than defects of will or lack of good intentions. But lack of means adequate to needs is fully as important as either; and perhaps most serious of all as a direct cause of the present crisis in our culture is the fact that, as is typically asserted of Christianity, we have developed ideals which are beyond our reach and have lost patience and become inclined to act rashly.

The great moral tragedy of life is not that people fail to act in accord with their ideals, or with right ideals, but that "love is blind," that goodness, good intentions and good people so commonly do harm instead of good because of failure to *understand* social and other conditions and the consequences of action. In particular, they do not see and face the limitations of life, choose between possible alternatives and find satisfaction in attainable progress at a speed consonant with a reasonable degree of order and security. Of course, justice and intelligence, on their side, must avoid being blind—to love. But the supreme lesson of modern thought is not only that ideals must be approached gradually but also that they change progressively, by intelligent redefinition in the process of their realization by rational action. Consequently, the objective itself can be formulated only as the *direction* of moral progress, not as a goal to be ever finally achieved. This conception in this form seems to be a new and distinctive product of modern thought, first appearing in the Enlightenment.

Discussion of the general problem of conduct naturally falls into two parts. The first has to do with the meaning of the good life from the standpoint of the individuals who live it, the second with social organization. Under the first head, again, a double division is to be made: We must explore the meaning and the limits of ethically good or valid ends or purposes (in contrast with what is merely desired) and the means or procedures of effective action. And we have to consider the social relations which are at once a part of the good life for the individual and necessary conditions for its achievement. Man, even as a being with personal desires, is both social and individual, while his values are inherently social. Beyond this relatively informal aspect of society is the political and economic organization, which will be considered in the two succeeding chapters.

The heart of the modern social-ethical problem is to be found in the premise of freedom in a form distinctive of our culture. This premise, rooted in the elementary notion of freedom of social intercourse or discussion, means the right of individuals to associate voluntarily (and not to associate otherwise) and to form and follow their own ideals as individuals and free groups. However, the conditions of human life on the earth require many groupings accepting common ends, and common activities for their achievement, or formally organized living. Freedom requires that such organizations, based on compulsory unanimity (whether called political or not), be as free as possible and restricted in scope to a right balance with literal individual liberty and strictly voluntary association. Freedom in this conception is the essential meaning of democracy, which, so conceived, is a unique feature of modern Western civilization and gives a unique character to its problems. Every other culture known to history has rested on more or less stable "classes" and hereditary status, with different norms for different classes, and with leadership or government vested by prescriptive right in an individual or a limited class. We assume here that the change to the ideal of freedom and equality represents a moral advance, and not a retrogression.

Even a brief discussion of the problem of social freedom must begin by recognizing the nature of purposive life and of individual freedom as a fact. The displacement of the center of the social-ethical problem from will to intelligence and power, and the prestige of modern science and technology, have engendered a disposition to regard the methods of natural science as exhaustively valid for man himself. This would make human beings simply a part of nature, and their lives a detail in purely objective natural process. It is possible here only to say briefly that this position involves contradiction in thought. It reduces both morality and discussion itself to an illusion. Thinking, both theoretical and practical, must regard nature as inert material which is to be understood and used by man as in part a free, active, purposive being. This antithesis between the fundamental "nature of nature" and the nature of man is implied in science itself, as definitively and as clearly as it is in all rational conduct and in ethics and value theory.

We need undertake no philosophical essay on the age-old controversy over free will versus determinism. The fact of freedom must be taken for granted because it is presupposed in making any statement about any subject and in thinking itself. Without freedom, defined as problem-solving activity, there is no difference between saying something or making a statement and making (mechanically causing) a noise. The scientific view of nature implies a positive or logical-empirical philosophy of nature, while purposive action, in which man understands and uses nature, implies a pragmatic view of the relations between man and nature. But all intellectual operations, beginning with knowledge in its most rudimentary, common-sense form, are based on communication and imply values which are final and not merely instrumental. And social intelligence, which is presupposed in social action, implies also a creative, critical-evaluative interpretation of human nature, over and above desire and satisfaction, and still further removed from the content of scientific psychology and sociology.

It is from the standpoint of group thinking and action that freedom, presupposing the validity of moral distinctions, has vital significance for the purpose of the present discussion. The possibility of effective democratic society depends on the capacity of men at large to *agree* upon super-individual norms for the guidance of action in and by groups. Any society, to the extent that it is truly free, is based upon the voluntary and consciously critical acceptance of common social ideals as guides for progressive improvement. Thus, for the interpretation of democratic society and for statement or discussion of its problems, freedom is not the opposite of determinism but of coercion, which itself implies that both the coercer and the coerced are active and free entities; men do not coerce inert objects, and they do coerce one another.

Activism versus *quietism* is perhaps the best expression in a single pair of words of the general antithesis between the liberal-ethical view of life and the religious view; but such categories or genera necessarily include various species. Active freedom presents a sharp contrast in meaning with the use of the term in John 4:32: ". . . ye shall know the truth and the truth shall make you free." (The meaning of truth in the expression will be referred to later.) Any problem implies the existence of alternatives of belief, judgment or action, among which intelligent choice is to be made. Any problem of action must root in some conflict between the nature of things as they are and as some purposive subject would like to have them—and must imply the possibility of change through action. And any ethical problem, or other discussable problem, roots in an opposition between reality and ideals or values which are real or objective, in contrast with mere desires.

The statement that human freedom is to be defined in terms of purposive, problem-solving activity must at once be qualified by taking account of a twofold division of conduct which is characteristic of the modern ethical world-view. This is the separation and opposition between serious activity and that which is non-serious, irresponsible or frivolous, i.e., between work and play. No feature of the modern conception of the good life presents a sharper contrast with the religious view than the recognition of play, humor and fun in general as ethically legitimate interests or motives. Play, in a wide range of forms and meanings, is characteristic of all known human societies, and doubtless of all individuals, as well as some of the higher animals. For man it seems to be a necessity for both mental and physical health. Yet this vast category of activities and interests is not recognized by religion as a part of the moral life, and is slighted by secular writers. The word "smile" does not occur at all in the standard versions of the English Bible; "laugh" and its derivatives occur as expressions of ridicule, irony or satire; "play" appears a score of times in several meanings, but not in a sense which recognizes games, or any sort of fun, as worthy activity and enjoyment.

Play involves several paradoxical features important both for the understanding of play itself and for its relation to ethics. Though it has serious value, up to necessity for normal healthy life, yet if its functional meaning is present in the mind of the player, both this value and its distinctive mental quality or tone of pleasure are lost. A characteristic feature of play is a feeling-attitude of irresponsibility; yet in any play which involves thinking or clear awareness there is an end or objective. The peculiarity is that the relation between this and the activity is the inverse of what it is in serious conduct or work. In the latter, the activity is undertaken for the sake of some end, intrinsically desired or valued, while in play the end is rather arbitrarily set up to make the activity interesting, and is instrumental to the latter. This means that the economic or efficiency interest has a different role, while foresight of the consequences of action is largely replaced by curiosity. Actual achievement of the objective has chiefly symbolic value, as a mark of success. Yet play always has rules and standards, which bring it into close relation with the serious matters of ethics and law.

Most play is social, and in social play the interest largely centers in emulation or rivalry—another essential human interest for which the religious view of life seems to have no place. (This applies to our own, late-Semitic religious tradition, in contrast with most other religions; the Greek and Roman gods were as playful and as contentious as human beings.) The relation between the spectator interest and that of the player is also highly important for ethics, but it cannot be explored here. Even more significant is the self-assertive character of social play. There is no place for the ideal of self-abnegation, "service" or benevolence except within narrow limits, in connection with generous interpretation of the rules in doubtful cases. In sport it is just as necessary for the player to play his own hand and to exert his powers to win as it is for him to obey the rules. It is noteworthy that games are like our competitive economy in that the "rewards" are distributed in accord with capacity and the exertion of capacity; the power factor is on a level with that of will. However, there must not be too much inequality in capacity; this would destroy the game, partly because it would remove uncertainty as to the outcome. The moral attitude toward the opponent in sport is better designated as "respect," with friendliness, than as "love." The meaning of good intentions is highly impersonal; the player must be interested in the game, and not, again, too much interested in winning. As in all conduct, ethics means a right balance between conflicting values.

Finally, it must be recognized that some games are better than others, and that some may be positively bad. This brings out another paradox in the nature of play, especially social play, but also solitaire. A very little argument (or even serious thought) about the game destroys the spontaneity essential to the play spirit. In social play, this may lead to strife—or one party may adopt a self-sacrificing role as a matter of duty, including the duty of dissembling his real attitude. In fact, play often resembles economic co-operation in that a person feels compulsion to associate though the terms are not satisfactory. The question as to the intrinsic value of a game must be discussed in serious terms, though discussion itself may be playful. The serious value in play is largely to be found in the development of the individual faculties which are useful in serious activities. But enjoyment is also a factor in the value of serious activity (work) while the final value of both is "cultural"—individual development and social progress. For civilized men biological values—life, health and comfort—are for the most part taken for granted, or even sacrificed to cultural norms and social interests. Cultural activities in the ordinary meaning present a mixture of play and work and are hard to classify between the two.

It seems to be correct as well as customary to consider "values"—restricted to the serious side of life—under the three heads of truth, beauty and goodness. It is evident from what has been said that only the serious values can be a subject of discussion, beyond narrow limits. In this field the contrast between liberal and religious ethics is largely bound up in the conception of truth. The two opposed conceptions carry with them correspondingly different

interpretations of other normative concepts, especially freedom, activity and progress. In religion, truth is to be had
by an act of will—by faith—a voluntary acceptance, embracing or taking possession, which is explicitly antithetical
to inquiry and investigation or critical judgment. The content of religious truth is ostensibly a matter of revelation,
originating through prophecy, which for any established
religion belongs to a past age. The religious mode of belief
is defined by the fact that the critical attitude toward serious
matters is sinful. This view of truth means in practice that
for any individual, whether priest or ordinary citizen, truth
is a matter of cultural inheritance. (The prophet is an exception; but he also is non-rational, and until he is "accepted" he is a heretic.) Thus, as to major distinctions,
religious truth is a matter of geography, while smaller sectarian variations are also for the most part socially inherited.
In our own tradition, intolerance is integral to religious
belief, as it must be, to some degree, in a religion claiming
universality.

In the liberal view of life, all this is of course reversed.
To begin with, liberalism repudiates the idea that any truth
is final or absolute; all concrete beliefs are in varying degree
subject to reinterpretation, revision and eventual rejection
and replacement, in the light of new knowledge or insight.
Truth is an ideal rather than a reality, something never
possessed but to be approached by criticism and critically
directed effort. The presupposition of even relatively valid
belief is a skeptical attitude—not absolute skepticism, which
would negate all belief, but a reasonable reluctance to accept
any belief in the absence of intellectually valid reasons. The
modern mind recognizes that this attitude is necessary because human nature is essentially romantic; it is characterized by the will to believe, on innumerable irrational
grounds, including avidity for the marvelous as such. The
liberal view makes truth inherently dynamic and progressive. Ultimately, we confront the paradox that the interest

in truth itself (apart from its utility) is romantic rather than strictly rational; it is an emotional interest in action, change and achievement, as well as in knowledge as such. The truth interest, when not instrumental to other interests, centers in novelty, and to a large extent in conflict or controversy. A truth is the answer to some question, and a question once answered is no longer a question. "Mere" truth, which is not somehow in question or controversial, is commonplace, uninteresting, even a bore. Truth, like other cultural interests, has the qualities of play and work in unanalyzable combination.

The intellectual significance of truth, as provisionally established, centers in the fact that it is instrumental to the further pursuit of truth. The importance of new truth, beyond the momentary interest in its novelty, or as a symbol of success (largely competitive), lies more in the new questions which it raises than in the old questions which it answers. The antithesis is apparent between this attitude and what is undoubtedly the essence of the religious view, that truth is to bring "peace," final satisfaction, cessation from effort—"salvation," as a kind of freedom. (This recalls what was said earlier about the passage on truth and freedom in the Gospel of John.) The intellectual liberal cannot desire or imagine life without unanswered questions and effort to find the answers.

In the liberal view truth is also instrumental to other activities and interests. Knowledge of means and their properties is the prime requisite to intelligent action. Knowledge is power. The means-end relation, in thinking and acting, raises hard problems. Two major difficulties call for mention here. The first is the virtual impossibility of defining any end which is really final, which does not under critical scrutiny become a means. The only ultimate end is the good life, which is merely a name for an undefined, vague, diverse and shifting complex of qualities of activity and experience. It is to be defined in the process of realization.

The second difficulty centers in the ambiguous relations between the physical human body—and even, in a certain sense, the mind—and the active, purposive, choosing "self." The body or person resists unambiguous classification between the categories of means and ends; it may be either, in different contexts.

A distinctive feature of modern ethical idealism is frank recognition of the role of power—including physical means and knowledge—in the good life, and of the need for the increase as well as the use of it. In this respect, again, the liberal is opposed to the religious view, meaning any moralistic theory, which makes the difference between good and bad conduct essentially a matter of arbitrary will. Power, or capacity, is recognized as not merely an indispensable means but also an intrinsic good, as an attribute of personality and a social possession which ethical conduct must conserve and develop. It is primarily in connection with power relations between individuals and groups that the distinctively ethical aspect of the value problem arises. Difference of opinion about ends is doubtless the fact which underlies the misleading term "materialism," so much used as a term of opprobrium, a survival from the time when the gentleman did not have to think about means or economy. It is obvious that power itself, as an attribute of personality, is not physical but metaphysical, and also that any end, as an end, consists in the *meaning* of physical things and events for personal enjoyment and cultural life and growth, not in the physical condition itself. Intrinsically, one configuration of matter is as good as another—with some reservation as to esthetic values, a problem to be touched upon later.

Truth itself, or intellectual value, is also a moral value, in the broadest meaning of the latter concept. In liberal ethics, intellectual integrity, the obligation to believe the truth because it is true, and for no other reason, is the primary and in a sense the all-inclusive obligation of the person to himself; and to tell the truth is the basic obligation to others. It is essentially unarguable, for acceptance of this two-fold obligation is presupposed in any argument or serious discourse. This view of truth as the ultimate value or norm is often opposed in modern thought by a view which makes it a derivative from utility. The worker in positive science often verbally takes this position, and explicitly denies objectivity to moral (and esthetic) judgments. (Interestingly enough, the defense of belief on grounds of expediency is also a common practice of religious apologists.) It is self-evident that science itself (and all intellectually honest belief) rests on a high and austere morality; there could be no such thing as science if scientists as men were not disinterested, if they were mere self-seekers or charlatans. Truth must be sought without knowing concretely for what one is searching; to view it as an end, given in advance, contradicts the idea of a problem.

The ultimate premise of the pragmatic philosophy was stated by Hume in the interesting dictum that "reason is and *ought* only to be the slave of the passions," and more explicitly in his accompanying denial that the working of the intellect is itself affected by emotion. (The use of the word "ought," italicized by us, obviously makes the whole statement self-contradictory.) It is also expressed in the familiar adage that there is no disputing about tastes (*de gustibus non disputandum est*). The plain fact is that all discussion is ultimately about matters of taste, or judgment. Real problems of fact are problems of the worth of evidence. Still more absurd, and vicious as well, is the theory that practical problems of personal relations and social policy are to be solved by utilitarian application of positive science. An effort of men to manipulate and use each other (however intelligently) would literally realize the war of each against all. This is the worst of all romantic oversimplifications, the worst form of original sin, rationally defined.

Recognizing that truth is a value means recognizing that it is a social category. Truth is known, tested, and practically speaking defined, by agreement in some community of discourse. Ideally, in the liberal meaning of idealism, agreement is reached on the answer to any question as a result of rational discussion, a co-operative intellectual activity. It goes without saying that in fact many other processes and interests are important factors in what passes for discussion and in agreement. Actual unanimity of belief is largely a matter of tradition and the fact that no question has ever been raised, or that questioning has been suppressed, mechanically or deliberately, or else it is the product of a mass emotional reaction. Entirely apart from repression of which either party is aware, intellectual freedom is narrowly limited. Beliefs of every sort are necessarily in large part institutions; they grow and change in any community through non-rational and irrational processes which it is the task of anthropology and social psychology to investigate; and rational change in social opinion must be slow and gradual. All this, again, is opposed to the liberal idea and ideal of truth, for which mere tradition cannot sanctify belief; and it is of the essence of the liberal view that truth or valid belief cannot be imposed by any form of force. Moreover, persuasion is a form of force, in contrast with intellectual conviction. It might be defined as coercion so subtle and effective that the individual is unaware that he is not moved by his own free or arbitrary choice. Persuasion rests upon deception; and ethically speaking deception or fraud is the lowest form of coercion.

In the liberal view of life this conception of truth as the ultimate norm with its social-ethical corollary of truthfulness in communication, defines the ideal and the limits of free association. The democratic ideal is well described as "government by discussion." But we must remember that little of what passes for discussion conforms closely to the ideal of disinterested intellectual co-operation. Apart from the role of tradition and authority, most of it is rather controversy, a phenomenon which is hard to analyze. Its motive is competitive persuasion rather than co-operative pursuit of truth or rational conviction. Even in quite informal "discussion" of the most intellectual (scientific and philosophical) questions and problems, opinions are interests; difference of opinion always goes with conflict of interest, as both cause and effect. And in human nature emulation and rivalry contend with the love of truth. Moreover, discussion in large groups has to be organized; and organization, in this field as elsewhere, must recognize inequality and must sometimes enforce its recognition. Thus it raises problems of discipline and power. (The relation between the play and work interest is an important aspect of the problem of truth through discussion.) The faith that "truth is mighty and will prevail" implies belief in an implicit rationality and intellectual morality underlying the processes of controversy. The tendency of controversy to degenerate into strife, irrespective of the importance of the issue, is a danger in all forms of associative life, and particularly in democratic politics. (But we must also have some faith in the arbitrament of war—in a natural connection between truth and crude power.)

Passing over the complex problem of the limits of freedom of expression and teaching, we must refer as a final point to the ethical limitations of the ideal of truthfulness. It is impossible to deny altogether the rightful place of the will to believe; for example, one "must" always be optimistic and trusting, beyond what experience justifies. Everyone also recognizes in practice that telling the truth must often be subordinated to other values, such as personal kindness, courtesy (even peace!) and various institutional loyalties. Within limits everyone will lie, and hold it right to lie, for love's or mercy's sake. In war, deception of the enemy is of the essence of strategy, and espionage is a virtuous activity. Strategy is also involved in competitive games, and deception plays a large role in humor, especially in the practical joke. These conflicts are important in large-scale free society, where the standards of conduct in organized economic and political life must be impersonal, i.e., loyalty to truth and

principle must take precedence over personal and group loyalties, which are the primary basis of order in feudal and monarchical society, and play a large role in small face-to-face
groups. Conflict between these standards gives rise to much
discrepancy between profession and practice.

We must pass briefly over the other two values in the
familiar triad, and particularly esthetic value or beauty,
which is especially interesting. In a sense, beauty and goodness are species of truth—truth "about" the one or the other,
to be reached and determined intellectually by discussion.
It is, indeed, possible to define each of the three so as to include the other two, though in concrete cases they are conflicting values. With respect to truth and beauty, the familiar
words of Keats—"Beauty is truth, truth beauty," etc.—
illustrate the point, since the statement itself is beautiful but
not true, except in a figurative sense.

Any desirable social life calls for a wide range of agreement
as to what is beautiful—though to be interesting, it also calls
for some disagreement. Disagreement as well as agreement
implies that beauty is real, not purely subjective and individual—not solely a matter of "mere" taste but also one
of "good" taste. To an even greater degree than in the case
of purely intellectual disagreements the question of what
is really beautiful can be left to informal social intercourse—
assuming individual tolerance—without compulsory social
action. Both fields differ sharply in that respect from personal, and especially from political, ethics. But, as with all
general principles, there are important limits. Monumental
public buildings and the esthetic features of a neighborhood,
including the physical plan, must be the same for all who
live in any community. Consequently, agreement on such
matters is necessary, and it is often neither spontaneous nor
easy of achievement. Everyone is familiar with heated controversies over such matters as statues, mural decorations, etc.,

between the public and various schools, and between the latter among themselves.

The relation between beauty and truth suggests the role of expression in art, and the relation between the beauty of art and that of nature. Great art does not have to be beautiful at all, and is often ugly, if the words are used in their common-sense meaning. The perception of beauty in nature, pure or affected with supposed meaning, is the product of a high degree of both esthetic and intellectual culture and sophistication. In this cultural sense, natural beauty is as artificial as art itself. Nature, viewed objectively, in the raw, is lacking in beauty as well as morality. In the intellectual life nature of course sets the problems of science, and affords the values of mystery and wonder. There is no place here for a discussion of the relations between the traditional schools of esthetics and types of art, classicism, romanticism and realism. It is perhaps a commonplace that all are romantic in different ways; but as already pointed out, this is ultimately true of the truth interest itself.

Two aspects of esthetics bring it into particularly close relation with ethics. The first is craftsmanship in human handiwork. This is especially important analytically because the standards or norms involved in its peculiar imperative present a mixture of esthetics and instrumental science (economics in its technological branch) and ethics, while conflict between the different norms is also present. The second aspect is the costliness of beauty or even of avoiding ugliness in human surroundings; this brings it still more directly into the sphere of economic discussion. Any intelligent approach to the problem of economic value must recognize that ultimately its content for the individual is predominantly esthetic and cultural, specifically as measured in terms of cost.

We come finally to goodness, or moral value, the third member of the triad. Of the three types or modes of value, it is at once the one most in point for the theme of this essay and the hardest to define in any satisfactory or relevant way, or to interrelate with the other two. For logical analysis, ethical value seems to be largely secondary to the other two forms, a matter of the attitude toward values as such, rather than a separate species. Moral obligation, then, consists in recognition of norms whose content must be defined in non-ethical terms. It seems to be impossible to define or conceive goodness merely as action in accord with an obligation to be good, without some intelligible content. This is the error of moralism, the general position to which liberalism is opposed in this essay. It is characteristic of the Christian ethical tradition but is a survival from primitive thought; it was formulated in secular philosophy in the Kantian dictum that nothing is absolutely good but the good will.

Kant himself attempted to give content to morality in his other two principles: that one should act in accord with principles which could be treated as universal (meaning for human beings) and especially that every human being should be treated as an end and not as a means. The weakness of the first of these has long been recognized. The second is without concrete meaning, since it leaves unanswered the essential question as to what is good for any human being, the actor himself or others affected by his conduct. The moral good is a distributive principle. It may be taken to mean that the good (undefined) of every human being should be given equal consideration, equal in particular with one's own good. But equality cannot be determined without defining the good itself, and in terms having quantitative meaning. This greatly increases the difficulty, specifically in view of the question as to whether the good is identical in kind for all individuals. A formula which ignores such questions can be construed to fit one social philosophy as well as another. It sheds no light on the main problem, which in practice is: who is to be the judge of what is good for any individual, he himself, or the person acting and affecting him, or some outside authority, and if the latter, what authority it is to be.

The liberal solution of the problem takes the form of a major principle and a corollary (both mentioned early in this chapter) which together define the ideal of freedom as the supreme value. The principle is that each individual is to be the final judge of his own ends as far as possible, i.e., reasonably expedient. The corollary is that all associative relations must be based on mutual consent; every individual should be free to refuse any relationship with another unless the terms are satisfactory to himself, i.e., agreed upon as reasonable, while of course everyone is free to offer terms of association to others. Anyone may, if he chooses, reject the activistic ideal generally approved in liberal society, the maintenance and creation of cultural values, combined with play. Instead, he may pursue the quietistic life of intellectual contemplation or religious devotion, even in a monastery, as far as he wants to do so, and can—i.e., if he has the means or can get them from others without overt force or crude fraud, and can secure the voluntary assent of all other persons directly involved in his program in any other way. Yet this principle (and corollary), as literally stated, is subject to sweeping limitations. In practice these embody the modern social problem, since the abstract principle of individual freedom has been formally accepted in our society. The more important limitations center in the fallacy of viewing the individual as given; they will be discussed in the two chapters which follow.

It thus appears that (to repeat) the distinctively ethical aspect of the good life is to be found not in a particular content of value but in a twofold principle of distribution of value. The first distributive principle is that the individual balance among goods should be such as to achieve a maximum; the second runs in the same terms for the distribution between different individuals and groups living at any time, and especially between those living and those who are to live in the future. Even intellectual freedom, as we have seen, presents a problem of distribution; it cannot be absolute for anyone, or equal for all. The role of spontaneous enjoyment, irresponsibility, or the play interest, and the balance between this and "duty" in all forms is also a major problem. Only one proposition in ethics is more important than that life, and specifically duty, is not to be taken too seriously; that one is the proposition that it is to be taken seriously enough.

Finally, the interrelations of the three traditional types of value are further complicated by the fact that the ideal quality of personality as a whole is a kind of beauty—the "beautiful soul," as expressed in conduct. There is in personality and conduct a relation between form and content similar to that in any other human creation, and (as always) the two elements in value are partly coincident or complementary and partly conflicting. The formal or esthetic side of personality value is etiquette in contrast with ethics—manners versus morals. The relations of harmony and conflict between these two categories are manifestly complex, and no more need be said here.

To conclude this chapter, we should recognize a certain weakness of the liberal-activist ethic of creativeness combined with recreation, and the appeal of the religious or quietistic view of life to the modern mind. The latter view has simplicity and finality in contrast with the confusion, the perpetual flux and change and especially the inevitable frustration which certainly characterize life under the liberal ideal. Our discussion of truth as the crucial and inclusive value makes it clear that the ideal of progress and a life of action means a striving after the unattainable, of "ever climbing up the climbing wave." It is inherently, even in principle, unsatisfying, and so in a sense unsatisfactory. This is as poignantly expressed in the English Victorian poets, who speak for the apogee of liberal culture, as it is in the thought of India, the classical home of the religious view of life. One need only mention lines from Tennyson's "The Lotus Eaters," or Swinburne's "Garden of Proserpine," or from Shelley, or Burns, which everyone has memorized. Even Browning, the

arch romantic, the poet par excellence of struggle and achievement, occasionally strikes the opposite note, as in "Old Pictures in Florence."

That this craving for finality, for peace and rest, is the
essence of the religious spirit, may of course be disputed, and
will be, particularly by modern Christians. But apart from the
impending consummation of all things clearly assumed in the
Gospel teaching, the later tradition of heaven as the abode
of the saved also points to the ideal of a state of existence
free from effort and uncertainty as well as conflict, a life in
which there are no problems to be solved. Heaven is like
Nirvana in this essential respect, whatever the role of more
active or sensuous enjoyment. And the same is true of the
monastic ideal which dominated Christian thought in the
age when Christianity itself was dominant, and thought
practically meant Christian thought. One also thinks of such
modern Christian hymns as "Abide with Me" and "Peace,
Wonderful Peace," though "Onward Christian Soldiers" may
express the Christian spirit for the present life, where the
church is militant. Literal passivity or quietism is of course
impossible for men on earth and can only be approximated
by relatively small, segregated and parasitic groups. The religious life in this interpretation must be a compromise unless
the devotee elects to die shortly from starvation or exposure,
as some Hindus are said to have done in ancient times. The
Christian compromise of monasticism (notably in the West)
made a place for action, for "doing good" and useful work.

The opposite, activistic ideal, if carried too far, also runs
into impossibility, hence it also faces the necessity of compromise. The best general designation of this extreme is
romanticism; and the best literary expression is doubtless the
Faust story, particularly in Goethe's version. Interestingly
enough, it stems from a medieval European setting. The ideal
expressed in Faust's contract is limitless and completely irresponsible power. It is true that in Goethe's version Faust
finally compromised upon achievement with an aspect of

"worthwhileness." This may be because Goethe was a modern man, or more likely because as a sound literary artist he recognized that men grow old. At the ultimate extreme (sometimes referred to as Dionysian in contrast with Promethan), romanticism runs into a craving for intoxication and madness. One of the most interesting literary expressions of this theme, in view of the cultural setting, is from the American poet Walt Whitman: "One hour to madness and joy! . . . Oh, to drink the mystic deliria deeper than any other man!"

The modern liberal view of life is a particular form of compromise. Its ideal is action, but power is to be disciplined to good ends, and to the conditions of effective action prescribed by the facts, both of the world and of man. The liberal view is closer to the romantic ideal than it is to the religious conception of a final reconciliation of man and universe through quietistic acceptance. Life is pictured as effort; and while effort is justified by good results, these are not expected ever to be satisfying. The experienced reward is more the joy of pursuit than of possession. It is recognized that the solution of any problem will raise more questions than it answers, so that man is committed—"doomed," from the standpoint of the quietistic ideal—to strive toward goals which recede more rapidly than he as an individual, or even society, advances toward them. Thus life is finally, if one chooses, or if one's temperament so dictates, a sort of labor of Sisyphus.

If this is condemned as unsatisfactory, the modern mind is at least committed to comparing alternatives; and the alternative, to the modern vision, is simply annihilation, death, as the only state of perfect peace. Thus the final issue, or dilemma, or predicament, is that of believing in life or not believing in it—optimism or pessimism. The religious view is pessimism, absolute in the Hindu version, and as far as earthly life (the only life we know) is concerned, in that of historical Christianity. Moreover, the facts of life seem to make it clear that the compromise of a "stationary" social life and culture, which was the working ideal of medieval thought, is not open. We must apparently move in some direction, either forward or backward. And we probably do not have the choice, in any rational sense, of going backward to barbarism and a brute existence. If civilization is destroyed, it will be through misdirected effort to make it better and not through passive indifference or deliberate rejection. There is a story of a man who persuaded the human race to bring the sorry tale of history to an end, painlessly, through race suicide. Being an exceedingly tough individual, he was the last human being left alive. As he was walking along a beach, waiting for his own final call and contemplating with great satisfaction the consummation of his life endeavor, he looked up and saw a large gray ape walk out of the woods upon the sand and proceed to build a fire.

CHAPTER FIVE

Politics and Ethics in Free Society

THE ideal of active individual freedom gives a highly distinctive form to the problem of political order and political life. In the modern period of history, roughly the past two centuries, our culture has developed political freedom, embodied in representative institutions; we have become committed to democracy as an ideal on its own account and as a prerequisite for other freedoms, religious, cultural, social and economic. The relations between economic and political freedom will be the topic of the following chapter; the present chapter deals with the meaning and problems of democracy itself, with only incidental reference to the particular tasks and dangers confronted by it, which happen to come from the side of economic life.

The meaning of democracy, in one view, is that social-ethical problems have come to be recognized as social problems in an entirely new meaning. They are problems *for* society—conceived as made up of the whole body of its members or citizens—problems to be solved by as well as for the people, in Lincoln's familiar words. Free and equal participation, or voice, in dealing with social problems follows from the basic modern ethical conception of active autonomous and responsible personality, in contrast with the older ideal, and specifically the historical Christian ideal, of obedience to whatever law and authority are established. Thus a part of our present task is to consider the meaning of a social problem, or the nature of social action, in what is finally the only proper meaning of these concepts. The ideal of government

73

by the people carries with it a new conception of government for the people, namely that people are their own judges of what is good for them, in contrast with the most benevolent authoritarian rule. Non-democratic systems, including modern totalitarianism, also claim to govern for the people; but apart from the fact that such governments are more likely to treat the people as instrumental to the purposes of the rulers, liberals regard self-government as ethically superior.

In the nature of the case, any social problem arises out of a combination of conflicting and harmonious interests of individuals. Men could not be free, or really human, until they felt unfree, until they consciously raised questions about their pattern of social life, based on custom and authority; and this questioning entails disagreement. It is disagreement which gives rise to social problems. But, on the other hand, there can be no social problem apart from agreement, or recognized unity of interests. For in the absence of the latter each individual could simply "go his own way in peace." (We assume that peace is preferable to violence.) It is also essential to the conception of a social problem that it arises out of conflicts of *ideals* which are more than mere interests. If the problems presented to individuals by conflicts of individual interests are to be dealt with by any form of social or joint, yet free, action, this must be of the nature of *discussion*. But discussion of conflicts of interests is impossible unless they also reflect differences of opinion, with respect to some conception of objective right, and truth about right. Discussion, envisaging agreement, is conceivable only in relation to some super-individual norm, in contrast with individual desire. Mere assertion of individual interests, in propositions beginning with the words "I want," is not discussion and cannot possibly tend to establish agreement, reconcile differences or eliminate conflict. The norms presupposed in discussion of conflicting interests, looking toward harmonizing them, must be at once ethical and intellectual; what is good must be a question to be answered by intelligence.

The "terms of association" form the content or subject matter of any disagreement which gives rise to a group problem. It is self-evident that if any number of individuals are to associate in any way, for work or play or even casual conversation, the pattern and terms of association must be the same for all. All the parties to any association must agree upon "rules." Agreement may be passive, even unconscious, or it may in varying degree be forced; and where there is no awareness of disharmony, an outside observer may still think problems ought to arise. We have already sketched the relations between three great principles of human social order—custom, authority and free association. It must be kept in mind that even the freest social order presents a combination of the three principles, and in particular that the social pattern must always be largely customary and undisputed. Freedom to change is necessarily limited. For the most part social forms have just grown up (as already remarked), or they have been established by force. (The theory of an original social contract is not now taken seriously, if it ever was; but the phrase has meaning for characterizing democracy.) And when any change is effected, by force or democratic action, the result must become established as a custom. Only a limited amount of serious questioning is possible without destructive disorganization.

In fact, the great bulk even of the most purely individual behavior must be habitual. Freedom in the metaphysical sense is conceivable only within a narrow range of choice, within limits set by the nature of the chooser, his established responses or the principles which guide his choices—all fixed in the past—in relation to the given conditions of action. And the scope of freedom is much narrower in the case of group choice, or individual choice where relations with others are involved. To act intelligently in any social situation the individual must know how to expect others to act. One individual can choose or plan intelligently in a group of any size only if all others act "predictably" and if he predicts correctly.

This means, *prima facie*, that the others do not choose rationally but mechanically follow an established and known pattern, or else that the first party has coercive power, through force or deception. (Persuasion is a species of force, based on deception; and all coercion presupposes metaphysical freedom in both parties.) Without some procedure for co-ordination, any real activity on the part of an individual, any departure from past routine, must disappoint the expectations and upset the plans of others who count on him to act in a way predicted from his past behavior. Change in group life can be rationally directed, from the standpoint of all members, only if all either plan jointly, in advance, any particular action or if they agree upon rules and obey the rules until they are changed by common action or consent. Such change in the law is the meaning of democratic legislation. Ideally, all members of any society participate equally in this activity; to the extent that any individual is denied participation, he is not treated as a member of the group.

Democracy, in this modern interpretation, is the unique achievement, in ideal and in fact, of modern Western civilization. As already observed, our modern European world must be understood as an evolution, involving a two-stage revolution, from the medieval social order of feudalism and ecclesiasticism. While more or less representative legislatures, estates or parliaments go back to the thirteenth century, they were not really democratic; and the product of late medieval and Renascence changes was absolute monarchy based upon divine right. Modern democracy is to be dated—as nearly as any great change has a historical date—from the revolutions of the seventeenth century in England, and the eighteenth and early nineteenth in the rest of the European world, largely influenced by contemporary developments on several frontiers, geographic and scientific-technological.

The historically unprecedented character of the modern situation and of its basic moral and political ideals means that the political theories of the classical writers of the past, like the teachings of religion, have little direct relevance for our problems. Greek city-state democracy in particular has little significance as a historical prototype of modern free society. The states were extremely small; they were really oligarchies, with citizenship (and culture) restricted to a limited upper class, and, notably in the case of Athens, economic prosperity was based on imperial tribute and on silver mined largely by state slaves; and finally, they were short-lived. These tiny, ephemeral and only semi-democratic states, based on slavery, class distinctions and the subjection of women, and without true representative institutions, contribute little to an understanding of the problems of democracy today, in which differences in status are obliterated in ideal and largely in fact. Apart from the tradition of government by law embodying accepted moral standards rather than personal fiat, the ideals of modern free society were not acceptable to the political thought of Greece or Rome, nor yet to Judaism or later Christian Europe prior to the age of the Enlightenment. Even later and in our own country, progress was gradual. Both slavery and a severely limited suffrage were generally taken for granted in the states when the Constitution was adopted; slavery was abolished in the second half of the nineteenth century by civil war, and the last step in the establishment of universal suffrage, the abolition of the sex qualification, was taken only in the twentieth century, after the First World War.

The general problem of democratic society is the problem of law. We are concerned here with the formal problem, in contrast with that of the right content of the law, in relation to any particular conflict of interest. The ultimate meaning of the democratic ideal would be "anarchy," in the sense of the absence of compulsion. Democracy, in Lord Bryce's famous definition, is government by discussion; and discussion, correctly defined, excludes coercion; it means voluntary agreement, by rational process. It follows that within wide limits self-government is ethically preferable to good government—though all such general statements are valid only within limits, and the limits are a matter of judgment, not of formal rule. But democracy is also strongly supported by the argument from expediency; for if the masses are not trusted with power over themselves, some individual or limited group must be trusted with arbitrary power over them. In practice, the authority will be self-selected, confirmed by force. In any case the evils of arbitrary political power are now recognized, and there is no need to argue that within wide limits abuse of freedom is preferable to abuse of power.

To say that ideal democracy is anarchistic does not mean that it is "antinomian," that there is no law, in the most general meaning of the term. Social life is hardly conceivable without established stable and accepted patterns of individual and associative behavior. Even under ideal anarchy questions may arise as to what the pattern ought to be and how to effect desirable changes. The ideal requires merely that in such cases the membership of the group shall be able to come to agreement through free discussion, without coercion or deception (persuasion) and without disorder and disorganization.

It should be emphasized that this ideal is approximately achieved in reality in modern democratic states, though in an indirect way. There is general agreement on a constitution, defining a procedure for making law, i.e., for changing the established law, including the constitution itself. And most men accept and obey the laws, as lawfully and rightfully made and administered, even when they disagree as to what the law ought to be in its concrete content. Actual coercion, through the threat of punishment, is in question chiefly for a small fraction of the adult population classed as criminal or defective. It is a serious error to view democracy as meaning that any majority has the *right* to rule the minority by coercion; subservience of any part of society to the interests of another part is utterly contrary to the democratic ideal. The principle of voting and majority decision is a method of forming and expressing the general will, based on a general opinion as to what is right, or as to right methods of adjudication of differences. And the reality must undoubtedly approximate this ideal if democratic institutions are not to break down.

The first and major problem of free society is not what, specifically, the law ought to be in particular situations, or which of the possible alternatives should be adopted; the prior question is whether there should be a law at all, or in general, what is to be the scope of law, relative to the sphere of individual freedom and voluntary association. The primary function of law is to define its own scope, to draw a line of demarcation between the region of behavior which is to conform to explicit uniform rules and that which is left to the unrestricted choice of the individual, to agreement upon rules or to *ad hoc* agreement among the individuals who may be concerned in any activity. It is a matter of the right limits of toleration, or freedom to disagree.

Freedom in society is to be defined not merely by antithesis to coercion (never to mechanistic determinism) but by antithesis to *wrongful* coercion. It is inherently an ethical concept; such coercion, which is really the concept to be defined in defining political freedom, means some violation of the *rights* of the individual. But since all law, in the ordinary meaning of rules which include provision for enforcement—i.e., all law which gives rise to serious problems—is formally coercive, the minimizing of such law is a norm and objective of right social policy. However (apart from the ordinary criminal code), intelligent people do not object to such obstructions to free movement as a strong fence along the edge of a cliff, to legal protection against their own gross ignorance or negligence or to rules clearly required to safeguard the rights of all. Such measures include sanitary laws and restrictions on the practice of medicine, requirements as to the quality of foods offered for sale, safety appliances on dangerous machinery, and the like. Few object to prohibition of drunken driving, whatever they may think about the right to become intoxicated where important interests of others are not involved. It has become a proverb that freedom in social life must mean freedom under law. The practical moral-political problem is that of giving the law such scope and content as will achieve "maximum freedom" on the whole. Or, it is to minimize mutual interference and the arbitrary use of power by individuals and by the political authority itself. (This is the problem with respect to freedom for given individuals; as the next chapter will show, there is another side of the problem, a long-view task which is at least equally important, namely, the endowment of individuals with both power or "capacity" and interests or "taste," specifically in economic relations.)

There is another way of looking at law which is useful in clarifying its primary function of defining and protecting a sphere of individual freedom. This is to view law as fixing the terms or conditions of membership in any group. In this sense, the law of any group is the content or meaning of the group itself, as a unit, a society or an association. Thus the freedom of the individual as a member of any group is defined by three factors. The first is the law of the group, which he must obey as a condition of continuing to be a member; the second is his freedom and power to leave the group; and the third is participation in making—accurately speaking, in changing—the law of the group to which he belongs. Together, the three factors measure the degree to which any organization approximates the democratic ideal.

In the discussion thus far, dealing with social freedom, the implicit reference has been to political society, political freedom and political law. What has been said should make it clear that every organization having any degree of permanence and stability has more or less coercive power over its members and might logically be described as a political entity, or as "sovereign," to the degree that its members lack effective freedom to cease to belong to it. In extreme cases, this freedom may be practically zero, even where the organization is not nominally a political one. This may be the case with an economic organization, a business enterprise or a labor union; the individual's opportunity to make a living may even depend on his being a member in good standing of a particular church or fraternal order. What is usually called political society in the world today is exemplified primarily by the sovereign state. It is distinguished from other associations by this sovereignty (*de jure* or *de facto*) over a territory with definite geographic boundaries. The individual is a member of a particular state, and subject to its laws, chiefly through residence within its territory. (Qualifying conditions may here be ignored.) For various reasons one's effective freedom (freedom and power) to leave his country is subject to special limitations, and the power of the state over its citizens or subjects is in that degree peculiar.

The actual working of any institution depends at least as much upon the character of the men who live under and operate it as it does on its structure and laws. Consequently, the nature of democratic social change may be either moral or politico-legal, and the relations between the two types may vary widely. Accordingly, discussion, or propaganda, or preaching, may be directed toward either form of free change, while in reality most social agitation for change is largely quest of power. The principle that formal law is to be minimized creates a presumption that the moral type of social change is to be preferred to the legal type, as far as the former method is practicable. This runs contrary to a tendency in human nature to assume that the way to effect any change is to "pass a law" and apply compulsion.

Our account of political ethics has recognized two forms of moral obligation: obedience to law and custom, and co-operative participation in the effort to improve them. The second obligation is not contained in the older conception of political duty, specifically the historical Christian view, which enjoined obedience to any existing law and established authority. In our own discussion so far it has been tacitly assumed that democracy is of the most ideal and perfect form, in which all citizens are law-abiding and there are no serious conscientious disagreements as to what the law is or what it ought to be, in scope or content. In real life there are, unhappily, other aspects of the problem, which are in practice far more serious and which may become tragic. The member of any free society has the obligation to take part in the "dirty work" of enforcing the law in the literal sense. In modern states, the more violent aspects of law enforcement are, of course, delegated to individuals specialized to this vocation, the police. The citizen in kid gloves is not compelled to act directly, apart from rare emergencies, and so far in history it has been possible to recruit the police on a voluntary basis, i.e., by hiring the individuals in the free market. But even such obligations as reporting offenses, serving as a witness and jury duty tend to be shirked by most people, especially those of the upper classes, and compulsion often has to be employed.

Far more serious still is the ethical problem raised by occasions in which the individual finds his "conscience" opposed to the regularly enacted law, perhaps outraged by it. This situation gives rise to a conflict of duties—the major fact in the moral life in the rational view, as we have repeatedly observed. We may pass over the case, familiar enough in fact, where the formally enacted law does not actually represent even the will of a majority in the constitutional or legal sense but is the result of political manipulation, trickery or high-handed action. Even in connection with the most legitimate law, the individual may confront the duty as well as the right of quiet disobedience, ranging to open defiance, resistance and organized insurrection. There is no formula which will solve these problems. The individual can only use his best judgment and strive to make his judgment as good as possible. The student of political ethics must recognize that the whole principle of majority rule represents a compromise with the ideal, which would call for unanimity; the theory assumes that morally and rationally ideal men would never disagree. In fact, a popular majority may be nearly as irrational and as tyrannical as an individual or class despotism. On the other hand, it must be recognized that any really human life must be lived in orderly society ("order is Heaven's first law") and that order must be largely a matter of conformity to law and custom. Consequently these must, within wide limits, be given the benefit of the doubt.

In the realities of life, however, progress in the improvement of the legal and traditional order comes about largely through nonconformity and disobedience by individuals who have come to have "higher" standards—and in cases of acute crisis, through open resistance and armed conflict. The case of slavery in American history is perhaps a sufficient illustration, and its complexities need not be discussed. A contemporary Christian writer has pointed out that even in such a case as institutionalized cannibalism or head-hunting the consequence of abrupt suppression by force might well be the complete demoralization of the society in question.

The view that obedience is the whole political duty of the individual assumed that there would be no question as to what law or authority should be obeyed. Under the conditions in which Christianity was first promulgated it was not impossible to take this view. As noted earlier, this situation was changed, even before the end of the period covered by the composition of the New Testament, through the requirement of a formal religious sacrifice as a symbol of allegiance to the Roman emperor. Thus began the conflict between church and state, which became the central fact in the history of western Europe throughout the Middle Ages and into the modern period. With the separation of church and state the problem is merged into that of religious liberty, including freedom of religious association. In the Middle Ages, in consequence of the claim of the Roman Church to supremacy over the political order, and its contention that its laws were laws of God and its will the will of God, and that both must be obeyed rather than any laws or commands of men, a conscientious individual often confronted the two-fold problem of (a) whether to obey the church or the state or (b) whether to follow his own conscience rather than obey either. In the later Middle Ages many leading individual authorities in the church, including Dante and Aquinas (in contrast with Augustine), hedged more or less on the question of obedience to ecclesiastical law or mandate against individual conscience.

The discussion so far in this chapter has implicitly dealt with the ethics of political relations within a society or group reasonably homogeneous morally and culturally. At least it has assumed the absence of differences considered intolerable, or actually associated with sanctity and intolerance such as the historical Jewish-Christian (and Moslem) religious attitude, and many other features of social-cultural and political ideals held by various groups in the world today. For good or for ill, the human "family"—the inclusive class of those who are possible parties to political and moral discussion—is not of this character. Man as a human being is at once the creation and the preserver and progressive creator of culture. Culture, again, is a phenomenon of organized group life; and, whatever our ultimate ideals may be, the brute fact in terms of which we must live in the world and solve our political problems is that both society and culture exist in the plural. Moreover, societies and cultures are both enormously numerous and diverse, and they must live in a relation of competition for space (*Lebensraum!*) and the resources necessary for physical and cultural life.

It is also an essential feature of the problem of political

ethics that human character and life are high or low, good or bad, at least as much because of the high or low ranking of cultures as because of attitudes of will or any individual qualities. Man is a social-cultural being whose nature is for the most part determined by that of the culture in which he grows up. Whether we take the backward-looking view of history, facing the problem of interpretation and explanation, or the forward-looking view, in terms of problems of social action, human society is not so much an aggregation of individuals having certain characteristics and standing in certain moral and organizational relations, as it is a complex of groups, each of which perpetuates a social inheritance at the same time that it perpetuates itself biologically. This social inheritance includes the structure of social relations, the law and all material resources and artifacts, instrumental, esthetic or religious, and the knowledge and traditions they embody, and also personal ideals and capacities. In all of these, the social aspect bulks larger than the individual. The pattern of groups and of culture traits, even within a single major culture (in the anthropological meaning), is enormously complex. The smallest unit, for purposes of analysis and for action, is the family, in some institutional form. In our own society, it is nominally the "natural" family of a man and wife and their children, though its real scope is wider and less definite. Great differences in kind and level of culture exist between families, even those which are closest neighbors. This is partly because of "natural" traits, biologically inherited, but is largely because every family is a member of many and diverse communities. Even the different individuals in the same family are from early childhood members of various groups and inherit, or are influenced by, divergent culture standards.

Beyond the complex of communities to which any individual belongs by way of face-to-face association or written communication are larger complexes based upon stable customary relationships, partly embodied in formal law.

However, major cultural similarities and differences correspond in widely varying degree with politico-legal units, i.e.,
with the sovereign states of international law, and other
political divisions. The most serious difficulty, for discussion
of the problem of social policy and action, is the vagueness
and inconsistency of ethical ideals with respect to culture
differences. No one can say how far or in what respects
the conception of an ideal social or world order calls for
cultural uniformity or diversity. The practical problem is
especially difficult because culture, including ultimate standards, is practically speaking (socially) inherited; it is only to a
minor degree a matter of free individual or group choice,
but is for the most part determined by historical causes little
subject to control.

The primary fact in the distinction and classification of
cultures is undoubtedly language, with religion less clearly
next in order. The problem of ideals in both these connections presents many anomalies. Most students of language do not consider that one language is intrinsically
better than another. All languages have points of superiority
and of weakness. From a utilitarian point of view a universal
language is *prima facie* the ideal; but there are other considerations, for the project obviously is not to be considered
in terms of immediate practical politics, even for nationali-
ties with closely related languages, and cultures similar in
other respects. Language often seems to be the central
fact in the idea of cultural freedom over which modern wars
are fought. Apart from emotional loyalty to an inherited
language as such, the issue centers in the divergent national
literatures and traditions.

With respect to religion, the problem as to what is ideal
is even more puzzling. Most men, in our society, would
doubtless agree that ideally all should have a common religion—each meaning that his own religious sect should super-
sede all others! This attitude is due historically to Christianity, as a nominally monotheistic world religion and con-

sequently "intolerant." Its relation in this respect to its parent, Judaism, presents a complex problem, as the latter never became fully, evangelistically, proselytic. The third great Semitic religion, Islam, stood for indefinite extension by conquest, with incorporation into its theocratic political order. Historical Christianity was nearly or quite as political in character, and as politically aggressive, whenever and wherever it possessed the requisite minimum of organized unity and power. It required the terrible wars of religion of the sixteenth and seventeenth centuries to convince the European peoples that religious unity is (a) unattainable, at least by force, and (b) unnecessary for morality and political harmony.

It would be impossible to say how far any existing Christian church, or its membership, is really tolerant in spirit, or how far political freedom of religion, as it prevails in Western states, is the product of religious indifference, in comparison with other interests. And it is problematical how far the spirit of brotherhood, humanitarianism or mutualism as it exists, within any sect or across sectarian lines in larger social areas, has any connection with religion. *Prima facie*, religion plays a minor role in the internal politics of states and in international relations; the latter fact is shown by inspecting the religious line-up in modern wars and especially in the two twentieth-century world wars. However, to whatever extent our religious tradition stands for any working individualism, and its logical correlate, cosmopolitanism, the theory presupposes religious and ecclesiastical unification. This is still clearly the position of the Roman Catholic Church, and at least some other large and effectively organized Christian bodies. This is the major change wrought in the mores of inter-group relations by Christianity, and the principle or presupposition is a large negative contribution to the problem of having peace and order within states and in the world.

It should be noted that religious differences, in theological belief and ritual practice, are much greater than differences in the ethical principles of ordinary human relations, either as taught by the different religions or as embodied in custom and law. Yet the adherents of any religion commonly hold that particular one to be indispensable to morality and social order; the one point on which practically all religious men are agreed is antagonism to any suggestion of replacing religion by rational ethics. But cultural differences, in the narrow sense, and the accidents of political organization, are actually far more important than either religion or ethics as ultimate causes of antagonism and strife.

Irrespective of religion, men should undoubtedly agree on major ethical ideals, and they must do so as a condition of living together in peace and harmony in any society, whatever its nature or extent, including world federation. But there would be little agreement as to either the scope of the ethical ideals on which agreement is necessary, as opposed to tolerance, or their concrete character. With respect to the content of social and political ethics, three possibilities are conceivable. The first is the perpetuation of standards solely by social inheritance (with the relations between morality, authority and religion as a side issue). The second abstract possibility is rational discussion leading to agreement. And the third is settlement of conflicts by force, eventually by fighting, and the absorption of the weaker by the strongest. However, as soon as any moral question is raised and recognized as a question, the issue lies only between the second and third alternatives, discussion and force. It is practically impossible for social discussion, once started, to turn itself off; a culture cannot go back to the traditional basis after this has ceased to function and serious differences of opinion, and controversy, have arisen.

One great and permanent lesson of modern history and modern thought is the inevitable role of force in the relations between free individuals and groups, backing up tradition or arbitrary will. The modern world has in fact passed beyond the stages of tradition and of authority traditionally accepted. But the area in which men and groups can reach agreement voluntarily, by purely intellectual methods, is limited. Consequently, war can be avoided only if one party to any serious dispute—either the weaker or the more pacifistic—will yield without fighting. Of course both might agree upon an arbitrator and give him the vast power required to deal with serious issues, but this would usually be ethically undesirable. The advent of democracy, in limited regions, has not changed this situation.

The lesson referred to has been made clear by the discovery of biological evolution. Human life is not only a struggle against nature on the part of man to achieve his desires and realize his ideals; it also involves struggle and conflict between human individuals and groups. This follows inexorably from the three facts pointed out above: (a) that man is a social being whose human life is based upon intelligent use of means—to live and to rise or to remain above the brute level; (b) that human life is lived in groups characterized by cultural diversity; and (c) that culture groups compete for the limited means of self-preservation and expansion. Groups could not voluntarily change their culture rapidly if they would; and in fact, each thinks its own is best and wishes to preserve and propagate it, and in this wish, this loyalty, most human moral values are bound up. There is always co-operation between groups, as well as competition, but the combination of the two relationships only complicates the moral problem and makes it the more acute. Any group, from a family to an international alliance, must finally choose, consciously or unconsciously, between increase and decline, and ultimately between survival and extinction, along with all distinctive features of its culture—and/or its race.

In the main, biological and cultural survival and increase are so closely connected that we may pass over racial differences as chiefly an accentuating factor. The important partial exception is race prejudice and restriction of cultural opportunities practiced toward colored people of lowly origin who live in predominantly white societies and now have no distinctive culture of their own. Of course race and culture are separable in theory, and to some extent in fact; one group may expand biologically in relation to others while taking over an alien culture in place of its own. But the separation is a theoretical rather than an actual possibility (apart, again, from ex-slaves, or conquered aborigines, in states of European culture). Exceptions are more apparent than real. Japan is the outstanding example of a folk nation which has deliberately adopted important features of a foreign culture. But it was mainly the instrumental side of Western civilization that was taken over, and the change only intensified the competitive group struggle. In general, a group will fight, to exhaustion if not to biological extermination, to perpetuate the features of its culture which it regards as essential to its distinctive group life; and it is hard to contend that it ought not to do so.

The struggle for existence naturally has a different character and meaning at the human level, in contrast with that of the infra-human animals (or plant species). With some possible exception for colonial insects, man is the only animal who carries on war with groups of his own species for the resources, natural or (in the human case) artificial, and material or spiritual, that are necessary for life (or culture). In most sub-human forms competition does not seem to take the form of direct conflict, but the details of the process by which one type is replaced by another in the course of geologic ages are little understood. In man there is always a "state" in some form, an organization with the twofold function of keeping the peace internally and exercising power in relations with other states. Existing states rest on some degree of cultural homogeneity, and usually create a degree of emotional loyalty, if they function and endure.

Civil war is unusual. Competition between families—and between other and larger groups, classes and organizations within the state—is restricted to non-violent and largely to indirect forms. One form is the economic endeavor to live at a high standard and to accumulate wealth; and another is the political struggle for control of the machinery of the state. Success in the internal contest for power, and for a high standard of living, seems to have little positive relation, or even a negative one, to biological increase—a cause of concern which has given rise to "eugenics" agitation. But the relation of individual success in life to cultural advance cannot be discussed here.

In modern war it has not been the objective of states to deprive other peoples of life or the means of physical life or a fair level of culture. They may be forced to give up substantial economic resources under the name of indemnities, or to transfer sovereignty over territory; but beyond political subordination the extreme imposition in the case of "civilized" peoples is, or has been hitherto, gradual compulsory adoption of the culture of the conquerors, primarily their language. The treatment of minorities and of colonies, as an internal problem for the state, or one of international law, can only be mentioned here. The real issues in modern war are notoriously a puzzle to students of the problem. We confront the paradox that war is more or less plausibly viewed as defensive by both sides, but it is difficult to discover just what injury or threat of injury either party is defending itself against. Wars arise directly out of some diplomatic impasse, immediately centering largely in the question of who is the aggressor. Practically everyone, regardless of religious professions, admits that aggression is wrong and defense against aggression right; but no one offers an acceptable definition of aggression.

The substantive issues in international relations, which are recognized and discussed, center chiefly in the right of an ethnic and cultural group to cultural and political freedom or autonomy, and in trade relations. The actual distribution over the earth of such groups on the one hand, and of essential natural resources on the other, makes complete autonomy, combined with unrestricted control by each people over the resources of the areas it inhabits, patently impossible, or incompatible with the maintenance of civilization in the modern interpretation. This applies primarily to the world of European civilization, but that has come to mean, for practical political purposes, the habitable globe. As to trade, the policies which the states attempt to carry out cannot be justified in terms of economic interests. For the most part they are protectionistic, and protectionism is clearly anti-economic and rarely serves any other intelligible purpose. In comparison with free trade both war and colonies are also economically unprofitable, and the explanation of international rivalry and war must run in terms of political or cultural antagonism, or sheer partisanship.

The problem of a right to life and to cultural autonomy on the part of political units is inseparable from that of the right to expansion, growth or progress, geographic, economic, political and cultural. The claim to this right may rest on population pressure or alleged cultural superiority, including devotion to the one true religion. Only in recent times have nations begun to claim the right to have their people emigrate without loss of cultural connections or political allegiance, or the right to extend their culture over "backward" regions and peoples—the "white man's burden" (or that of the superior white or yellow "race").

Religion has been, until recently, an exception, for Christianity and Islam, justifying enslavement as well as conquest. With respect to these problems, we can only point out that they are vital for rational political ethics as well as for practical politics, and note the large element of unreason and hypocrisy in political and literary utterance relating to them. The lack of accepted standards is more glaring in international morality and law than in internal politics, while there are much more definite norms for relations between persons. It seems impossible to find in modern ethical common sense any accepted principles which give much help in judging the merits of an actual case of conflict of "rights" between nations or cultures.

The competitive struggle between human individuals and groups is made complex and subtle beyond the possibility of clear analysis by the capricious and arbitrary character of individual and group motives and ideals. In so far as these are at once stable and concrete, they are cultural rather than biological in origin and content. In a broad sense, the final ethical problem centers in the relations between quantity and quality of life, and between different "qualities" held to be good or bad, or better or worse. Both ethically and practically, the problem raises the issues of military power. In modern ethical thought, the obligation to be good, centering in having a "good" culture, is inseparable, for any culture group, from an obligation to be strong, economically and politically, and to use power in promoting the survival and extension of the highest civilization. Any attempt to renounce physical power is equivalent to suicide. In principle the police force is as much military as the army—a fact which pacifists usually find it convenient to ignore. Undoubtedly, conflicts of interests between men and groups should be settled, as far as possible, by discussion; and persuasion, while a form of coercion, is within limits preferable to violence as a technique —as far as it can be made to work—to the same result or one not too much worse. But in fact that is not very far, particularly in international relations; and where "higher" forms of technique fail, and the end is imperative, recourse must be had to "lower."

To the problem of group rights principles of ideal ethics offer no solution. Undoubtedly, conflicts should be adjusted, as far as practicable, first by rational procedure and then by such methods as will entail a minimum of destruction, or sacrifice of essential values. This tells us only that we should adopt the compromise which seems best on the whole. Those who find themselves in a weak position, and believe in what they stand for, certainly need to be as wise as serpents and as gentle as doves while they strive to build up strength, internally or through alliances. As to the "sticking point," of tolerance on the part of the strong and of submission on the part of the weak or pacific, no formula can supply an answer; it is a matter of individual and group judgment, involving many considerations of abstract right and of expediency. As to individual pacifists, a state can tolerate refusal of military service, as in the case of any other imperative social obligation, only to the extent that it is not a serious danger, or to the extent that toleration is socially more expedient than compulsion. Men also have conscientious reasons for refusing to support their families or do any productive work. Both the state and individuals need to recognize that a certain amount of nonconformity on idealistic grounds (but not too much) is a precious value in national or community life. This lesson is most needed by religious bodies.

It should be noted that, in principle, the moral issue of the right to a tolerable existence and to increase extends to the relations between human beings and the animals. In some religious traditions all animal life is held sacred, and some Christians interpret their religion as enjoining vegetarianism. (Dr. Albert Schweitzer, surely an enlightened Christian, confesses scruples against killing noxious insects in equatorial Africa, and even against using screens to prevent them from feeding upon himself and giving him dreadful diseases. Do microbes also have rights?!) In general, of course, Christianity has followed the Jewish tradition, which gave man unlimited dominion over all lower orders of creation; the Bible says little about even cruelty to animals. The rightness of eating and enslaving animals for human ends, and rearing them for this purpose, is now hardly questioned in our society; even opponents of vivisection are usually rated along with pacifists as anti-social cranks, happily not numerous enough to be a menace. In the abstract, it is hard not to sympathize with the view which assimilates the animals to man to the extent that any species clearly manifests pain, the fear of death or other conscious interests, and the feeling of disappointment.

In general, modern Christians do not carry their professed belief in universal love and non-resistance to a point where it does or threatens serious damage to their country and civilization. Inconsistency between profession and practice, and the practical consequences of the discrepancy, is another matter, but a topic on which we need not add to what has been said in other connections. Some exception as to Christian teaching being harmless might be made for pacifism, in the immediate background of the present world conflict. But the motives back of the appeasement policy in the democracies, and their neglect of their military establishments, which in effect caused the war, were not primarily religious or even unselfish; they were as complex and inconsistent as human motives typically are.

The greater danger from Christian ethics lies in the tendency to carry the sentimental, brotherhood morality of primitive tribal life—more especially the condemnation of differences in wealth and power, which are organizational conditions of efficiency—into practical measures of internal social reform to such an extent, or in such ways, as to work serious injury. The economic problem is the subject of the next chapter. In the field of international relations, which is our concern here, the main reason why there is little danger from the side of religion is doubtless the fact that exclusive national patriotism itself has become a kind of religion, and that group loyalty and inter-group antagonism seem to be impulses entering into original human nature. The issue of religious pacifism as a principle is perhaps disposed of by the fact that religions, and specifically historical Christianity, have openly stood for the use of force to resist efforts to convert them or to limit religious indoctrination of their children, and until recently for its use to convert others.

CHAPTER SIX

Economics and Political Ethics

THE conflicts which seem most important as a concrete source of discontent and a threat to peace and order in modern society are those which center in economic interests, and specifically in economic relationships regarded as unjust or ethically wrong. Discussion of the topic within the compass of a chapter in an essay of this sort can stress only a few of the most important general truths; and this will best be done by contrasting them with fallacious beliefs or presuppositions which are currently accepted in popular discussion and by religious and other agitators for reform.

The situation in popular thinking in the field of ethics and economics may be illustrated by brief reference to protectionism in international trade, the dominant economic issue in all modern politics. The outstanding fact is contradiction between what men do, or advocate, and both the economic and the ethical principles in which they profess to believe. Few will deny either that division of labor increases efficiency or that specialization is particularly advantageous for dwellers in different regions who possess different natural resources and differ in knowledge and skill. Moreover, an attempt to export without importing, to sell abroad without buying abroad, is patently an attempt to get rid of goods and get nothing in return. Yet for the most part, people talk, write and act, politically, as if they believed it good economic policy (for the nation, state, city or neighborhood) to encourage exports and to restrict imports, by taxation, "regulation" or outright prohibition. Again, the motive is that of profiting at the expense of the foreigner, and this is as flagrantly contrary to the rather mundane ethical idea of mutuality, to say nothing of the brotherhood of man, as the policy is contrary to the economic norm of productive efficiency. Yet those who advocate the protective policy are undoubtedly sincere in their professions of belief in brotherhood, as well as in economic co-operation for mutual advantage. The vast range of phenomena typified by this example makes rational discussion difficult and causes it to seem unreal and futile.

The first requirement for an intelligent discussion of economic issues is an understanding of their meaning in relation to other problems. To begin with, "economy" means the "effective" use of any means to realize any end. Ends are taken as "given," as not in question or already decided upon; that problem is left to other inquiries. The problem of economy is to use the given means so as to secure a *maximum* total achievement. Second, the problem calls for economizing all means, natural and artificial, not merely human effort or capacity. The more serious fallacy, however, is the restriction of the economic interest to some limited class of ends, usually designated as "lower," in contrast with the "higher." The pursuit of any end calls for economy of means, and in fact the standard of living is almost entirely a matter of the level of cultural life. Finally, the main subject matter of economic discussion is not individual behavior but the *organization* of economic subjects for *co-operation* with a view to increased efficiency. The conflicts of interest which give rise to social economic problems relate either to the terms of co-operation or to the rights of individuals to the possession and free use of resources. These two issues make up the general problem of economic ethics.

The notion that our serious social conflicts center in economic life, or seem to do so, calls for some qualification. In connection with war, the most serious problem of all, the limitations of this view were earlier touched upon. It was also shown that within a state conflicts of all kinds arise between groups, families, communities and classes far more than between literal individuals. Reflection will reveal, further, that it is rather an accident that internal social conflicts take the economic form. This will be clear if one pictures the situation which would result if every adult were granted the power to work physical miracles, and could bring about any desired physical result simply by wishing, thus eliminating all problems of production and distribution. Problems of associative life would then arise only in the other two of the three main forms of interest and activity we have recognized, i.e., in play and culture. But without some revolutionary change in human nature, conflicts in these fields would be fully as acute as those to which economic interests give rise, and they would not be essentially different in form. It is probable that the necessity of economic activity and co-operation actually reduces social conflict on the whole. Man is by nature self-assertive and competitive, and is also disposed to gang up in conflicts and contests, whether or not any real advantage is at stake.

Still less, as a little use of imagination should reveal, is social conflict in the field of economic activity bound up with the particular method or form of economic organization which prevails in the modern world, i.e., the market or price economy called, or rather miscalled, "capitalism." The essential features of economic conflict as we know it would be present in a society in which economic activity was not organized at all, or was organized on any conceivable pattern. The former fact will be clear if we think of a society entirely without co-operation, with all production conducted on a basis of "individual" self-sufficiency. The term "individual" is placed between quotation marks because the individual cannot possibly be the real unit in social structure. We shall later stress the importance of the fact that "individualistic" social order is really familistic, and also rests upon innumerable larger institutional groupings. In a society based on family self-sufficiency, then, economic conflict would arise, in the essential form in which we know it under the "capitalistic" system of organization, and perhaps to an equal or greater degree. There would be economic inequality and insecurity, along with injustice, as judged by the same standards; and inequality would also tend to increase cumulatively, both during the individual life and from generation to generation.

The facts of life in relation to liberal ethical ideals and other values force us to recognize poverty as a world affliction. Even the wealthiest regions lack the material means, the power of man over nature (in fact largely spiritual in content) which would be necessary to a "good" life, affording everyone either effective freedom or a humanly satisfactory standard of living, defined in cultural terms. Individual freedom from poverty is possible only for a few, and through inequality and exploitation. General poverty can be reduced through (a) the rational—in the sense of economic—use of means, and (b) the gradual accumulation of more means than are now available, including more knowledge and better organization. Of course, increased production on the whole must be accompanied by an equitable distribution of the immediate means of life. Liberal ethics is distinguished by insisting upon the diffusion of cultural life and opportunity for free activity and development among the masses, in contrast with using them as means for providing a high material and cultural standard for a small social élite.

The first axiom of liberal ethics is freedom, in the active meaning of rationally directed activity. Freedom is always regarded as good, intrinsically as well as instrumentally, but liberal thought has overemphasized the instrumental aspect of freedom as the best way to secure economic efficiency and progress. Men actually prefer freedom to efficiency, within limits; and both our highest ideals and our laws and institutions recognize that they ought to do so if they do not, and may even rightly be forced to be free. No one is allowed to contract away his freedom, to sell himself (or his children) into servitude, even if he believes that other advantages to be gained outweigh the value of freedom. A more serious weakness of liberal thought, at least in the early modern period (one in which it resembled the Christian tradition) was relative neglect of the fact that effective freedom calls for control over means. Freedom proper, or formal freedom —mere absence of coercion—is empty without *power*. Effective freedom must have both these dimensions, and the power dimension must include both personal capacity and external means; both are largely the historical creation of society and culture.

The principle that the problem of conduct is one of compromise and balance between ideals, as well as between interests, is strikingly valid for the social-economic problem. The conditions of productive efficiency, particularly the necessity of large-scale organization, limit individual freedom. The requirements of economic progress are in part inimical to both freedom and efficiency, while in some respects they are harmonious. Progress also depends on conditions which give rise to insecurity and to some extent interfere with efficiency. There is at any time a direct conflict between a high standard of living and provision for economic growth. Increase of the resources (of all kinds) necessary for cultural life requires *diverting* resources in hand from use in maintaining a higher standard at the moment to the use of creating additional resources. This is the meaning of saving and investment. Finally, all the more strictly economic objectives in part run counter to the ideals of equality or justice (in some meanings) and of "fellowship." The economic conflict between present and future is especially important because an individualistic or free society leaves the choice and compromise in the main to individuals—always meaning to the family, the primary social unit. Individual and family accumulation tend to progressive growth of inequality, as already noted.

Any program of action must start from the situation as it exists, here and now. Consequently, the first major step looking to intelligent action is an understanding of the modern organization of production and distribution. Adequate treatment of this phase of the problem would call for a treatise on economics. We can here only point out a few major fallacies commonly accepted as the basis for action, with results which are unquestionably bad. For the most part, such fallacies are due to thinking romantically instead of objectively.

The main function of economic organization, in liberal society, is co-operation in production for the purpose of increasing effectiveness in the use of individual means to realize individual ends, freely chosen. Consumption remains relatively unorganized, the natural family being the principal unit. (It must not be forgotten that activity and co-operation have intrinsic values apart from resulting consumption.) Any co-operation between individuals performing specialized functions may be viewed as an exchange of services. But where individual ends differ, free co-operation of a considerable number of persons is possible only through exchange organized in markets. A free market establishes a uniform price, over which no individual has any appreciable control. A free market means a competitive market, but there is no psychological competition, no feeling of rivalry between buyers or sellers; if there is rivalry, it is because emulation or dominance is preferred to efficient co-operation. For the most part, the economic motive prevails in reality; the purchaser at a retail store has little or no competitive feeling toward other purchasers, and on the side of the sellers such a feeling reflects a desire to restrict the market by securing a monopoly.

The modern organization of production and distribution represents an advanced stage in the development of exchange economy. In contrast with a more primitive form, individuals no longer produce and exchange goods or services, directly or through the medium of money. Production is organized in large units or enterprises, which typically have the form of a business corporation. The corporation, again, is an advanced embodiment of the principle known as entrepreneurship. A limited number of individuals (roughly the owners of common stock) take the initiative in production and assume responsibility and business risk. This collective entrepreneur replaces the single individual of the more primitive stage—with the partnership as an intermediate type. The entrepreneur buys productive services from the other participants, laborers or property owners, and sells the product at prices determined in both cases by market competition, always more or less imperfect. The entrepreneur form of organization gives rise to the problem of distribution in its familiar monetary form. Laborers receive wages, property owners interest or rent. The entrepreneur also receives *virtual* wages, interest or rent at market rates for the services he himself furnishes to the enterprise; and in addition he makes a *profit,* or incurs a *loss,* depending on his success or failure, in comparison with his competitors, in directing production in accord with consumers' demand and in achieving technical efficiency. Direct management is largely delegated by the entrepreneurs to agents who work for a salary and are thus in the position of laborers; but the entrepreneurs carry the ultimate responsibility and take the risk of the managerial decisions of these employees being good or bad. It is an essential fact, well known but generally ignored or flouted, that on the average entrepreneurs' losses equal or exceed their gains. This is in accord with theoretical expectations, and statistical investigation discloses no aggregate net profit, over substantial periods of time, as a share in the social distribution.

A perfectly competitive economy would realize for each individual the ideal combination of freedom and efficiency, in the meaning which these principles would have for an individual acting under the condition of complete self-sufficiency. That is, the meaning would be the same as for a Robinson Crusoe (or a Swiss Family Robinson) living entirely apart from other human beings. To the extent that competition prevails, the only difference between organized and self-sufficient economic life lies in the enormous gain in efficiency which results from specialization. In effect, each individual uses his own resources in his own way to satisfy his own wants. To be sure, he is free to make wrong choices (through error or prejudice) as consumer or producer. But he is likewise free to place any of his activities under the direction of any other person whom he may judge more competent than himself, subject to agreement with the other party on the terms of the arrangement, which is like any other exchange of services. Finally, any two parties are free to buy and sell on any terms other than those ruling in the market, upon which they can agree as being better on any ground; this amounts to freedom to give and to receive gifts, since nominal exchange on terms other than those of the market is a mixture of exchange and gift.

Before turning to an ethical appraisal of the enterprise economy—specifically corporate enterprise—it is in order to refer briefly to the historical experience of modern society under this system of organization. Roughly speaking, the nineteenth century was the age of liberalism. It is proverbially known as the "wonderful century." It was the age of freedom, religious, political and social as well as economic. It was characterized by unparalleled progress in science, pure and applied, in the mastery of mind over matter and the elevation of the general standard of life, cultural as well as in terms of the so-called material values of health, comfort and leisure. Its most distinctive achievement was the diffusion of personal freedom and cultural participation over the whole mass of the population. This applies not only to the advanced nations; the benefits (and attendant evils) have also spread widely to peoples who had little to do with the creative advance. Ethically, the age of liberalism was also to an unparalleled degree one of humanitarian idealism and benevolence, and of respect for the dignity and rights of the individual—"A man's a man for a' that." Yet this century eventuated in unprecedented self-criticism and discontent, in growing internal class conflict, threatening war, and in actual international war, on a world scale, threatening universal destruction. This paradox is rooted in growth of ideals and expectations beyond achievements; it sets the problem which we have to investigate in terms of economic ethics.

The statement that under perfect competition the free-enterprise organization of economic life would achieve for everyone the best combination of freedom and efficiency does not at all imply either that the actual system is ethically ideal or that nothing can be done to improve it. The results diverge from the ideal for two main reasons. On one hand, perfect competition is not present in real life; many necessary conditions are absent, and individual freedom does not tend automatically to establish them. On the other hand, the evils imputed to the economic order, especially inequality and injustice, are by no means due merely to the failure of market competition. This idea is one of the major fallacies in popular and reformist economic thinking. A little reflection would show that any close approximation to theoretically perfect competition would be intolerable. As to mechanical defects, without going into an extended analysis in terms of technical economics it is possible only to make a few brief assertive statements about two of the most serious.

By far the most serious problem arises out of the tendency of a market economy under real conditions to fall into oscillatory changes or cycles of expansion and contraction. These occur in most fields of production, but of course the main source of hardship and insecurity is the alternation of boom and depression in economic life as a whole which is known as "the business cycle." Only two observations can be made about this phenomenon here. The first is that practically no one profits by it; hence conflicts of interest are not a factor in the problem. Remedial action is a matter of scientific understanding and political and administrative competence. In the second place, the causality of the cycle centers in large-scale organization, with the use of capital and especially of money, which could not be abolished without both destroying freedom and throwing society back to primitive barbarism. We cannot here go into the technical problem of controlling the flow of money and the differential price changes which make production now excessively profitable and now unprofitable, causing boom and depression.

The second mechanical criticism centers in monopoly. It is the evil of which most is made in popular and reformist thought in connection with inequality in the distribution of the product and of power. It is often said that "competition might be all right if it worked," but that it is unreal and impossible, a myth; and realistic discussion of monopoly and competition is viewed by reformist critics as propaganda on behalf of vested interests. Monopoly is indeed a serious problem. But consideration of well-known facts would show both that the amount of monopoly is fantastically exaggerated in the public mind and that a substantial amount is functionally necessary in a free and progressive economy. Analysis is difficult because "arbitrary" power is the only distinction between monopoly gain and legitimate profit, while profit itself cannot be empirically separated from entrepreneurial income, which represents normal earnings of personal services and of property. Profit is an occasional and temporary monopoly gain due to imperfect competition and associated with loss. It is typically (not always) connected with innovations which lead to social economic progress. Everyone knows that innovation and exploration sometimes yield a return disproportionate to the outlays incurred, and also that these activities frequently involve enormous losses to their promoters. As we have seen, theory predicts an excess of loss over gain on the whole, and this result seems to be confirmed by statistical inquiry. To see the functional role of temporary monopoly, it is only necessary to think of patents on inventions; other monopoly normally works in the same way, and most monopolies are in fact relatively short-lived, though there are exceptions and many are serious evils while they last.

Without going further into the theory of entrepreneurship and profit, it should also be evident that neither society nor the workers (nor any other group) could appropriate the gains without also assuming the losses. Business cannot be conducted on the basis of "heads I win, tails you lose." Social abolition of profit would force the government to control all production and distribution in detail, by methods of politics. The result would be collectivism or socialism, to which only a few words can be devoted here. It may be defined as producers' co-operation on a national scale, ultimately that of the world. But producers' co-operation has been repeatedly tried, and its history is one of failure, even on a small scale where the difficulties are relatively minor. Moreover, the recent history of Russia, and of other states which have adopted socialism, on the basis of different ideologies, has made it clear that a socialistic state must be a dictatorship. Moreover, destruction of freedom is probably accompanied by loss in efficiency (except perhaps in war) and by little or no gain in equality or justice.

The general conclusion must be that already stated: In any free and effective large-scale organization, the terms of co-operation must take the form of prices fixed by market competition. Business must be separated from charity. In work as in play each participant must stand on his own feet, play his own hand and reap the consequences of his conduct, the fruits of his own capacities. (The role of property will be considered presently.) The ethical side of the relationship consists in obeying the rules and in striving to improve the rules in any way which will lead to a better game on the whole. Popular and reformist thinking, under the influence of romantic moralism, seems unable to grasp this elementary idea. It runs to one absurdity or another—either a purely mystical fellowship without rules or fixed objectives of action, or a fight, similarly without rules, or finally that to have order and peace, every move in the game must be planned in advance by some authority. If any organization is to be improved, action to this end must first of all be based upon an understanding of the existing rules and the way they work. Without this, the consequences of action, grounded in romantic impulse, however well meaning, will usually be the opposite of what is intended or will entail new evils indubitably worse. Moreover, it is necessary to have a reasonably clear conception of the ideals which are to define the direction of improvement. We turn first to this latter problem.

While criticism of the enterprise economy has usually run in terms of injustice, critics have rarely tried to formulate any explicit norm of distributive justice to be applied in place of the market norm. Except for a few economists, no one has seriously tried to understand what this norm is and what it means. Critics have rarely implied that the ideal would be absolute equality, and in fact this could not be given a definite meaning, and in any meaning it would be repugnant to ethical common sense.

We have said that the principle according to which a competitive market economy distributes the joint product is that each individual receives the amount which is attributable to his activity in production, the amount which the use of the productive capacity he possesses adds to the total. That is, rewards and incentives are as they would be in the case of a Crusoe or of an individual (or family) living in society but acting economically on the basis of self-sufficiency. The effect of organization is merely to increase the productive efficiency of all (relative to given wants and capacity) while maintaining individual liberty (again in the sense in which a Crusoe is free). All relations between individuals have the form of exchange of equal values or what has been called "commutative justice." This principle is "just," in a kind of natural sense, and in the most primitive and universal meaning of the term in human society.

However, it is easy to find arguments to the effect that the results of competition, assumed to be theoretically perfect, have no ethical justification, even in terms of the individualistic ideals as stated. First, equality between productive contribution and its remuneration, or between what is given up and what is received in any exchange, depends upon the market measure of values, on both sides. This measure, the pecuniary demand, depends upon the scarcity of the particular type of productive service which any individual is in a position to furnish. Sufficient abundance will reduce the value of any service to a low level or to zero, while sufficient rarity alone will place a fantastic value upon nearly any activity, making it correspondingly "productive," apart from any rationally defensible "utility." The one extreme is illustrated by the starvation wages commanded by the lowest unskilled labor, and also by many creative artists; and the other by the incomes of various stunt performers (including some who are popularly called stars) down to human monstrosities on exhibition in side-shows.

Consumers' demand also depends on two other factors besides scarcity—taste and purchasing power. No one would say that either factor is ideal or that the two together measure the ideal desert of producers. Large incomes must be secured chiefly by rendering some special service either to the rich or to great numbers of the populace. Finally, the earnings received for any type of service are enormously affected by contingencies, accident or luck. And beyond all these facts, it must never be forgotten that the family and not the individual is the real unit in society, in economic relations as in other connections. Whatever may be thought about the relation between performance and social desert for those who directly produce and receive income, it can hardly be held that the dependent members of families deserve to participate in the fruits of production in proportion to their fraction of the earnings of the breadwinner.

The principle of distribution on the basis of productive contribution has typically been defended in terms of two different or even contradictory premises. On the one hand, it is held to be ethically right, on the basis of primitive natural principles, as already suggested. Even according to Scripture, a man should reap what he sows. (A more logical moral defense, less often met with, is that it is an implication of the ethical ideal of freedom, but serious limitations of this reasoning will be pointed out later.) On the other hand, it is commonly admitted that the productivity principle is contrary to ethical ideals but is held to be expedient, even necessary, for efficiency and the progress of civilization. It is argued that without the direct personal incentive of enjoying or suffering the consequences of his own acts (for himself and his dependents and heirs) the individual would not use power or means effectively or strive to achieve the ends most desired by others, and especially that he would not make the efforts and sacrifices involved in the maintenance and accumulation of capital or assume the risks of entrepreneurship. Again, the most important argument from expediency is commonly ignored because it rests on principles of economics, which the educated public passes over for more romantic notions. This argument is that no way of directing production rationally is conceivable except to have the individual act as producer and as consumer in accord with the price measure of product value, through an interest in maximizing an income measured in price terms. After an income is earned, it may be put to any use more important than consumption by the earner or addition to his capital; and this may be done through free choice of the earner himself or through social compulsion, and market competition will direct the use of productive capacity accordingly. In recent years we have seen a most remarkable triumph of the will to believe, among reformers and the articulate public, in the notion that automatic natural forces bring about adequate accumulation and growth in production; it is even argued that they cause excessive output, capital formation and technological advance.

The problem of distributive justice has been strangely neglected in the literature of modern ethics, and our political discussion and laws and court decisions are rarely explicit as to ultimate moral premises. The problem cannot be seriously discussed without going beyond the simple norm of "commutative justice" (exchange of equal values) on the one hand and the naive ideals of love and brotherhood on the other. Many other principles are implicit in political and legal action. One reason for the neglect of the problem in modern speculative thought is to be found in a confusion of morals with science, which defines the correct attitude in economics and the other behavior disciplines concerned with explaining what actually is or happens. Objectives come into discussion by economists in connection with problems of social policy, i.e., applied economics, not in the pure science.

In a democracy, the premises of social action are derived from public opinion, as sensed by the politicians and ultimately tested by election returns. Science can only explain these attitudes, and such explanation amounts to justification. Thus liberal thought paradoxically comes finally to coincide with the logical position of theistic religion, that "whatever is is right"; for, to be inevitable, as a consequence of given conditions, is for practical purposes the same thing as to be ideal. Both these positions would eliminate all possibility of action if men in acting paid serious attention to their professed theories; but this would be self-contradictory in either case, so that only the absurdity of the theories, and the greater rationality of men's acting than of their thinking, need be pointed out.

In an attempt to break out of the vicious circle of commutative justice, which largely vindicates whatever happens, it is necessary to find other principles. This quest will take two lines; first, obligations of given individuals which go beyond mutual respect, and giving for every benefit received a *quid pro quo* satisfactory to the other party; and second, an investigation of the assumption that the individual is to be taken as "given," with respect to his interests and his endowment with means or capacity.

In primitive society, there are ideals of right and of rights within the tribe which go far beyond justice or equity as defined by equality in exchange. There are obligations of helpfulness on the part of those in a position to help toward those in need, and also rights and obligations between the individual and the group. All these are more or less clearly defined by custom and generally understood. In primitive and later pre-democratic society, these rights and obligations are defined by social rank and status. In modern democratic society, peculiar difficulties arise because the notion of status has been formally repudiated in favor of individual equality, while actual differences are nearly as great as they ever were, though no longer definite or permanent. The great change is that the individual is now formally free to improve his social position, and such action is regarded as meritorious; but his *power* to do so ranges from zero indefinitely upward.

Dissolution of the "crust of custom" has left the individual free to form his own ideas of his rights and obligations, except for minimum legal requirements. The natural result is that the duties which he recognizes toward others and toward society fall far short of the rights which he claims at the expense of both, and a wide gap is opened for controversy and conflict. The replacement of custom by law, made by democratic process, carries controversy and struggle into the political arena, where the conflict is more acute. It is further aggravated through the replacement of the small tribal unit by the great national state, and especially by the fact that efforts to get ahead on the part of individuals, families and institutional groups give rise to the tendency to cumulative growth of inequality, already mentioned. A further source of confusion, in fact, is the role of a nominally monotheistic and universal religion, which purports to view all human beings over the whole earth as brothers in one vast family.

This brings us to the second line of inquiry, the idea that ethical obligation is a matter of relations between given individuals. From the standpoint of social problems of today, the major concrete defect of the liberal social philosophy is that of taking the individual as a datum with respect to his endowment with economic power or productive capacity. This includes his ownership of external things or property, on a parity with his personal qualities of strength, skill and knowledge of modes of using means, or technology. Under effective competition, the distribution of the product corresponds with the ownership and use of economic capacity, regardless of its nature; but this carries no implication of ideal distributive justice. That depends on the extent to which the distribution of capacity is either ideally just or actually beyond human control. There is general agreement that the actual distribution is not just, though little indeed as to what ideal justice would mean. It is also evident that imperfect competition is a source of injustice, and that the distribution of economic capacity, the character of competition and the distribution of the product are all subject in some degree to individual and social control.

Of the two main components of productive capacity, the qualities of man himself are partly innate, partly acquired and largely determined by factors external to the individual. Innate qualities are of the nature of potentialities, which are of no value until they are developed and given opportunity for expression and use. Both development and opportunity for use are partly the result of the activity of the individual himself during his own (earlier) life, but are far more largely effects of the activities of other individuals and of social conditions and culture processes beyond his control. Thus personal capacity itself is for the most part artificial,

in a threefold sense. To the extent that its creation is deliberate, it is a "product," and in economic terms is the result
of "investment," and is essentially "capital," like non-human
agents. The sharp distinction made in popular and reformist
thinking between labor-power and property in external means
of production is for the most part spurious. All forms of productive capacity are ultimately capital and are to be traced
back to the same complex of factors—inheritance, the activity
of the individual owner and other persons (primarily his
parents), social processes and accident. Property is practically
as much, or as little, as personal capacity, an attribute of personality. In either case, a moral claim of the owner to the
fruits of its productive use rests on dubious grounds. From
the standpoint of the individual, the whole situation is largely
a matter of good or bad luck.

There is no visible reason why an individual should be
ethically more entitled to the earnings of inherited personal
capacity than to those of inherited property. The problem of
social action to remove or offset inequality would be only
formally different in natural and institutional inheritance.
The individual's own activity in creating economic capacity,
and that of his parents in creating it for him, is of the same
kind, causally and ethically, whether the result is internal
or external to the individual himself. In any case, the investment is made by the use of economic capacity previously
possessed. The devotion of economic capacity to investment
use rather than to production for immediate consumption
must be regarded as socially and ethically meritorious, but the
precise extent to which it is to be treated as the basis of an
ethical claim is problematic. It must be kept in mind that the
result of deliberate economic activity is always largely affected
by unpredictable factors, hence again by luck as well as foresight, facts which create distinct ethical problems.

Thus the ethical problem of inequality, or of just and
unjust inequality, must be analyzed into three or four
main factors. These include inheritance, natural and social

(through the family and other communities); the employment of capacity possessed at any time to create a useful product (either for immediate consumption or to add to existing productive capacity); and finally the factor of luck. Luck, again, cannot be separated analytically from foresight, which is a form of capacity and involves effort. The most important practical problem centers in the natural tendency, already pointed out, for inequality in economic capacity to increase cumulatively in all its elements. The individual who at any time has more productive capacity is in a better position to acquire still more—in fact, more than proportionately so. And the fact that the family and not the individual is really the primary social unit (while other institutional groups operate in the same way) means that this cumulative tendency does not cease with the individual life but goes on from generation to generation unless it is offset by some accident or by individual or social action.

The argument brings up the economic aspect of a proposition stated earlier, that if society is viewed as an entity continuing in time, it is a complex of institutions rather than an aggregation of individuals interrelated in various ways. Institutions are the medium or channel of social inheritance. They make the individual what he is; and social continuity and progress, and all cultural values, center in the preservation and improvement of institutions. Economic ethics must take account of the fact that it is through institutions that the individual comes into possession of his economic attributes. This applies not only to his endowment with economic capacity, including internal capacity and external means, his knowledge of the use of means and his economic opportunity, but also to his wants, tastes and preferences as a consumer and as a producer. Of course these are also partly dependent on his own activities, but the social factor clearly predominates; and it is this factor which is chiefly in question for the problem of social policy and action. From this point of view we are concerned primarily with the family as the most important channel of inheritance and with the state as the principal agent for deliberate social action.

Moral obligations cannot be regarded as ending with the boundaries of any group or class or neighborhood, or with those of the national state, particularly as such boundaries have been drawn in the course of history, chiefly by brute force and accident. Inequality and injustice, and the tendency to cumulative increase in inequality, are as real between states as between individuals and families. The ideal of individualistic ethics, both liberal and religious, is an undifferentiated community, the organization of the whole human race as one vast mutual-aid association or family—the latter of an ideal sort, of course, in contrast with the diverse realities which characterize actual brothers since Cain and Abel. The practical difficulties in the way of realizing this ideal are clearly insuperable, and the theoretical problem which is presented for ethical idealism itself has no definite solution. The struggle for existence and expansion between cultures and groups not merely seems to be inevitable but is also the only process by which civilization can expect to advance to higher levels. And acceptance of this fact is apparently a condition of belief in the validity of a real moral distinction between the higher and lower in human life.

The ethical problem centers in the scope or boundaries of society, a matter more or less equivalent to the scriptural question as to who is one's neighbor. In a rational view, this is a question of degrees and kinds of neighborliness or its counterpart, self-seeking. It is unrealistic to define selfishness in individual terms; family and state selfishness, and perhaps others, are in fact more important. The injunction to love one's neighbor as one's self presents relatively little difficulty in the case either of members of one's own family or of other adult human beings; the serious difficulty is to love other families, beginning with one's neighbor's children, as one's own. The difficulty is multiplied when the neighbor belongs

o an alien nation or culture or race. It is not only a matter
f will but a profound moral issue to the extent that the
questions of natural or cultural superiority and inferiority
re felt to be involved; and in practice this is the heart of the
natter. Beyond the fact that "love" is not impartial, we must
recognize that by rational ethical standards it ought not to be.
Superiority has an obligation of self-preservation and ex-
pansive propagation. In practice, every kind of being will and
must assume that it has a right to life, self-perpetuation and
growth.

In short, since human life is social and human society cultural, ethical love or devotion must be directed to cultural
values as well as to individuals, and in case of conflict the
former love must commonly take precedence over the latter.
In the moral life, as conceived in modern thought, devotion
to the future maintenance and progress of civilization is a
different thing from personal affection, and conflicts with
the latter, and must be rated above it in the scale of values.
When competitive cultural expansion leads to the appeal to
force, as we have seen must inevitably happen occasionally,
the use of force is a moral obligation, as a threat or as outright
violence.

These facts destructively undermine the ideal premises of
both liberal and Christian ethics, since both are individualistic and ostensibly cosmopolitan, though neither is so in
practice. In terms of individual rights and duties there is a
sharp and unavoidable conflict between the individuals of one
generation and those of the next, within any continuing
society, from the family to the state and the world. The individual of the generation which is adult at any time certainly
has both the right and the duty of providing for his own
children the best he can, along with due regard for broader
social obligations. Just what is meant by the best provision
and by a right balance between obligations in this connection
is a question which has no simple or definitive answer but is
always a matter of judgment. Moreover, no sharp separation

can be made between right and expediency; that also is ethically a question of balance and a matter of judgment. For there is no sharp distinction between ends and means, and both are affected by value judgments. It must be assumed to be better for the world, and within wide limits better even for the disadvantaged groups, to have civilized life maintained and advanced than it is to have it decay or be destroyed. But civilization and progress rest on inequality because the world is so poor, relative to its population, that means are not available to provide for all a decent level of life, defined by cultural requirements. Rational ethics cannot even absolutely condemn the emulative interest, getting ahead of others, as a motive to action.

But the right and duty of the family (or other group, including the state) to provide first for its own future or that of its own posterity conflict sharply with any abstract right of all the individuals of the oncoming generation (within any group, up to the human family, not to mention other species) to an equal or fair start in life, to an equal opportunity to realize their potentialities or to equality in any interpretation. Even equal reward for equal performance is excluded; for, as we have seen, there is no possibility of defining equality, either of reward or of performance, without using existing conditions as data, including prior inequality.

Liberal and Christian thought are alike in professing to treat the individual as he stands, as the absolute moral unit. Yet both teach that the family is of right the basic social institution. This is particularly in point in connection with the inheritance of property. In terms of the primitive assumption that economic justice consists in a natural right to the fruits of one's own efforts, spokesmen for both liberalism and Christianity assume tacitly, and often say explicitly, that this includes the fruits of inherited capital, which is assumed to have been produced by the "labor and abstinence" of the individual's parents or ancestors. In fact, capital is never produced by labor without the co-operation of pre-existing capital, and labor-power itself does not differ in any essential respect from physical capital.

A discussion of the economic aspect of the social problem should clearly recognize that inequality in the distribution of the cultural inheritance is not limited to the inheritance of productive capacity, even when all forms are included. The social inheritance of the individual also includes, or largely determines, both his tastes and wants for goods and services exchangeable in quantitative terms, and the general purposes, ideals and values which lie beyond specific wants and are the main content both of personality and of culture. It largely forms his interests in action apart from wants for the concrete fruits of action, his energy and ambition, his concern for progressive achievement for himself, his family, his country or its particular culture and the progress of civilization on the whole. It also determines his opportunities for action, along with the means of action and the ends to which action is directed. These facts recall what was said earlier with respect to the limitations of the economic view of individual conduct and of the conflicts of interest which finally underlie social problems. Ultimately, these conflicts of interest involve more of the psychology of play or of religion than that of economics.

The argument of this chapter is likely to give an impression of opposition to all positive social action, i.e., to anything beyond the negative activity of policing, or at least beyond measures which give rise to no serious disagreement. This is neither our meaning nor the correct conclusion. The tendency to draw this inference itself illustrates the romantic character of natural human thinking, which is the main obstacle to beneficial action because it obstructs a rational approach to the problems. Human nature is disposed to "do something" about any situation which seems unideal or annoying, to act or to demand action without much considering the consequences to be expected from acting in any particular way. And men naturally treat opposition to any particular suggested action as opposition to any change and defense of the existing situation—usually for selfish and immoral reasons. The uncritical disposition to act finds abundant illustration in the history of medicine. The treatment of disease has usually been based on magic or superstition, or on reasoning of no greater scientific validity, in terms of some suggestive analogy. Prior to the development of modern scientific procedure less than a century ago, even the practice of professional "doctors"—to say nothing of popular remedies —undoubtedly killed or injured far greater numbers than were cured or benefited.

In the field of social-economic therapy the difficulties are far greater than in medicine—beginning with that of defining health—and crowd thinking is still more romantic and irrational than that of individuals. Consequently, the first and greatest need is to understand the difficulties and grasp the practical certainty that measures adopted without careful investigation will do more harm than good. Ample illustration is to be found in the recent history of our own country. The main political phenomenon has been the organization of pressure groups for collusive action, both economic and political, ostensibly aimed at justice but actually more or less predatory. Bargaining, or "log-rolling," between such groups leads to action which causes loss all around, as in the case of protectionism, mentioned at the beginning of this chapter. The worst tendency of all is the demand of doctrinaire reformers that someone be "put in charge" of economic life to direct it in the way it ought to go; this policy would certainly destroy freedom and probably reduce efficiency as well, or direct action to bad ends. However, as we have been equally concerned to show, it is not true, either that effective open-market competition would produce ethically defensible results, or that this can be achieved without extensive social action. In fact, the "classical" defenders of economic freedom have always stood for a wide range of state action, and have in general advocated such action wherever it reasonably promised a balance of good over evil.

Only the briefest indication of what are sound and unsound measures can be given here. In general, the sound measures run along lines already explored and developed in liberal states. The first requirement is to "make competition work," wherever this is feasible, by dealing with the business cycle and predatory monopoly and other recognized evils. Excessive inequality in distribution can be corrected through taxation and the use of the proceeds for socially desirable ends, especially for relief and giving the children of each generation a fair start in life. For excessive insecurity the main remedy is social insurance, in so far as the cure is not effected by the measures already suggested.

In view of the trend of events as showing natural ways of thinking, it particularly needs emphasis that most procedures of regulation, and specifically all or practically all arbitrary fixing of prices, is to be condemned outright. The simplest principles of economics, well known to every competent person without special study, show that price fixing is equivalent to restriction of output and hence to monopoly. It is immaterial whether the effort to increase the incomes of the members of any group by raising prices is applied to services (wages) or to products (of farmers) and whether it is carried out as direct restriction of output by organization and collusive economic action of the groups affected or by public authority. The result in any case is decreased production and economic loss—and also the special evils of unemployment, possibly more or less alleviated by wasteful use of labor and other productive agents. An effort to increase real incomes by artificially lowering the prices of consumption goods would call for the same judgment, but such action is practically unknown (in time of peace). Public opinion in economic matters considers it "immoral" even to allow prices to fall in consequence of natural and desirable market adjustments.

The monopolies established by arbitrary fixing of wages

and prices are vastly worse than any which result from large-scale organization of production or business combination not directly encouraged by public policy. Monopoly which is not the consequence of governmental action—including unwise provisions in the laws affecting patents and the powers of corporations—is a serious evil chiefly in certain areas long recognized in economics as "natural monopolies." In such industries as the municipal public utilities effective competition is virtually excluded or palpably wasteful. In such areas (identification of which is a matter of judgment in marginal cases) the industry should be operated by a public authority, not subjected to regulation. If governmental operation is not extended over too large a part of the whole field of production, the inherent weaknesses and dangers of political management may be largely avoided, since standards of efficiency and of remuneration will be set for the public bodies by competition in the larger area left to the control of that process.

It is always to be kept in mind that the major social problems of economic organization do not arise out of economic conflict, accurately defined. They are rooted in social and activity interests of the sort involved in play and culture, in contrast with work. But it is the combination of all these types of interest in the same activities and social relations which gives the economic problem its actual form and its extreme difficulty.

In the long view, the major social problem is that of creating ideal individuals—and limiting the number of people in relation to resources. The good society can only be built out of people with appropriate tastes and capacities and adequate external means. This problem presents enormous difficulties for analysis as well as for action. There is a circular causal relationship between individuals and institutions. The individual is largely made what he comes to be by social life and culture, and the traits and endowments of men must be changed through the remaking of institutions. But this remaking must be done by the individuals who have themselves been formed by the institutions which it is proposed to change. This means that action must be gradual, and the problem is also conditioned by the ideal of freedom. It is relatively easy, and tempting, to picture social change through the arbitrary remaking of institutions by some individual or group with unlimited political power. How far this process would really be effective in the long run is a dubious question, to say nothing of the desirability of results to be so achieved. Infinitely more serious is the problem presented by social change under democratic auspices, where a consensus must be established through free discussion, both as to the ideals to be realized and as to the methods and measures for effecting change. Redistribution of the economic product and of economic power through the agency of political power within any political unit is not difficult if the bulk of the people are agreed on what is to be done. But institutional repercussions are difficult to predict, and still more obscure is the relationship between forms of organization and men's tastes and dynamic interests. Unfortunately, when such questions are raised, rational discussion is likely to turn into a struggle for power, resulting either in chaos and strife or in the establishment of a dictatorship.

The ethical problem of the unequal inheritance of economic capacity, while neglected in scientific discussion, has been recognized in practice in modern liberal society, and extensive action has been taken to counteract the tendency to increasing inequality. Inheritance of property has been more and more limited directly by taxation of inheritance (and of anticipatory gifts) and differential taxation of income, with use of the money to throw the ordinary costs of government upon the well-to-do and to provide relief and more extensive and prolonged education, general and vocational, and other services for the poorer families. All such measures tend to equalize opportunity for the oncoming generation and (in some degree) to reduce current inequality in consumption.

But it is a serious question how far such measures, which transfer the functions of the family to the state, can be carried without undermining the psychological and moral basis of the family as an institution. Here we must think not merely of the sanctity of the family but of the difficulty of devising any substitute which would be workable, or which would not involve the same evils, with others. Differential inheritance of property and culture through the family is the basis of high civilization throughout history; and the effort to eliminate inequality, insecurity and injustice must not be pushed to the point of menacing the continuity and progress of accumulation and the growth of technology, and of knowledge, insight and good taste.

At the present juncture in our civilization, the crying need is for more straight thinking, specifically on the part of academic and literary leaders as educators of the public, far more than it is either for better intentions ("changing men's hearts") or for increased knowledge of facts and techniques. This applies particularly to critical objective discussion of value, with a view to agreement upon social ideals. Romantic voluntarism (sentimentalism toward people and absolutism toward principles) and instrumentalism (utilitarianism or pragmatism) are the twin, or polar, vices of modern intellectual life. Both involve naive dogmatism about ends, as well as indifference to means, with the result that our body politic does not rationally use the knowledge it possesses even at the level of everyday observation and common sense. The great danger is the romantic urge to action without taking the trouble to understand or to reflect and to reach agreement on ideals and with respect to given conditions, the possibilities of action and the effects of different procedures. In the field of ends, too much idealism—in the form of the soft heart toward suffering, or in any other form—is in effect a vice; for it creates a tendency to rush into ill-considered action, aggravating the evils it is intended to cure or producing others that are worse. Idealistic reformers are perhaps a greater menace than the outright criminal, partly because idealism is usually combined with excessive self-confidence, a righteous pose and ambition for place and power.

As in individual medicine, the social doctor must not have too much feeling for the condition of his patient. The hard head must resist the soft heart; science and the instinct of workmanship must predominate as motives over the urge to relieve symptoms. The functional processes of the social organism must be kept going and improved, and to that end they must be understood. The statesman must know and adopt effective ways and means of getting things done, using the motives of men as he finds them until they can be changed for the better. Measures of betterment must be largely indirect, aimed more at upbuilding than at relief. Social justice, like individual enjoyment or freedom from pain, is to a considerable extent a luxury; and too much direct pursuit of the one or the other is not conducive to success, to genuine prosperity or to length of life, for it means interfering with natural processes which are not well understood.

It is important not to press the medical analogy too far; its limitations are equally important. To begin with, democratic society must be its own doctor, with a limited place for specialization of individuals to the diagnosis and treatment of social ills. Again, the ideal of health can be defined with reasonable accuracy in the individual, but in society there is no given or static norm. The ideal itself must be progressively redefined and improved, concurrently with treatment of recognized maladies. Ultimately, society is able to remake both its own organic structure and its "cells"; but the limits are not known, and the attempt involves a peculiar liability to self-injury and even self-destruction, through conflict between the units. Society confronts a major problem of self-preservation against internal conflict which has no parallel in the life of the individual.

More important still, it is doubly dangerous for a society to experiment on itself, though practically all action is in some degree experimental. It is as difficult as it is necessary to experiment intelligently, to avoid the simple method of distinguishing between mushrooms and toadstools by eating them and seeing whether one is nourished or killed. The prestige of instrumentalism and the experimental method in science and technology have made this one of the most serious of all the popular fallacies which must be combated in modern society, in the interest of a rational approach to social problems. This form of romantic oversimplification implies dictatorship or chaos and is doubtless more dangerous in fact than either the religious idea that love will solve all our problems or the kindred naive individualism of the liberal social philosophy. Both science and good will are required for intelligent social action; but both must be understood and directed by a critical intelligence different from that of instrumental science.

The first and last word of any sound discussion of social ethics is a twofold statement in which the main emphasis is negative. First, the problems have to do with the structure and laws of organized groups, *not* with relations between individuals in face-to-face or primary association; and second, the conflicts within any formal organization, particularly the business enterprise and the state, are conflicts between groups, also with some degree of organization, *rather than* individuals. It should be superfluous to observe that both statements apply in a peculiar degree to the problem of world order, which actually presents the most immediate threat of destroying civilization.

PART II

ECONOMIC IDEALS OF LIBERAL CHRISTIANITY

Thornton W. Merriam

CHAPTER SEVEN

Has Christianity an Economic Responsibility?

CHURCHES are more deeply involved in American economic life than is commonly thought. To some extent this fact is not the result of choice but has been determined by the nature of Christianity and by the kind of institution which the churches have become. The zone of choice lies in the discovery of ways by which the churches' relationship to the economic activities of our times may be made most constructive. For this task a clear understanding of the facts and a positive philosophy are required. There is no more urgent challenge confronting Christianity today.

To fail to recognize that this view is not held by a large and influential body of church members would be naive. They are convinced that churches ought not to concern themselves with economic questions. Their views are expressed in a statement by Josephus Daniels, former ambassador to Mexico, which was quoted in a religious periodical of recent date:

> The pew wishes sermons that are redolent of the whole Gospel. They tire of essays, discussions on economics, solutions to political problems, and the like. They have a surfeit of these on week-days and often are bored by half-baked solutions as they listen to the radio or read their journals. They go to church looking for something spiritual—for strength in the hour of endurance, guidance in the time of peril and temptation, and abiding peace of the soul.

While it is not my purpose to discuss specifically what clergymen should preach about, it seems reasonable to suggest that the "whole" Gospel must have economic content, and that peace of the soul in our times is not to be achieved, if at all, by closing the eyes to ugly if boring facts of economic maladjustment.

The basic issue is whether the message and activity of the churches shall have economic content. Recent events have tended to obscure but have not diminished the importance of the question. The tragedies of war, typified by casualty lists and the return of mutilated young men to local communities, have led churches to an understandable emphasis on a ministry of personal comfort for those bereaved or shaken by misfortune. Many a minister, facing such tragedies, feels that it is no time for discussions of economics. It would, however, be more tragic and erroneous to dissociate such personal ministry from its social context. The tragedy of war is in part the result and the concomitant of economic dislocation. Failure to recognize this fact is to deprive folks of the whole Gospel, a Gospel which must concern itself with the creation of societies in which resort to war is impossible.

Religion, like education, begins with people where they are and attempts to meet their needs. It must not stop there. It must lead to a deeper understanding of human needs and the social forces which underlie them; men must be stimulated to acquire the knowledge and competence necessary for intelligent mastery of the forces which now threaten to overwhelm us.

The thesis that churches must concern themselves with economic issues is sustained by three considerations. The first is that churches are social institutions. They, and related organizations, own property, raise, receive and invest funds, buy and sell, and employ men and women. In 1940 American churches were reported to have spent approximately $600,-000,000.[1] This is a large sum, though it may not impress a generation accustomed to expenditures of governments in wartime. The churches are a large business. They require

---

[1] *Information Service.* Federal Council of Churches of Christ in America. Vol. 20, No. 26.

expertness in financial and economic affairs. The amount of time spent by officers and boards of churches on financial and property matters has become great.

Such boards and officials have to decide how funds entrusted to their keeping are to be invested. As employers they must decide what wages and salaries are to be paid; they determine policies regarding hours of work, employee tenure, retirement. In determining such matters shall a church follow the prevailing standards, if any; or does its ethic demand another standard? Shall the church lead or follow the procession?

The moment churches consider such questions they have become participants in our economic society, whether they like it or not. To conduct their business well is a primary obligation. It is their initial opportunity for influencing the society of which they are a part, in deeds rather than in words. In a society in which there is economic conflict the churches will inevitably find themselves taking sides by their decisions in these economic questions of their own. What side they ought to take is not "given" in their creeds or in the customs of the economic groups from which their governing boards are drawn. Their practices, like those of any other institution, must be determined on the basis of their objectives and the practical alternatives offered by the economic culture in which they operate. This task requires devotion, courage, intelligence and practical knowledge.

Churches, furthermore, cannot ignore economic questions because of the kind of Gospel to which they are committed. Christianity is an ethical religion. Its God is a God of love. Christians believe that the love which they owe to God must be expressed in human relations if it is to mean anything. These relations are in part economic. "How can ye love God whom ye have not seen if ye love not your neighbor whom ye have seen?" is an authentic and fundamental statement of the Christian faith. For better or worse, churches are committed to that kind of religion. On what possible grounds can economic aspects of human relations be excluded? Love of

God and love of neighbor are inseparable aspects of the religious attitude which requires that attention be given to the ways in which human beings relate themselves to one another in all activities, including their efforts to secure food, clothing, shelter and the means for play, study and the enrichment of life. To proclaim love of God and of neighbor and to confine it to the orbit of ecclesiastical behavior, leaving out of account the ways by which the individual earns his living, not only would be untrue to the basic insights of Christianity but would condemn religion to a message of futility in a world whose major evils arise from the economic situation. The logic of the churches' message demands application and implementation in economic relationships. What love of God means in terms of the actualities of an economic society is a question which every generation of Christians must face.

A third consideration is that a Christian fellowship generates a *concern for persons* in their total relationships to reality. Christian fellowship is the name given to a certain kind of human relationship which exists when a group of people seek to worship God and to discover a mode of living that expresses God's love. Such a concern for persons is not restricted to particular aspects of the individual's life and activity. All the needs and possibilities of development of any member of the fellowship are the interest of his associates. If he is hungry, he must be fed; if he is sick, ways must be found to heal or relieve him; if he is lazy or fails to carry his share of the burden of the common life, his difficulties must be understood and his spirit and energies restored. No concern of his is alien to those with whom he shares the fellowship. As will presently be pointed out, this concept of human relations and its embodiment in actual group life gave vitality to early Christianity. Experience in such a fellowship is the seedbed for ideas and ideals for all human society.

The motive-power for change generated in the Christian fellowship is not to be minimized. If existing social arrangements negate and frustrate the concern for persons produced in the Christian fellowship, a force to change the social order is released. This concern is not focused merely on individual need or remedial measures. Depending on the depth of understanding of the individual and society possessed by the participants in the Christian fellowship, there is no limit to their efforts to seek social causes and social remedies for the personal problems of their fellows. There is a common fallacy that the *religious* approach to human need is individualistic and restricted to relieving the distress of individuals. This is not true. In so far as the social basis of personal problems is apprehended, social causes and social action will be sought. Thus the Christian is compelled to become economist and to seek an economic strategy for making his concern for persons effective.

The Christian fellowship is not identical with churches. Within the churches, to be sure, the best expression of the fellowship will often be found. Frequently, however, many people will fail to find it there. When a particular church does not concern itself with the whole person and with an economic and social order which brings persons to poverty, unemployment, crime, disease, it ceases to express Christian fellowship. Then men and women who seek this kind of relationship with their fellows are compelled to go outside the churches. They then become the real conservers of the Christian faith for their times and for generations to follow. It is encouraging to note that within the Christian churches today there is arising again a determined call for an experience of fellowship with other persons who share a common allegiance to Christ and who without equivocation attack the economic injustices of our society as an authentic expression of the Christian faith.

There have always been people within the churches who interpret the meaning of Christian fellowship differently. They turn their eyes from the economic conflicts of their times and find comfort in the thought of a better life beyond. This view has required men to suffer while they must, in the secure knowledge that peace and justice will be granted by God if and when He sees fit. This way of looking at religion is contrary to the Christian tradition. It is also contrary to insights derived from experience in the fellowship which Christianity fosters. When it is genuine this experience generates a responsible concern for persons which seeks economic implementation because many of the causes of human suffering and frustration are found to be economic.

There are also Christians today who despair of ever shaping economic forces to correspond with the Christian ideal and have given up the attempt. Sometimes they seek a social embodiment of the ideal of the Christian fellowship in a form of group life which artificially simplifies living by giving up the inventions and conveniences of modern life. This seems like a retreat from the challenge which modern life presents to Christianity. Such retreats often benefit individuals but contribute little to the solution of the economic problems of society. If these problems are to be solved, the economic powers inherent in modern industry and finance must be understood and used to improve the common life and meet the longing of men for fellowship of the type envisaged in Christianity.

The "tough-minded" attitude often found among economists and businessmen regards this talk about realizing the values of Christian fellowship in economic relations as sentimental twaddle. It believes that the two interests do not mix, and that it is best to recognize that fact and keep them apart. There is a certain realism in this attitude. Religion has not been successful in influencing economic life in our society. When this has been attempted, religion has often blundered and sometimes been misled by a false psychology concerning the relation between ideals and action. It has sometimes thought that the regenerated individual who has embraced Christian ethics could be trusted to translate these sentiments into appropriate practical action. Thus in time, it was thought, the evils of an industrial society would be eliminated through individual action of Christians, and a Christian social order would be achieved. The task of the churches was regarded as the transformation and conversion of individuals to Christianity.

It is now increasingly accepted that individuals, however lofty their sentiments, can do little as individuals. Their effectiveness depends on their associating themselves with others in joint action directed toward Christian goals with a philosophy of social action based on facts as well as wishes. Christian social and economic action has at long last arrived, and an increasing number of Christians are prepared to move into the social situation with a realistic strategy. They are attempting to accomplish directly and collectively what they had formerly thought to accomplish indirectly and through individual activity.

Thus implemented, the Christian sentiment of love may well prove to be as "tough" as the situation demands. This is a fact which was well known by the prophets in Christian history but is often lost sight of. Under these circumstances Christian groups cannot claim exemption from severe criticism, which comes when inflammatory social issues are attacked. These proposals for action cannot be presented under a halo as if they were the final word of God. Custom tends to say that a group's religious beliefs are its own business and entitled to respect. When, however, religion enters the arena of economic action, as we believe vital religion must, it must give up the notion that its proposals are sacrosanct. They are to be examined and open to attack like proposals emanating from any other source.

If Christianity ceased being an institution of society, if it gave up its belief in an ethical God and if it no longer tried to create fellowships of folk devoted to discovering ways of making their concern for persons effective in the complex life of modern times, then and then only would Christianity be justified in excluding economic issues from its teaching and activity. But it would then cease to be Christianity.

CHAPTER EIGHT

The Outlook for Collaboration Between Economics and Christian Ethics

CHRISTIANITY requires economic implementation. Economic activity involves the well-being of persons. The objectives of the Christian fellowship cannot be achieved unless there is an economic structure which supports them.

If these points be granted, an important question arises concerning the kind of relationship which ought to exist between religion and economics. What is a desirable pattern of interaction between churches and business? How should Christianity relate itself to the processes by which our society feeds, clothes, shelters its members?

In approaching this question, it is well to dispel certain misconceptions which lead to unnecessary misunderstanding. When speaking of the churches dealing with economic questions, it is frequently assumed that one refers to the role and ideas of clergymen. Since they are generally supposed to be untrained in business and economic matters, it is argued that the churches' judgment will not be good. This is then offered as a reason why churches should not concern themselves with such questions.

A church is the people who compose it. The clergyman is often its leader and spokesman, but in its membership are businessmen, clerks, housewives, economists, financiers, laborers and representatives of a great variety of occupations. A wise churchmanship will utilize the variety of talent thus at its disposal. When dealing with economic matters, a church will draw on the knowledge and experience of its members. Its proposals need not be uninformed. If they are the result of the collective thought of its members, they are entitled to careful consideration. The clergyman has a distinctive contribution to make. He should be a stimulator of the consciences of his membership; he should bring together men and women of varied experience from the membership of his church when economic issues are to be discussed. His training should have equipped him with the skill essential to helping such groups think their way through these problems and to reconciling the differences sure to emerge when important economic issues are discussed.

Churches are not condemned to dilettantism when dealing with economic matters. Their membership includes specialists in that field as well as persons of general experience whose wisdom on many aspects of these questions would be an asset in any group.

Another misconception concerns the attitude which churches take toward their own proposals on social questions. Enlightened Christians do not now believe that they can turn back to the Gospels and discover the answer to questions of social and economic practice. They do not believe that in the Gospels or the creeds or the traditions of the church, or in the writings of St. Thomas, Martin Luther, John Calvin or others, is to be found a blueprint which can be proclaimed as *the* Christian social or economic plan. Christians must be granted a sense of the meaning of history. The past, it is believed, can shed light on present problems but can never be conclusive in determining what should now be done. Finding a way through social and economic difficulties is an arduous responsibility which cannot be shirked by appealing to the past. Christians believe that economic plans and ideas must be developed in the crucible of present experience by men and women now living who intelligently and sensitively seek an appropriate social embodiment of their faith. This, essentially, is their reading of Jesus' words concerning the "Spirit of Truth," which, He said, could be depended on to make new disclosures concerning the Christian's faith and duties.

This teaching has rightly been called the Magna Charta of intellectual freedom in Christianity, but it also implies responsibility for seeking the truth, which may not be dodged by a slavish following of intellectual and spiritual landmarks.

This statement carries the implication that enlightened Christians do not identify particular economic proposals, however noble, with an authoritative will of God. They tend to view with distrust people who affirm that a particular way of organizing the economic life of a nation or a specific reform is *the* Christian way. The attempt of finite minds to translate spiritual values into conduct, and even to think up the right ideas for doing so, is fraught with infinite difficulties and must always contain a large margin of error because of the limitations of human capacity, the intractability of the material to be dealt with and the sheer magnitude of the problem. The Christian is well aware of the fact that under the guidance of the Holy Spirit he can discern ways of living and values far beyond his capacity to formulate, much less incarnate in his own person and in the life of society. Thus he regards every specific plan of economic action *critically*, for he knows that it has within it the seeds of its own undoing and, in the hands of men limited in capacity and in the quality of good will, is sure to fall short of the hopes which gave it birth.

This view has often led to so profound a pessimism regarding man's attempt to incarnate Christian ideals in social action that Christians have turned away from the attempt and have regarded the world as lost beyond redemption. This reaction seems like blindness to the essential meaning of the doctrine of the incarnation in which the absolute and infinite take on the limitations of the relative and finite, and portray both the tragedy and the possibilities of human existence as a lesson and inspiration to men. Men glimpse the eternal; they live in the present; they seek to incarnate the eternal in the present; they fail, but they do not give up, for the attempting is the meaning of life as the Christian sees it.

Thus a critical mind is an essential part of a Christian attitude and approach to social action. Criticism is a check on dogmatism in the area of social practice where the discovery of the most effective means is the basic question. Criticism provides a safeguard against an excess of optimism which frequently turns to despair and bitterness when the means used fail to achieve the desired goal.

Enlightened Christians do not believe that they have a short cut to economic wisdom. Methods of incorporating spiritual values in individual behavior and social practice must be sought through whatever means the environing culture offers. From the religious-ethical impulse and dedication may come the goal and the will. The pattern and the way must come through intellectual discipline, patient gathering and weighing of facts, experimentation, checking of results and, in short, through as profound an understanding of the principles of economics and of human behavior as science and human experience make possible. Social inventiveness cannot be predicted or planned; it emerges under a variety of circumstances. The common-sense view is to look for it in those societies where there are many persons who have clear social vision, believe in the possibility of making a better order and discipline themselves in the acquisition of knowledge.

The modern Christian embraces this view and thus supports and utilizes modern scientific approaches to economic wisdom. He does not seek a short cut. It requires to be said, however, that a Christian must view with distrust any specialized branch of learning or activity which cuts itself off from related fields and from consideration of values and goals. He distrusts it because a discipline so circumscribed tends to lose its sense of direction and get bogged down in its own precious pursuits and interests. It loses a sense of social relevance and purpose which alone can make it useful in providing insights and methods for lifting the level of social effort.

The actual relations which exist between economics and Christian ethics are easily characterized. There is and has been an absence of effective communication. The gap between the two fields is not easy to explain. Many economists are active and professing Christians. The reason cannot be merely a difference in subject matter, focus of interest, methodology or even a temperamental unlikeness as between the ethicist and the economist. The attitude appears often like resentment, as well as distrust. Economists sometimes act as if they thought that too close contact with ethics or religion would sully the purity of their work or soften them in their attack on their own problems.

This attitude is perhaps related to the economist's ambition to make his field a science and his fear that others may not accept this appraisal at face value, particularly if there were the least suspicion that he were consorting with religionists. Perhaps the economist himself has misgivings that his work may not and cannot be a science.

The desire to be scientific seems to have led the economist to restrict his field in many ways, notably by excluding moral or ethical considerations. Whether justified or not, this attitude has tended to isolate economics from religion and ethics. It has given the economist a mind-set against issues of social philosophy and purposes. Economics has not thus far been markedly influenced by the view now widely accepted that science operates on the basis of assumptions regarding man and society which need to be taken into account by the scientist qua scientist. These assumptions determine the economist's selection and interpretation of data regardless of how refined his instruments may become. What he calls "facts" are colored by these assumptions. Values enter into his selection of problems to be studied and facts to be emphasized. His estimates of relevance are influenced by his social and ethical orientation. Conventional economics has not been greatly concerned with such considerations. The economist seems still to be pursuing a model which is increasingly being discarded by the physical sciences.

The result has been an ever widening gap between economics and religion. There have been individual economists who have attempted to cross the gap, but they have generally been looked down on by their colleagues. Even economists who were themselves personally religious have succeeded in maintaining an effective separation between the two interests.

A similar absence of effective intercommunication has characterized the relationship between religion and the world of commerce, finance and industry. The cliché, "business is business," expresses the idea that business conceives of itself and its operations as governed by necessities or principles arising wholly from *within* that context, in which moral or ethical considerations are out of place. Attempts to introduce religious considerations have been deeply resented. Many a businessman has been quick to support churches and interpretations of religion which guaranteed to keep him from being disturbed by any reference to the social gospel.

It would be unfair not to recognize that this separation between business enterprise and ethical or religious considerations has "paid off" in certain tangible results. It may be argued that the rapid economic expansion starting from the invention of the steam and internal-combustion engine was in part due to the fact that business was relatively free from checks by church, state or conspicuous ethical sensitivity. While the human cost was heavy, success in "conquering the continent" came in part because the economic pioneers and freebooters were uncontrolled and were free to do anything they could get away with.

On the whole American business has acted as if it were above ethical responsibility. It has claimed ethical autonomy and has refused to acknowledge the justice of any checks on its activity which came from outside its own sphere. Even the right of social and political institutions to judge it on the basis of ethical values has not been admitted.

The results are now to be seen. The state has moved into the situation and set up controls based in part at least on ethical considerations. Business has fought such limits on its autonomy. A livelier sense of moral responsibility might have made political action unnecessary. But it is now too late. More and more business is becoming an instrument in the hands of the state for achieving ends which the state and not business determines. Business has lost its autonomy.

Recently, academic economics also has seen its claim to moral autonomy and social irresponsibility challenged. Its desire to pursue its own ends, determined by internal considerations alone, to interpret its function independently of broad ethical and social aims, was a possibility in a stable society. It is an impossibility in a society like ours in which the ethical foundations are crumbling. Such a society must re-discover the common values which have sufficient cohesive power to hold together its component parts. It cannot afford to permit the kind of autonomy and independence which economists seem often to assume are essential to the existence of their subject as a science. Economists have more and more been forced to think politically and socially and to relate their activity to the total problems and aspirations of American society. Their role, their methodology, their specific activity are not determined by unchangeable "laws," nor are they given in the nature of things; they are functions assigned by specific social and political interests and agencies.

Thus one is forced to the conclusion that in many respects economics, as it has existed, is ill suited to an effective relationship with religion or ethics. It has a bias against that trenchant re-examination of assumptions which liberal religion demands; it is anti-philosophical for it prides itself on knowing nothing about ethics; it is attached to an outmoded psychology regarding the relation of fact and value; it has little in the way of social morality and is afraid of getting any.

Within religious institutions the effort to build up a *rapprochement* between religion and economics, especially in Protestant circles, has been stubbornly resisted. It took fully a half-century of agitation before there was any considerable body of opinion in the churches to support the view that the church had responsibility for social conditions. There is a persistent tendency, never entirely absent from Christianity, to look on the world as bad; too close contact with it will defile the church. Some churches find it more comfortable to dwell in the realm of abstractions than to face the conflicts which result when principles are applied. There has been, however, throughout the history of the Christian churches a demand, often of a minority, for a socially applied interpretation of religion. From such groups has come a spirit of social pioneering. Today the responsibility of the churches to deal with economic issues is accepted by significant groups in most denominations. Many of the churches have active social-action organizations whose primary task is to stimulate the conscience of church members, provide them with information and build lines of communication with business, labor and the social sciences.

If there is to be an alliance between economics and religion, it is obvious that readjustments on both sides are necessary. Religion must lose the feeling that it has some peculiar method of discovering truth about mundane matters. Economics must get rid of what almost amounts to an anti-intellectualism in the field of values and irresponsibility in the moral realm. No marriage of these interests, or any effective communication, is possible until both have modified their outlooks.

The suggestion that religion "deals with ends" and economics "deals with means" is a facile but unsound statement. Many people assume that the religionist has access to some authoritative source of information concerning goals of economic life. This is not true, and is furthermore the wrong attitude to take in a collaborative enterprise. Both economist and religionist are human beings who should be seeking light on the problem of ends or values and trying to discover effective ways of achieving them. Objectives have to be worked out in the crucible of experience and reflective thought and must be the result of collaboration of many minds. Knowledge of desirable objectives arises in experience, economic as well as other. All persons closest to the arena of experience must have a part in determining what the objectives should be.

What, then, may the churches and other Christian groups be expected to contribute to the alliance of economics and religion which is here recommended? Without attempting an exhaustive list, we may present five resources which Christianity offers.

Christianity will (a) proclaim an "impossible ideal" of human relations. This will be based on its belief concerning the destiny of man. It is an impossible ideal because it embodies visions of human relations never yet achieved or, given man's limitations, fully achievable. This ideal will not take the form of a pattern of social arrangements but will provide the ethical base and the atmosphere wherein such ever changing patterns may be evolved. Christianity need not be greatly disturbed when people criticize it because its ideals are impractical. It can rest assured that this is only a half-truth. How practical its ideals are no one knows. The importance to society of having such ideals continually expressed in vigorous form to entice men and women into new adventures in social action is so great that the churches need not become too concerned by charges of impracticality.

Christianity will, further, (b) propose criteria for judging contemporary economic practices. In the next chapter these criteria are suggested. The important point here to be emphasized is that the vigorous proclamation of these standards will make it difficult for men to be contented with existing achievements. By providing society with a transcendent point of reference, on the basis of which it will criticize existing society, Christianity will furnish a dynamic for continuous growth. It will help keep men's minds open to new possibilities often requiring new economic arrangements. It will help prevent complacency. These criteria will also give Christianity a basis for appraising plans and programs which are put forth in its own name. Toward such plans it will have an attitude of optimism and critical detachment because of its commitment to a goal which no human plan will ever fully achieve.

Christianity may, further, (c) be expected to provide a situation in which men and women of widely varying backgrounds may meet for discussion of ethical issues in economic activity from which patterns for social endeavor may be evolved. Churches are perhaps the most widely representative of all social institutions. Men of business, finance, labor, science, economics and plain workaday folk make up the membership. These resources for creative intellectual and ethical discovery in the field of social action have scarcely been tapped, largely because of lack of an appropriate methodology and a vision of possibilities. This is the churches' great opportunity.

Such discussion, no matter how well informed, will, however, be relatively fruitless unless the participants act on the basis of their insights and convictions. That alone can make discussion responsible. A common ground of belief concerning the ends of human living is also essential. Only "committed" men and women who have dedicated their lives to an all-embracing responsibility, viewed as a transcendent obligation, can make such discussion more than a beating about in egoistic zeal to prove one's neighbor wrong and to maintain personal prestige. Participants can rise above self and group interests when they are committed to something larger and more inclusive than self or group advancement. They are then in position to adjust differences and produce effective social ideals and plans which can intrigue the loyalties of their fellows and guide their society through the maze of economic and social changes.

Christianity offers such transcendent loyalties. What are the alternatives? Nationalism? Racialism? Communism? Secularism? None has the possibility of unifying and fructifying creative ethical discussions of the type described.

Christianity to many people means knuckling under to authority and accepting beliefs that insult the intelligence. If we dare hope that economists will overcome ethical inertia and come out from their protected towers, we must also expect Christianity to offer them a different basis of fellowship than it has usually done in the past. This converging of the religious and economic forces is so important for the future of our society and the churches that it is of the utmost consequence to make a place for it in Christianity either by readjusting church life or by creating fellowship outside the churches.

Groups of this type now in existence have a tendency to exclude the very elements essential to the task. Their methods are often pietistic; their social action symbolic and remedial rather than realistic and reconstructive; their attack on social issues limited to personal adventures in human relations; their emphasis mystical rather than rational. New fellowships need to be created in which people of varied technical and ideological orientation with common commitment to Christian values will share in the task of discovering social patterns expressive of basic Christianity. Such groups must also utilize the highest degree of skill which our scientific and technological development makes available. This is the way that men today may discover the new spiritual orientation and fellowship for the reconstructive social task.

Christianity, again, (d) will emphasize changing the lives of individuals, and this *in* the social situation in which they are placed, rather than *outside* it. The "wants" with which the economist claims to deal are in their most significant aspect not "given" at all as he has been prone to assume. They are socially produced and determined by custom. Christianity proposes to have a hand in the shaping of these "wants" and through them the personalities of the individuals. Persons can be oriented to the Christian culture as well as to any other. They can be made socially responsible as well as socially irresponsible.

Christianity, finally, (e) may be expected in the future to carry on an educational process which may mean that the next generation will accept economic discussions as part of Christianity. They will not feel the tension that the older generation feels when economic references come into religious observance. Christians will then be able to pray with better grace and more understanding, "Give us this day our daily bread."

CHAPTER NINE

Christian Social Ideals

IN THE long history of Christianity the desire to shape the social order into conformity with Christian ideals is an ancient and recurrent motif. A competing theme is the determination to ignore society's ills and to restrict Christian responsibility primarily to individual or other-worldly interests. Both movements have always existed in Christianity. Which is the authentic expression of the Christian's faith is still today a matter of disagreement.

This chapter deals primarily with the first motif—the social thrust of Christianity—and examines the content of its social ideals. Little attention will be given to the counter-movement which always and everywhere attempts to check the progress of social Christianity. It is important, however, to recognize that both movements exist, are a part of Christianity and to some extent tend to cancel one another.

What is the content of the ideals from which Christian social directives are to be derived? What values are posited concerning human relations? What is the meaning of a "Christian" society? What is the religious significance, from the Christian viewpoint, of man's struggle to secure food, clothing, shelter and the material basis of existence during his brief span of life on earth?

A summary of the answers proposed to these questions is as follows: the Christian social actionist seeks to establish forms of human relationship and of social and economic functioning which express the values of freedom, collective responsibility, equality and universality. The basis of his action is in a theory of the universe. In this theory man's economic and other

148

activity is viewed in a supra-human dimension. It is held that as men seek to develop these four values in their social activities and relations with other human beings they fulfill the meaning of existence. So to act, in other words, is to do God's will.

Obviously these are "mere words," signifying anything; they serve only to indicate the direction in which this discussion will move. We shall now attempt to give them positive content and briefly to indicate the historical setting out of which they have emerged to become key concepts in Christianity.

Before proceeding, we shall indicate the point of view from which the whole question of religion and Christianity is approached. These presuppositions are necessarily stated in condensed form. The main purpose of this chapter precludes elaboration of them.

The task of religion in any age is to *bind together* man's fragmentary knowledge and his aspirations in a coherent and dynamic world view. This world view must do justice to what men know and to what they believe to be true, desirable, urgent. If in any generation a particular religion fails in this function, it ceases to be a genuine religion. People will then increasingly look to other sources for an integration of their knowledge and aspirations.

Christianity has been a vital force because it has had this critically synthetic power of valid religion. Christianity is a constructive force today in so far as it demonstrates the capacity to face new facts, new conditions of life, and to express the longings of men for the best possible living. A definition of Christianity expressed primarily in terms of a world view and beliefs worked out in a previous age is untrue to the genius of Christianity. In the dawn of Christianity Jesus bade his followers to expect new disclosures of truth. That is precisely the expectant attitude which ought to characterize His followers today if they are to be true to His spirit. They must expect new world views and new ethical ideals relevant to the facts of life in our present technological culture. When they cease to expect the new, they cease to follow Him.

Christianity today has many enemies. They are within the fold as well as outside. From within, in a day of rapid social change and disintegration, they summon weary folk to a haven of refuge and bid them close their eyes to the realities of life about them. Outside the churches, these enemies insist on defining Christianity according to statements of belief worked out in a former period to prove to themselves that Christianity ought to be rejected. Both misunderstand the function of religion and the genius of Christianity.

The integrity and continuity of a historic religious movement do not depend on the continued survival of particular forms of belief, particular definitions of duties, particular observances. Integrity depends rather on whether there is present in the movement a vital and persistent effort to integrate knowledge and aspiration into a coherent and dynamic world view, and to work out the social correlates of that world view on the basis of achieved understandings. These understandings are derived both from past and from present experience. Integrity further depends on whether the adherents of the movement are today *acting* individually and collectively in the light of the world view which they have achieved. There must always be a sense of history, but never sheer imitation. In this respect Christianity does not differ from other human movements. The integrity of the scientific enterprise does not depend on present-day scientists' holding the views of eighteenth-century science.

Authentic interpretations of Christian social ideals must come from within the Christian movement from those who participate in attempts to achieve them. The nonparticipant in Christian social action—even when he is a weekly occupant of twenty-five inches of church pew-space—is in no position to interpret the meaning of social Christianity. He, like the outside critic, persistently misses the point: namely, the needs and urgencies of contemporary society around which Christian concern is mobilizing. That is the dynamic point of Christian social idealism. Ideals emerge from the experience of attempting to put Christianity into the social process, and then change with that experience.

The values which the Christian attempts to preserve are rooted in the experience of the Christian community and its culture. These values are not inert ideas to be picked up here and there from books and pieced together in an intellectually pleasing pattern, then to receive the label "Christian." They are the product of *living* in the Christian fellowship and are regarded as claims on the loyalty of the person as a member of this fellowship. They "hang together" and have power because they are related to a total experience and view of life as seen through the Christian fellowship. Apart from this culture content, Christian social ideals may often sound banal, silly or ethereal, and inevitably will lack power to incite to action. The all-important stimulus comes from a group connection which the Christian calls the community, the fellowship or the Church.

Christian social ideals are based on a theistic world view, but that does not mean that Christians possess any magical methods of changing men and institutions. Christianity's techniques of action must be derived from the general culture and civilization of which it is part. Through its particular form of group experience it may develop methods and contribute them to the common fund, but, in turn, it draws on this common fund for light on human nature and the social process. In the past Christianity has often erred in its selection of techniques, been misled, gone up blind alleys and failed. It will doubtless continue to do so. But, like scientists, Christian social actionists learn by their mistakes and seek constantly to improve their techniques as human wisdom advances. Hence Christianity has a vital interest in the advancement of what is sometimes called secular knowledge because such advance enables it to discover ways of implementing its ideas and deepens its understanding of the social situation in which it exercises its aspirations for a better society.

Anyone who attempts to formulate Christian social ideals soon discovers that he is working with highly complex materials. Not only have these ideals changed from period to period, but at any particular moment in history it will be found that Christianity presents conflicting phases and expresses itself in a variety of ways which baffle comprehensive formulation. Even when apparent common ground is discovered, it often turns out to be specious, consisting of verbalisms which conceal fundamental disagreements.

Yet this situation is not without its advantages. Even if he found a precise and integrated formula the Christian would be obligated to criticize it, perhaps add to it. Expressing Christian social ideals is a "prophetic" function. It can never be done by adding up the creeds, pronouncements and teachings of various branches of Christianity. These ideals in any period must represent the responses of men's consciences, nurtured in the Christian faith and community, to the social needs and urgencies of the age in which they live. Thus there must always be divergencies in view, which, however, the Christian is obligated to communicate to his fellows; and from this process there may emerge a conviction which is in some sense a group product.

Something of this kind is now in progress. Individuals within churches and the churches themselves officially have seldom been so actively aware of the importance of formulating their social ideals. Before the war such world conferences as Oxford and Madras were an expression of this movement. In the reports issued by these gatherings will be found clear indications of the directions which Christian social thought is taking in these times. These reports, supplemented by similar statements from other conferences, the *Social Ideals* of the Federal Council of Churches and certain papal encyclicals, might well be taken as sources for a formulation of essential principles of Christian social ideals. Certain emphases will be found to recur again and again in varying phraseology which indicate with reasonable clarity the directions Christian thinking is taking when confronted by the evils of war, unemployment, persecution of races and nations and the breakdown of traditional political forms.

For various reasons it has seemed best not to approach the question in this way. Instead, we shall seek to discover the rootage of Christian social ideals in the historic movement of Christianity, particularly the life and teachings of Jesus and the experience of the early Christian churches. The major emphases which appear in the social pronouncements of recent ecumenical conferences were established in the early stages of Christianity. Through the vicissitudes of twenty centuries these emphases remain to challenge the Christian. They have become the characteristically Christian way of regarding man in his social relations. First let us consider briefly the influence of Jesus on these concepts.

There is social "dynamite" in the Gospels. This fact will not be missed even by the casual reader. He will hear Jesus saying that he came not to bring peace but a sword. He will read a denouncement of riches of considerable vehemence. "It is easier for a camel to go through the eye of a needle than for a rich man to get into the Kingdom of God."

Elsewhere in the Gospel Jesus appears to advocate almost an attitude of extreme passivity toward external social conditions. He emphasizes the importance of accepting one's lot, rather than attempting to change it, in the faith that God takes care of His own. As Mr. Knight has said, Jesus appears to believe that if a man's heart is right toward God, the material things necessary for existence will somehow be provided. Jesus further counsels love for people and neighborliness, but does not discuss the problem of how such attitudes may be expressed in social-organizational terms and become instrumental in bringing in the Kingdom. This task, some would argue, Jesus conceives as primarily God's responsibility.

The reconciliation of these two apparently opposed themes, in so far as they can be reconciled, is to be found in Jesus' treatment of the idea of the Kingdom of God. This is a central concept in his teaching.

The Kingdom of God, as has been said often, was for Jesus the criterion of all values. Modern scholars tend to believe that it meant to him a good and just social order in which God's will would be done and men would live the kind of lives God intended them to live. The Kingdom was the end toward which creation moved. The ultimate meaning of being alive was so to act that the Kingdom of God would come.

For the modern man, Jesus' teachings on this matter are vague. Probably they did not seem vague to his contemporaries who listened to him with a richness of background in Hebraic prophetic thought that gave a precise connotation to terms which to us are indeterminate. Modern scholarship has done much to recapture some of the meanings which Jesus and his contemporaries found in the concept of the Kingdom of God. It symbolized the Jews' long-frustrated hope for freedom, justice and a place of pre-eminence among the nations of the world. This tradition carried denunciation of the powerful and wealthy who misuse their positions to subjugate human beings and deprive them of bread. Jesus' attack on riches is in line with this tradition; when his words are read aloud to a wealthy congregation today, they have a startlingly "radical" sound and seem out of place. The prophetic tradition carried the belief that those sitting in the seats of power are to be turned out, and their places taken by God-centered men who will govern under God with justice, love and regard for the weak.

Jesus was the inheritor of this tradition. When he made the Kingdom of God central in his message, such were the ideas which came to the minds of his listeners. Jesus emphasized the universal character of the Kingdom. All mankind was included in its outreach, Gentile as well as Jew. The Kingdom of God was a universal reign of justice and love.

Jesus also stated that the Kingdom was to come through the intervention of God. While there is much for men to do, the Kingdom is not to come to pass primarily through man's initiative. This belief formed the basis of his hope in an unjust and harsh world. Events, despite superficial appearances, were on the side of those who attempted to live the good life. When God would intervene, Jesus said no man could tell; that was in the providence of God. The question did not interest Jesus, but apparently he did believe, like other Jews, that divine intervention was imminent and would occur within the lifetime of some of his hearers.

Another facet of Jesus' thinking about the Kingdom of God emphasized its "inner," spiritual meaning. The Kingdom is not a future social state but a spiritual attitude. The Kingdom "comes" whenever men enter into right relationships with God, the Father, and express love in their relationship to other people. This inner life of man was perhaps Jesus' dominant concern, as far as one can judge from his words and activity. A man ought to live in the presence of God, and commit his life to Him. This means making the concerns of His Kingdom primary. Evidences that a man has done so, Jesus taught, were to be found in the kind of life he lived: his capacity for renunciation of conventional standards concerning what is important when these standards conflict with the demands of love; his care for his neighbor and his readiness to help the poor and dispossessed. When a man so acts, the Kingdom of God has already come within him. Only in this way could a man be prepared for the kind of living required in the future state. Jesus spent the few years of his active ministry in challenging men to this kind of living.

Jesus also required that the interest of the Kingdom of God be placed first among the loyalties of his followers. Property and riches were condemned because they had a way of ex-

cluding other, more important interests. The poor and dispossessed, Jesus observed, heard God's voice and its challenge
to radical righteousness more clearly than those who were
tied to their age by great possessions. Such a change of mind,
he observed, was difficult to achieve when a man's security
was based on the property he had, by hook or crook, extracted
from the existing social order. Institutions which maximized
ritualistic observances to the neglect of personal righteousness
were likewise condemned along with conventions which
assigned status on the basis of wealth, power, office rather
than the quality of devotion to God's Kingdom.

This brief statement concerning Jesus' teachings obviously
fails to do justice to many aspects of his thought. It may serve,
however, to indicate some of the contributions to Christian
social ideals which are derived from the Gospels:

The human scene and the struggle for social righteousness
ought to be viewed in a supra-human context. "Being good"
is rooted in the meaning which is found in life as a whole,
namely, that God is working in the universe trying to develop
men of good will who act toward one another as sons of one
Father. Eternal values are at stake and are present in the
urgencies of human relations.

Reformation of the mentality and attitudes of the individual are inextricably bound up in the problem of social
reformation. Change of personal standards of evaluation and
neighborly action in all human relations must go together.

The search for food and for justice are alike divine urges.
Efforts to satisfy them in all men are a part of man's effort
to live in the presence of God.

While man should work for the coming of God's reign, he
should be modest in his estimates of what he will be able to
do. Jesus had no superficial optimism concerning the coming
of the Kingdom of God. Man's role is important and essential, but limited. Jesus' view is more realistic than that of
many of his followers, who have often believed that continued
improvement in human affairs was inevitable. Jesus enter-

tained no such view. Even when man is living in an age in which the values inherent in the Kingdom of God are on the decline, as was the case in Jesus' time and perhaps our own, it is his teaching that men ought still to live by these values. The germ of the Kingdom will thus be preserved when other forces seem to overwhelm. There will be witnesses to something better, to a way of life that carries in it the meaning of being human.

The early Christian communities are of great importance in understanding Christian social ideals. The historian of the Roman Empire first encounters Christianity in the form of numerous small groups scattered through the Mediterranean world. He sees these groups increase in numbers and move from insignificance and obscurity as a minor sect at the beginning of the modern era to a position of power. How explain this vitality? At the time of Constantine, Christianity had achieved a place of dominance among the religions of the Roman Empire. It did not at that time seize political power; it was seized by the powers that be because it had become the outstanding religion of the people. In that period of social disintegration, in which the political state was slowly crumbling, this obscure and "illicit" movement, competing with scores of other religious sects, suffering from persecution, handicapped in numerous ways, suspected of disloyalty to the state, grew in power and vitality until by the opening of the fourth century shrewd politicians saw it as the only possible cohesive spiritual force which might successfully counter the forces of disintegration.

Why? What did Christianity offer men in that age of "fading hopes"? The answer is not primarily new teachings. Rather, it presented a new group attachment which became for individuals a sustaining force, the most important fact and relationship of existence, and their final authority in matters of belief and conduct. While these groups, called "Christian," differed from one another in many ways, they developed a community life with a common object of loyalty and characteristic modes of human relations, observances and ideals. Within these communities were developed the basic principles of Christian group relations and the norms of the Christian's outlook on society.

The Christian community was a relatively close-knit group of people united by devotion to Christ worshiped as God and by a common sense of need for salvation. Its members were drawn from all classes, including the wealthy and cultured, but predominantly came from the lower economic and social stratum and included, at least in the first two centuries, many slaves, freedmen and laborers. A variety of beliefs developed. The process of unification and standardization was long and never fully achieved. Within these Christian groups was sustained a type of living and of human relations which profoundly influenced the outlook and conduct of the members.

The needs, frustrations and weaknesses from which individuals sought freedom in the Christian community were numerous and varied. Hunger, disease, loneliness, despair, insecurity resulted in a ministry which offered food, medical service, comradeship, hope. The interests of these communities were more inclusive than some modern definers of religion would call religious. They ran the gamut of human experience, and in the Christian community the individual found his needs met more adequately than in other groups which competed for his allegiance.

The total needs of the person were the concern of this community. If in any case the environing society did not meet those needs, the Christian community attempted to meet them.

In these groups there was gradually developed a texture of human relations which is most important for the present study. It included four major characteristics or principles. They were: (a) the equality of all believers; (b) collective responsibility; (c) freedom; (d) universality. Let us indicate briefly what these terms meant in the Christian community.

Belief in the essential and inherent *equality* of men was basic. Life in the Christian community was characterized by equality of status of all members regardless of the distinctions that prevailed outside. This meant that wealth, political position, racial differences, class distinctions or individual achievements, as judged by secular standards, gave no basis for preference within the community. There it was a matter of indifference whether a man was slave or free, rich or poor, Jew or Greek.

The foundation of this equality was in the belief that all men were made in the image of God and that all men were sinners and equally in need of God's forgiveness. No man was good enough in the sight of God to dominate other men in the Christian fellowship. Men were also equal in another sense. All were equally entitled to the resources of the community to meet their needs, whatever they might be. In a common human search for meaning in life, in the midst of want or futility, members were united.

It is not difficult to understand the appeal which the Christian community had for men and women who lived in a society shot through with economic and class distinctions. This community offered a type of human relationship which seemed to be what God intended life to be like. Such hierarchies of rank as developed within the community did not violate the principle of equality. There were bishops, presbyters and deacons, but these represented functional divisions of responsibility and conferred no special privileges.

Two further points should be noted. These Christians did not feel responsible for extending the principle of equality outside their religious community. They did not attempt to give it political expression. For example, slaves who became Christians and enjoyed equality with freemen in the community were apparently taught to remain in that status, to obey their masters and to do their work as a task set for them by God. Masters were taught to treat their slaves fairly.

These views of equality are not to be considered as uniquely characteristic of Christianity. The theory of "natural inequality" as represented in Aristotle had by the second century disappeared, to be replaced, in Cicero and Seneca, for example, by the doctrine of the natural equality of human nature. Christianity may have taken over this view from such sources; but from its own Hebraic antecedents it derived influences which must have led it in the same direction. Regardless of sources, the doctrine of human equality received in the Christian community expression as a way of life; men and women experienced a way of living in which all were equal.

The second basic emphasis of the Christian community was *collective responsibility*. One of the primary sources of the extraordinary strength of Christianity, enabling it to withstand the blows of official persecution and popular contempt, was the compactness of its group life. The feeling of brotherhood which appears clearly in the teachings of Jesus did not exhaust itself in sentiment. In each member there was inculcated a sense of personal responsibility for every other member and for the community as a whole. Care for the needy was an important part of the community's program. When one community fell on hard times, others, even at great distances, came to its rescue. Every member had a claim on his fellow members for whatever was essential in maintaining life. Persecution only increased the need and strengthened the sense of solidarity. Historians have noted that early Christian literature emphasized the duty and responsibility of believers but had little to say about rights. This is significant, and helps explain how the Christian community survived while many other religious sects, which focused attention on individual salvation through elaborate ceremonials or unimplemented philosophical principles concerning the rights of man, lost out.

This religiously inculcated sense of collective responsibility, which was the essence of brotherhood, also provided a check on individual tendencies to excess. Such tendencies are always introduced into human conduct when freedom is emphasized. Christians felt themselves free from Jewish legalism, but they were under a discipline which set the welfare of their brothers in Christ above personal gratification. They were not free to loaf or willingly to become dependent on the charity of others. They were not free to disintegrate body and soul through dissipation. There was for each an overarching responsibility to the Christian community which required that they live sober, industrious and righteous lives. Christianity thus provided a basis for personal discipline which was rooted in a community relationship and which enabled individuals to withstand the forces of spiritual decay accompanying the social, political and intellectual decline of imperial Rome. In time Christianity became almost the sole stabilizing and integrating power in that society.

Collective responsibility was the Good Samaritan principle given material and practical embodiment. Anchoring it was the belief that this kind of relationship between human beings was the pattern which God intended to prevail between men and between Him and his children.

The third ethical value expressed in the Christian community was *freedom*. Christianity grew up in a period of intellectual ferment. Because the moral foundations governing the conduct of men were crumbling, there was a kind of freedom in which every idea and religion had a hearing, provided only it did not attack the imperial authority. There was a receptivity to ideas which has seldom been equaled. This condition left individuals without those basic convictions concerning life values which seem to be essential for personal stability and for an integral political and social life. The power of Christianity lay in its ability to offer such a basis of character by means of which the individual found integrity amid a "changing and chaotic world." Once found, it gave the individual the basis of freedom, a set of values in which he believed.

In the Christian community individuals brought up in the

Jewish tradition often found another kind of freedom. They were released from the bondage of a complicated system of rules and observances which only the specialist could be expected to understand. For the "law" there was substituted right living, and this increasingly meant fulfilling one's responsibility to the Christian community. Doubtless there were many who did not find the "law" irksome, but those who did felt that in the Christian Gospel was freedom.

In an even deeper sense the Christian community offered intellectual freedom. This point has been often overlooked. The Christian believed that the whole of life belonged to God. "This meant that everything that made man's life wider, deeper, fuller; whatever made it more joyous or contented; whatever sharpened the brain, strengthened and taught the muscles, gave full play to man's energies, could be taken up into and become part of the Christian life. Sin and foulness were sternly excluded; but that done, there was no element of the Graeco-Roman civilization which could not be appropriated by Christianity."[1]

This gave the Christian community a power of assimilation which helps to explain its extraordinary growth and vitality. Without it Christianity, which began as a movement of the uncultured and the poor, could not have had the irresistible lure to intellectuals and the cultured classes that it began to manifest at the close of the second century. Failure to maintain this freedom has led in many a subsequent period to bigotry and an intellectual rigidity which has cost Christianity many a creative spirit. In its formative period, however, it became a power because it was a movement of freedom.

Based on the belief that God had created all men in his image, the principle of *universality* asserted that the Christian community was open to all men, regardless of race, color or social status. There was no "chosen race"; there was one human family. It was the function of the community to

[1] Lindsay, T. M. in *Cambridge Medieval History*, Vol. I, p. 96.

demonstrate this unity and to proclaim its message to all men. Its timeliness is apparent when one considers the vast mingling of peoples which was then taking place in the Mediterranean world. Through succeeding centuries, and despite the development of national churches, Christianity has never lost this belief in the universality and supra-racial character of its message.

As a competitor with unnumbered other religions in the Roman Empire, Christianity demanded exclusive loyalty. Unlike its competitors, it never admitted the right of the individual to be a member of several religious groups. It asserted that it was the one and only religious loyalty which a man might sustain. This brought it into conflict with the state, which demanded at least a formal bow to its gods. The Christian's refusal to accede resulted in official persecution.

Most of the non-Christian philosophic thought of the times emphasized the *common humanity* of men, as against racism or nationalism or the inevitability of classes. Christianity consolidated a principle of Stoic philosophy with the Hebraic idea of a common ancestor of all humankind and the belief in the fatherhood of God.

The principle of universality also gave Christianity a sense of world mission. It did not, however, prevent the development of a principle of exclusion through which those who were not willing to accept the principles of equality, collective responsibility and freedom in the community were rejected and excluded. To such and to others to whom the opportunity to join the Christian fellowship had not been given, the community had an ever present obligation to take its message. The principle of universality made Christianity an expanding movement.

The Christian social ethic is thus a community ethic in which the dominant emphases were and are: equality, collective responsibility, freedom and universality. This "fellowship" is the Christian's spiritual home, the generator and source of his ideals of human relations. In a real sense, the Christian does not "apply" an ethic, but rather participates in a community in which an ethic is produced which he is impelled to try to expand to include all society. In this community he both discovers possibilities of human relations and experiences a mode of life characterized by freedom and recognition of collective responsibility and the essential equality of all men. The Christian community is sometimes an actual human group; always it is a "kingdom of ends" toward which the believer looks for the ideals which shall govern his own life and toward which he hopes society may move.

Coupled with the idea of the community is Jesus' emphasis on a change of mind in individuals. Man must do something about himself if a "community" is to be achieved. He will not usually or naturally be "community-minded." Whatever he may be in his natural state, modern social experience is almost certain to have distorted his outlook, habits and ambitions by the time he comes to the age of understanding. While Christian social ideals require constructive action to change these formative influences, it is also recognized that most men must be re-educated in the ways of Christian living before they will desire or be fit for the kind of living required in a society based on the principles of freedom, equality, collective responsibility and universality. It is part of the Christian's social task to challenge men to a change of mind, even as Jesus did, and to transform the home, school, church and neighborhood into agencies where persons are made ready for living in a society which exemplifies the Christian values.

The next chapter considers the economic meanings of these values which Christianity presents to the modern world.

CHAPTER TEN

Economic Implications of Christian Social Ideals

CHRISTIANITY presents the challenge of building a *world community* based on the principles of *equality*, *freedom* and *collective responsibility*. Through education, preaching, worship and other appropriate means churches should attempt to develop in people understanding of and devotion to these principles, as well as a determination to incorporate them in the social and economic order.

It is the Christian belief that all men have latent capacity for free, co-operative, social living. However warped human nature may have become, it is still man's destiny to develop these potentialities; in so doing the divine image in which he was made becomes more clearly discernible in him. It is the task of Christians to seek a way of living which expresses the Christian values in the family, the community, the nation, and in a world society.

A way of living of this kind demands economic structure. The means of securing food, clothing and shelter must also serve the ends of freedom, equality and collective responsibility for all human beings.

What kind of economic organization accepts such goals? Unless it is possible in some degree to embody its ideals in an economic structure, Christianity is not entitled to serious consideration as a social ethic, since it would then fail modern man at the point of his most serious confusion. An ethic without economic implications is no ethic.

The early Christian community provided a social framework which expressed the values to which the believer was committed. His needs were met. Today Christianity is confronted with the task of creating a social structure which will meet the needs of men who are forced to live in a vastly more complex society.

The difficulties of the task should not be underestimated. To good will and ethical sensitivity must be added knowledge beyond the possession of any one individual. Collaboration of experts in many fields is demanded. Illusive motivational forces, which the economic system develops and on which it depends, must be understood. "Blueprints" are not enough. They often look well on paper, but may fail to release the human power and enthusiasm essential to the success of any social system.

American traditions contain elements which are akin to Christian social ideals. This is more than an accident. Into the building of the American nation went many of the ideals of the Hebraic-Christian ethic. If our present economic system may be said to be failing, it fails not merely because people cannot eat securely but because it is not expressing a basic aspiration of men for a mode of human relations which is both Christian and American. Our deeper selves, molded by our traditions, require a better system than has yet emerged.

In his criticism of the Christian ethic, Mr. Knight makes a point which merits careful consideration. He calls attention to the fact that the Christian ethic was derived from small, face-to-face groups. He questions its relevance for the gigantic operations of an industrial society in which many of the most important relationships are impersonal. In meeting this criticism, it may be pointed out that all human ideals seem originally to have been derived from small groups. The family and the community have always provided men with the basic experiences in human relations. In so far as men found them good they have tried to extend them into the larger and more complex society. This was precisely the course of development of the Christian ethic. Its source was the small Christian community. There men experienced a way of life which seemed good and became their ideal for all human relations. Our task is not to try merely to reproduce in their original form the sentiments and relationships of the small, familial group, but rather to discover the principles underlying these relationships and to see how they may be given the widest necessary application.

Consequently, the principles which we have presented are not dependent on face-to-face relations. One may, for example, find it impossible to feel the same toward Mr. Unknown in Tokio as one feels toward one's neighbor across the street. There is no reason, however, why his actions and the policies of his government should not express his conviction that there is a common humanity uniting the Japanese and the Americans, that both have a claim on the resources of the earth, are equally entitled to freedom and are mutually responsible for the common welfare. Experience in the family and community disclose *possibilities* for human relations which we must then try to realize in the larger relationships of modern life.

First the economic meaning of the principle of *human equality* will be considered. What would have to be done if this value were to be made an operating principle of our economy?

The early Christian community was under no illusion concerning the fact of inequalities in possessions, social status and privilege in the Roman Empire. Its members were drawn, as has been stated, primarily from the lower classes, on whom political, social and economic disabilities rested heavily. Nevertheless, the early Christians believed in equality in the sense that all men fall short of God's goodness, are equally in need of the salvation which the Christian Gospel proclaims and are equally entitled to the spiritual and material resources to be found in the Christian fellowship. A member has a "claim" on his fellows because he is a human being. The Christian thesis would thus seem to be that any group which fails to recognize this claim as a right of all members is doomed to disintegration.

The meaning of the principle of equality is revealed by a simple test. Let it be asked: Are there children in our society who because of unfavorable conditions start life with handicaps which tend to warp their entire physical, mental and social life? Such conditions include: inadequate food, demoralizing home and community life, inadequate medical care, poor education. If on inquiry we find that there are such children, while at the same time there are other children who start life under superior conditions, we can be sure that our society is violating the principle of equality. Its first duty is then to put its collective intelligence and resources to the job of providing the deprived children with a start in life that compares favorably with that enjoyed by the more privileged.

An economy or political, religious or educational institution which makes it impossible for society to do this task requires change. This is Christianity's first reconstructive proposal with which the economist is asked to come to terms.

To such a proposal an objection commonly encountered is this: "If equality has to be maintained by special props provided for the weak, lazy or improvident, the price is too great because you thereby discourage initiative and produce dependence. It is far better for society and for the individual to have equality as a goal or possibility to be achieved by industry and struggle than to have it guaranteed or handed out as a gift." It is further maintained that the stimulus to initiative and self-reliance is the mainspring of social progress, and without it life would stagnate.

A simple answer to this objection is that most of the good things of life have to be gained through collective action. If we desire a society characterized by equality of opportunity, we cannot leave it to individuals. Because of the collective nature of modern economy, if we want young people to start life without handicaps which may forever hold them back from their highest possibilities of achievements, the conditions can only be secured through collective action. The obstacles are socially produced and must be removed through social measures.

That there is a risk involved at the point of personal motivation may be admitted. It would, however, be difficult to convince most parents that their efforts to provide their children with proper food, medical care, education inevitably produce dependence; otherwise they would turn them out at an early age to shift for themselves. The Christian ethic asserts that the same kind of economic provision which wise parents try to make for their children ought also to be made for every child born into our society. Society has too great a stake in childhood to leave such matters to individual initiative.

The problem of stifling initiative and producing dependence is an educational and political one. The art of providing children with enough but not too much, and of creating self-reliance out of initial dependence, is not an insuperable task. As a political problem the difficulty arises not so much from the people receiving help as from those giving and administering it, who often enjoy the exercise of power over those whom they have helped. Politicians and social agencies have been known to encourage and exploit dependence for their own political advantage or egoistic satisfaction. It is possible to control them by enlightened political action which puts into office persons who combine intelligence with genuine devotion to human welfare.

The principle of equality also requires attack on those persistent social and economic conditions of our society which keep large groups of people in poverty and squalor, such as the sharecropper, and withhold opportunities to earn a living or learn trades or professions to which their talents entitle them because of racial or other considerations. Periodic unemployment may or may not be controllable. In so far as control is beyond the wisdom of economists, the principle of equality requires collective action to provide the material basis for living for those who are dispossessed of opportunity through no fault of their own. This is an inescapable "charge" on the resources of society.

No one who has seen a modern nation gird for war will be convinced that the economic problems involved in the Christian's concept of equality could not be dealt with far better than we are now doing if equivalent energy were applied to them. To undertake the task with similar all-out resolution is a responsibility of our society. Common sense dictates that a society which hopes to continue to exist must adopt something like the principle of equality, as conceived in the Christian ethic, if social disintegration is to be avoided.

The second principle—that of *collective responsibility*—is based on a vivid sense of group solidarity. It involves an awareness on the part of each member of the needs of his fellows and a readiness to do whatever is necessary to meet those needs. If such action demands a sacrifice, he is willing to make it.

Mutuality can be developed only by enlarging and socializing the self through education and social experience. The process must begin in the home and school.

The principle of collective responsibility comes into conflict with extreme individualism and the fierce competitiveness which characterizes much of present-day economic life. The theoretical problem of the merits and demerits of competition has long been debated; the debate has been largely outmoded by developments in the operation of business. Individual competition is not now an issue. Competition in our time is primarily a contest of groups—corporations within the state, and between states. The time-worn arguments concerning the benefits to the individual from competing with his fellows have been made irrelevant to the actual situation which is now faced.

If the principle of collective responsibility is to be implemented in economic affairs, the problem must be expressed in terms of the control of large corporations rather than of individuals. This control must be on the basis of responsibility to society; and responsibility is to be interpreted not by the corporation itself but by society functioning through its political agencies.

This raises the issue of state control. The ills to which state control is subject—bureaucracy, inefficiency, irresponsibility, political chicanery and self-seeking—are well known. Whether private industry is less subject to these evils may be questioned. The problem is how to make the state an efficient economic instrument and how to be sure that it is used for the common good as interpreted by the principles of the Christian ethic.

An urgent task is to devise a method of discovering and estimating the basic needs of the total population. This should be done by a political agency set up as a normal part of governmental organization and given the means for discovering and measuring needs for food, drink, shelter, health, means of communication and travel, education. In our wartime economy this is actually being done.

A planning group will also survey resources for meeting these needs. This might show the necessity of restricting or expanding existing agencies of production and distribution of goods and services. Whether such agencies should be publicly or privately owned and operated would have to be determined solely by the ability of a particular business to operate under the requirements set up in the exercise of the state's function to provide the basic necessities of living for all. It is conceivable that such a mechanism would be less responsive to new needs than was the system of "free enterprise"; also that the weeding-out process by which inefficient businesses were eliminated under the older economy would be lost. However, a flexibility and responsiveness to changing needs in the economic-political system is a possibility as long as people are free to criticize and to demand changes when they want goods and services which the system is not providing.

The people might conceivably elect a new President because he promised to get them better safety razors than those now in use. Memory recalls a presidential candidate who promised chickens and automobiles. Representative, democratic government is itself a competitive system in which we believe, despite well-known inadequacies, because parties compete for public support on the basis of improvements which they claim to be able to make in the conditions of life of the people.

It is impossible to take seriously "collective responsibility" for the basic economic needs of the people without collective action by our *political* agencies. The need for adaptations in the governmental mechanism to enable it to perform this task is clear. This is a major task confronting society today, and no one who is seriously committed to the Christian social ethic can escape it. Even if he prefers the good old days or is satisfied with his personal situation, he must be led to see that the Christian ethical demand for collective responsibility cannot be met unless adequate forms of political action are discovered. Improvement of the state as an instrument for achieving ethical values in economic relations is required if collective responsibility is to be a reality.

The "new day" which this development proclaims can come only as the outlook of individuals is enlarged and socialized. Egoistic individualism and provincialism must be replaced by a sense of collective responsibility and a capacity for mutuality in action. The education of the individual is a task to which religious and secular agencies alike must give themselves. Without it reconstruction of the political state is impossible.

The discussion of equality and collective responsibility has raised acutely the question of *freedom*. The two first-mentioned principles require limitation of the freedom of the individual for the sake of something else which is usually termed the general welfare. To secure a measure of equality requires some curtailment of freedom. Citizens cannot be free to exploit people, and everyone knows that exploitation occurs unless—and often in spite of the fact that—there are laws to curb it.

We cherish no illusions that this age-old problem is to be solved now. We must, however, find some means of balancing the dual values of an ideal of freedom which conserves and nourishes each man's distinctive capacities and individuality and an ideal of social responsibility which requires him, when he will not do it of his own accord, to abide by rules the purpose of which is to make the values of freedom available to all.

In the specific area of economic activity the system of "free enterprise" was an assertion of the right of the individual to produce and distribute whatever goods and services he wished, limited only or mainly by the inexorable circumstances of being able to find buyers at the price at which he was able or wished to sell. Never actually enjoying that degree of freedom and limited increasingly by laws regulating wages, hours, working conditions and "sharp practices," the businessman was nevertheless committed to a potent idea which, to his mind, represented ethical freedom in the economic world. He believed that the state ought to interfere as little as possible with his activity and leave the question of his professional life or death as man-of-business to the competition of the free market.

For a generation and with increasing rapidity, laws and regulations have been imposed infringing freedom thus interpreted. These restrictions have been devised "piecemeal" to alleviate ills resulting from business activity. Sometimes they have protected the business interests of one group against a competing group. The apparently inescapable tendency of businesses to amalgamate and to form huge combines with near-monopolistic power, quite apart from government interference, has further limited individual freedom. To protect himself against such gigantic concentrations the businessman has appealed to the government for help, and has secured the enactment of laws intended to limit monopolistic tendencies. This in itself was a restriction of freedom.

We have now reached the point where such piecemeal restrictions on economic freedom must add up to *something*, but no one knows precisely what. Many men feel that the answer is chaos in which it is almost impossible to conduct business. The only possible way out is to find a rational principle on the basis of which these laws and regulations may be revised and reformed. This requires a philosophy of economic and political conduct.

Such a philosophy requires a redefinition of freedom in terms of economic realities. To define it as the absence of restraint is naive and useless. To define it as a condition in which the individual is limited only by the principle that he shall not do harm to another is not illuminating unless harm is defined in something other than individualistic terms. A concept of general or social good is required. To find it, there is needed a new conception of the individual. He should be thought of not as a separate entity seeking satisfaction by establishing relations with other individuals but as a person whose individuality is a function of human association, custom, education and law. The individual is a product biologically and culturally of other human beings to whom he is related by unseverable ties. His ethic, his politics, his economic activity, his education, art and religion must express this fact of human relatedness. Whatever freedom he finds must not negate this fact. It can only be found in a condition which makes freedom possible for all in the measure that it is possible for him.

Freedom is thus "under the law" of a larger responsibility, which is: the creation of an economic culture in which there is opportunity for every man to earn a living for himself and his family and to have access to the culture in that measure which he is able to enjoy. The political state is the agency of the future which must take the leadership in arranging the conditions which will make this possible and will enable each man to develop to such heights as his endowments make possible.

To develop such an economy requires restriction of freedom at points which seem crucial to many people who have been habituated to the philosophy of "individual enterprise" or who through the present system of "ordered chaos" have reaped special advantages which they have no mind to give up. Increasingly such persons are coming to see that change is inevitable. It is to be hoped that they see it soon enough to develop a philosophy which will find new freedoms in an economically implemented sense of human interrelatedness.

One freedom which it is essential to maintain is freedom "to know, to utter, and to argue freely according to conscience." Finding a way through the difficulties of fashioning a collective instrument by which equality, social responsibility and freedom may be made a reality is a difficult task. Mistakes are inevitable. Public discussion and criticism are indispensable. However, even this highly important freedom must at times be limited to those who accept the basic values which society sets up as its goals. It is not easy to lay down a general principle for determining when such times exist or the types of criticism which cannot be tolerated. The ideal is complete freedom of criticism. In times of great stress when a society feels its existence is threatened, some limitation is unavoidable. There are those who regard freedom of discussion as an evil, and would limit it to a few; they are opposed to the view that a good society offers equality of opportunity to all, regardless of race, color or creed. There are occasions when such radical deviations from a liberal outlook may require restraint in the interest of social peace or freedom.

The economic implications of the fourth principle, *universality*, relate chiefly to the range or inclusiveness of outlook to characterize the approach of the economist. The Christian ethic recognizes that its life and message are open to all men regardless of race, color, nationality, social status or other accidents. These artificial divisions are subordinate to a common humanity seeking salvation, or perhaps just a chance to live without excessive pangs of hunger and without being stepped on by some frightened brother who is seeking the same thing. Christianity's outreach is humanity-wide. Its ethic is supposed to apply to all human beings.

Underlying the principle is the belief that a God of love has created man in His image. If this means anything, it means that every man has something within him that is like God, and this something is an ineradicable tendency to love —that is, to act in a way which may be variously labeled as co-operatively, with respect, brotherliness or good will. The vocation of the Christian is never to let men forget that fact, or permit them to think that this way of acting is foreign to their natures. This impulse toward fraternal action is an expression of ultimate reality. It is a fact of human nature in spite of impressive evidence to the contrary, such as attitudes of hate toward foreigners or the satisfaction which some men have in seeing other people suffer. There is in man longing for fraternal relationships and fellowship which any economic or political system frustrates only to its own ultimate destruction.

In the early Christian communities men and women of different backgrounds, including slaves, impoverished free men, slaveowners and government officials, seem to have found just that kind of fellowship. The social barriers did not make any difference within the fellowship. A man was taken for what he was—just a sinner trying to get ahead in righteousness and obedience to God. He found a life of helpfulness and mutuality.

This is the pattern which Christians at their best have always wanted to transfer to the world "outside," but it has not been easy. Thus they have often thought of themselves as actually living in two worlds, never completely separated—for after all a man had to earn a living—but the requirements of one world often negating or conflicting with the requirements of the other. Especially was this true of the requirements of universality. The slave was free in the community but he was not free outside and his fellow Christians could do little about it. Many thought it was not their business to do anything about it—not if they valued their heads and wanted to keep out of prison. The Roman government, like all governments, knew how to deal with people who tried to upset the system of private property.

But the principle of universality persisted in Christianity. The missionary movement was an expression of it, but now the principle seems to demand other implementation. It demands a world order and a world economic and political system which aim to secure, as far as any society can secure them, the benefits of equality, collective responsibility, freedom, for *all* humanity.

This is a large order. The world is at war. To the cynic, every nation seems to be mainly looking after itself, co-operating whenever it can find a partner in crime or some group naive enough to believe that its own interests will be served by working and killing for somebody else. Brotherhood and universality seem far away. But for once, time and circumstances seem to be with the Christian, who demands a society based on the universal relatedness of human beings. Even if he cannot feel himself bound by fraternal ties to the "Japs" and the "Nazis," modern conditions require that all his social problems—economic, medical, political—be viewed and solved as world problems. New methods of communication and transportation have knit all regions of the world together. Man of the future must be a world citizen whether he wants to or not. He cannot escape this condition; the ethic that will fit this future will be Christianity's creed of universality and not some kind of imperialistic nationalism or parochial racism.

The intervening conflicts will be costly, and many an unjust and temporizing armistice may ensue before a workable *modus vivendi* can be found which will make it possible for mankind to appraise the universal needs and resources of human beings everywhere and bring the two together through workable political and economic arrangements.

This seems like a dream, but there is a dynamic in the principle of universality which statesmen overlook. It contains an ethical potential that, because it is in line with the facts of modern life, is probably more powerful than racial fanaticism, which everybody thinks is pretty potent these days. When a man attempts to enlarge his horizon and sympathies and transcend his race, class or nation, something happens within him. He is then expressing that which is most "real" within him; the sources of the impulse are in the common biological and cultural heritage which he shares with all other human beings. When he responds to this impulse, he is growing into the manhood for which he was destined. New capacities, new and stronger incentives, intellectual vigor are released under the impact of an intelligent attempt to become a citizen of the world and to seek equality and freedom for all men, not merely for one's self, or one's family, or one's nation.

Today, as the Christian faces defeat of his most cherished hopes for world order, he ought to take account of stock, and if possible find out why he has not been more successful in translating his high community ethic into social actuality. There are doubtless many reasons. One is his refusal to take seriously the job of finding economic and political implementation for this ethic. A related reason, I believe, is that the Christian has failed to get a *philosophy of force*. He has assumed that love or freedom required that nobody be "pushed around." He has been sickened by the examples of terrible evils resulting from the use of force for bad ends or as a substitute for understanding and reason. He has been unable to see that even good ends require the use of force, and that the primary ethical problem, when ethics ventures into the market place or state house, is precisely the problem of the use of power over people: how much, what kind, when to be used and when discontinued; how to use power so that its use becomes progressively unnecessary; and how to relate power to the method of conference and the achievement of consensus. On the whole, the ethically sensitive Christian has tended to stay out of situations involving such issues; sometimes he has condemned without understanding the complexity of the practical issues. In instances where religion has entered the field of political or economic action—as, for example, in establishing legislative pressure organizations or conducting a publishing business—it has often failed to demonstrate that it understood the ethical use of power any better than business or political groups.

Unless the Christian ethicist can shed light on how to implement values through reason *and* coercion, he has little or no contribution to make to economic and political life. Perhaps his example as a person who never uses force or violence may do some good in keeping an ideal afloat in a sea of violence, but he is still avoiding the major problem.

The hope that the Christian ideals of freedom, equality, responsibility and universality can become the operating principles of a world order is based on the assumption that some group will understand the rational use of force or coercion in behalf of those ideals. Its use is dangerous to the ideals, and to the people using it; but refusal to use it to preserve ideals will postpone the coming of a society in which force and the threat of force is confined to increasingly narrow limits. But we have a long way to go on the pathway toward humane behavior.

CHAPTER ELEVEN

American Economic Life—An Appraisal

CRITICISM is a function of Christianity. To be effective, it must be based on a clear-cut set of values and a knowledge of the facts about man and the social order in which he lives. The Christian ethic is a statement of the values to which a Christian is committed. It has been suggested that these values include equality, freedom, collective responsibility and universality. It is now our task to look at the facts of American society, specifically in its economic phases. How good is our economic order from the standpoint of Christian ethical values?

The function of social criticism is not usually associated with religion. Generally religion is thought of primarily as a conservative rather than a critical movement. "Religious," for many people, is synonymous with "uncritical" or "conservative," especially in social and economic matters. The fact that religion criticizes personal conduct seems more generally accepted than that it ought also to criticize social conditions. In the latter case, religion is thought to be departing from its field and meddling with affairs in which it has no competence. That religion is frequently incompetent in the complex field of social issues is undoubtedly true. Its job, however, is not to quit the field, as many assume, but to become more competent.

When Christians do become social critics, they should be not only well informed but humble. In their criticism there should be the quality of confession. There should be recognition of the fact that the individuals and churches who criticize are participants in the social evils which they condemn.

They share responsibility for the injustices, maladjustments and stupidities of their society. To some extent it is their own inattention, ignorance, ill will and readiness to accept a lower level of social practice than the culture makes possible which are responsible for the conditions they criticize.

Despite this humility which ought to be a part of Christian social criticism, the role of the critic is not a popular one. Men do not take kindly to demonstrations of the evils of their society, especially when their own security is founded on these evils. Criticism is resented particularly when it comes from churches, from which, because of a serious limitation in outlook, men have come to expect docile conformity and preoccupation with so-called "spiritual" interests. It is not strange that social criticism has often been pushed outside the churches where it has maintained a precarious existence as a minority movement.

To some extent this is the situation today, but far less typically than many people like to think. Within most of the larger Christian churches today there are important and official movements engaged in active social criticism. They wield considerable influence, difficult to measure but in excess of their numerical strength. From such groups the criticisms which follow are largely derived. These groups are saying that the American economic system is failing men at a number of crucial points. These will be briefly reviewed.

American economic society fails to distribute economic goods and services with anything approaching equality. Some people have more than they can use, while the masses have less than enough to provide an adequate diet. According to the Brookings Institution as reported in *Social Action*,[1] 20 per cent of our national income in 1929 went to 8/10 of one per cent of the population. The 12,000,000 at the bottom of the economic scale received income equal to that received by 36,000 families at the top. The mere fact of differences in

[1] *Social Action.* Council for Social Action of the Congregational Christian Churches. Vol. VII, No. 10, December 15, 1941.

income is less impressive than the human costs which result. Adequate diet as worked out by the Department of Agriculture is reported as impossible for 74 per cent of America's urban and village families.

Regardless of how this inequality is explained or how pessimistic one may be concerning the possibility of changing it, the fact that it exists makes it impossible for a person who takes Christian social ideals seriously to be complacent about the economic system. The loss in potential human capacity which might serve the commonweal is great. Malnutrition, bad education, faulty care during childhood result in part from economic inequalities.

Obvious deficiencies in human capacities may be admitted. The fact is, however, that it is to society's interest to provide a better start in life for millions of people whose potentialities for a constructive contribution are blighted in childhood. Economic inequalities also mean that many people are condemned to culturally impoverished lives. It takes money to buy transportation, tickets of admission, good light for reading, comfortable rooms, and the budgets of all too many families won't stand such expenditures.

The point need not be labored. Christians live in a society of economic inequality. It is an offense against conscience and requires development of a program so to alter the economic system that inequalities are eliminated. This is plain.

What is the goal? How far is the ideal of equality to be carried? This is an important issue of theory. For the time being, however, it is sufficient to say that we need a great deal less inequality than we now have. As long as three-fifths of American families have incomes inadequate to provide them with the basic necessities of life, while productive capacity is adequate to provide those necessities, the ideal of equality indicates a change in the system. This task may be attacked while the debate goes on as to how far the idea of equality should theoretically be pushed.

Today it appears that millions of people have made up

their minds to build the kind of society that equalizes income and refuse to be content with less. They may be frustrated and misled in their efforts but they will not give up the struggle. This is the revolutionary state of mind of these times. The Christian may well interpret it as the moving of the spirit of an ethical God in the hearts of men. To attempt to build an economic order which will implement the Christian ideal of equality is one step in the direction of creating living conditions which make it possible for men to act as if they were made in the image of God. A full stomach is not enough, but it ill behooves men with full stomachs to dwell on that fact when about them are men, women and children who are too debilitated by physical privation or its threat to have much else on their minds beyond where the next meal is coming from.

A second point at which the economic system offends the Christian conscience is this: The system concentrates economic power in groups which are deficient in social vision and social responsibility or are ignorant of the ethical implications of their activities.

Concentration of power is necessary; the problem is how to control it for the general welfare. Too often the responsibility which financial and industrial leaders feel is based on a limited view of social and economic values. They often have a sense of obligation to make profits and to keep themselves and their organizations in the running with their competitors. Most of them also feel that somehow these responsibilities are related to the general welfare. But this is not enough. The economic power which these leaders wield gives them power over the lives and destinies of men, and commonly this power is not exercised with a sense of stewardship for the people as a whole. Business should not be a game for the competitive display of ability to outwit opponents. It ought to be regarded as an activity through which society seeks to perform certain indispensable functions. If a man because of ability, luck or hard work secures power, he thereby becomes responsible for the lives of people. He only distorts his function when he thinks of it primarily in terms of making money. But this, by and large, is exactly what the system forces him to do. To stay in the game one must play the game according to the rules. The rules, or rather the concept of the game which has produced these rules, are the root of the evil. The ability to make profits is an entirely inadequate but the most widely prevalent standard of a successful business. The ability to provide goods and services and to make them available to the largest number of people who need or want them is the social function of business and the only function that is acceptable to the Christian conscience.

Fortunately there are increasing numbers of men who are seeking to serve a social purpose through business enterprise. They appreciate the fact that without sound business and industry the community would disintegrate in a few weeks, or even days. Whoever possesses power in a business enterprise has a heavy social responsibility. The traditional conception of the way this responsibility is to be regarded is contained in the Christian teaching regarding stewardship. Our economic system, however, has distorted this concept by emphasizing it as a stewardship for profits.

Today the agency through which the *social* concept of business is being expressed is the state. Political power is being exercised increasingly to force business to perform its social functions. This tendency to look to the state to force changes in economic life has been resorted to mainly because business has been slow to read the signs of the times and has fought legislation intended to socialize its activities.

Christians do not believe that any person is wise or noble enough, or so consistently sensitive to human need, to be vested with power without providing definite checks on him. The checks must represent the broad functions which society expects him to perform. Checks arising from limited views of those functions will be no good. It is recognized that few even of the strongest financial or industrial groups have unlimited power. They are limited by the requirements of the economic system itself. These requirements, which may not be violated if the group is to stay in business, are not, however, moral principles. They are in many cases merely experience regarding what can be gotten away with in a system which assumes that production for gain is the chief end of business enterprise. In the Christian view, the end is the development of persons.

In so far as business has been limited by what is called government interference, it has come about both as an expression of social conscience, endeavoring to bring business into line with its essential function, and also as the result of pressure of rival economic groups or of labor to move in on the economic powers that be and pick up some of the gravy. To the degree that government activity in the economic sphere represents an attempt of the people to meet the needs of all people, and to force power groups to find their legitimate function within the total welfare, it moves in a direction which the Christian conscience can approve.

The Christian ethic requires an economic structure which will express *collective responsibility*. This responsibility is greater than the interests of any particular business or set of business interests. To accomplish this end power is granted—not inherited or seized—for the performance of specific functions determined by the society in which the business operates. In the Christian society the ends under which economic functions are carried on are the development of man in the image of God, the fulfillment of his possibilities, one of which is to live in relationship to his fellows so that they too may develop their highest potentialities.

Because in our society economic power has so often been held without a corresponding answerability for the performance of human functions, Christianity finds our economic system unacceptable and in need of changing.

At a third point the economic system under which we live is weighed in the scales of the Christian ethic and found unacceptable. It tends to bring out and foster the acquisitive impulses of men. It emphasizes the self-regarding and unsocial potentialities. Thus it shapes men. Business is conducted to make money. To succeed requires the suppression of humane and co-operative impulses. The system cannot implement the Christian's desire for a society based on the principles of freedom, equality, collective responsibility and universality. The system also assumes that the lure of profits is the most effective motive for getting the best out of men, and best is interpreted in terms of qualities which can be used by the system whose end is profits. Other motives are pushed into the background. The result is disintegration of the finer nature of men. Another result is seen in the kind of religion which is produced to minister to men dominated by that kind of economic system. It is a truncated misrepresentation of Christianity with a compartmentalized ethic, removed from effective contact with economic life and hence powerless to change it. That kind of Christianity in turn nurtures men who have no interest in changing the economic system.

To provide a measure of ideological support, a theory of man is produced which asserts that man is by nature self-centered, acquisitive. It overlooks the fact that his nature is produced by the social situation in which he is reared.

The fact that economic activities occupy so large a place in our society intensifies the problem. What a man is in his business he tends to become totally. Unless the Christian ethic can get itself expressed in and through the economic operations of society, it is doomed to futility and ineffectiveness. It will never be able to put the stamp of its love ethic on the men and women and children whom it must reach. To those who accept the Christian ethic and who try to live in a society in which economic considerations are as dominating as they are in our society, there will be a split between ideals and action. All standards tend to become subsidiary to the economic. Success comes to mean and to require the highest possible degree of clever acquisitiveness and this flows over into all departments of life. What should be a subsidiary function is exaggerated out of all perspective. The good man becomes the successful, i.e., the cleverest and most acquisitive, man. Thus the Christian ethic is transformed into an impotent dream-world into which the unsuccessful and successful retire for inspiration and reassurance that the sins of acquisitiveness are forgiven by a loving God.

The dominance of the economic in our society has led to the depersonalizing of human relations. In the growth of large-scale industry, relations between employer and employee, producer and consumer, management and labor have become formal and abstract. The personal contact and sense of co-operating in a socially important task have been lost. Tasks have become specialized and mechanized; it has become easy for industry to think of men as cogs in a machine. People are valued in terms of economic *power* and means, rather than as individual personalities. Their significance is in their power to produce. "The soul of man is treated as so many horse-power in the economic machine." Man, as such, has no monetary value; it is only his power to produce that is important.

The process by which man has become monetized is a responsibility which the economic system must bear. Money as a medium of exchange is vital to society. It provides a way of labeling material values so as to make possible the exchange of goods for other goods, labor for labor and labor for goods. Its effect is to reduce all values to a material or exchangeable standard. Men are *worth* so much in dollars and cents. Even a pastorate is often considered important or unimportant depending on the salary that the church can pay, the size of its contribution to foreign missions or the amount of property which it owns. So long have we lived in this monetized atmosphere that it has permeated our outlook and evaluations.

It is obvious that such a culture is antagonistic to the evaluations which are implicit in the Christian ethic. Love can mean little more than a sentimental and slightly assuaging influence. Man is made in the image of God and ought never to be treated purely as a means, but it is precisely as a means that our economic society is treating him—a means for the production of goods for the sake of profits. This is a social structuralizing of evil and of a view of man antithetical to the the Christian view.

With the depersonalizing of human relations which is increasingly a characteristic of modern industrial society has come a loss of ethical integrity and standards. Persons cannot feel the requirements of honesty, fair play, good workmanship toward a large corporation, industrial or political, that they feel toward persons whom they see, react to, enter into contractual and co-operative relations with. The result is loss of a sense of values which is required for achieving a stable society.

Our present economic system is further unacceptable to the Christian ethic because it condemns man to a "kingdom of fear." Ever around the corner for the modern man stalks the specter of poverty and the day when he will be unable to feed, clothe and provide shelter for those who are dependent on him. Fear of loss of job, fear of ill health and resulting inability to work, fear of old age, fear of being thrown on the industrial scrap heap when he can be replaced by a more powerful man or by a more efficient machine, fear of devastating wars which will wipe out his life and his business, if he has one—these are the fears which dog the steps of modern man. Surely no one can claim that it is inconsistent with or irrelevant to Christianity that men should join with their fellows to accomplish what they cannot accomplish individually, namely: the organizing of an economic life which will reduce the element of fear and insecurity. This determination has taken hold of modern men as perhaps no other cause in our times has done and will not be denied. It moves in the direction of effectualizing the Christian ethic.

Our economic system is further in conflict with the Christian ethic because it requires a way of looking at work which denies the traditional Christian concept of work as a "vocation." In the Christian view, work is a task which a person, given certain abilities, interests and potentialities, is called to do in order that he and his fellows may exist. Work is a responsibility through which one's social obligations are fulfilled. It is also a means for the expression of the desire to create and to secure the satisfaction from doing a job well. It is difficult to apply this view of work in our present system. The "machine" cannot be blamed solely. There is no reason why the help of machines should be antagonistic to the human desire to create. Degradation of the "calling" comes from the fact that men feel that they are not producing for social ends. Men are not "called" to work at a job to make profits so that other men may live in luxury. According to the Christian conception of work, the worker is a co-operator in a common enterprise which has a purpose approved by the Christian ethic in which he shares. Drastic revisions in the system are indicated when this view of work is considered. Many of the tasks which men now do and which seem to be required by our competitive system of distribution cannot by any stretch of the imagination or charity be regarded as "callings" in the Christian sense. They involve trickery, misrepresentation, victimizing of the weak and ignorant. In so far as these jobs are necessary to the functioning of an economic system, that system must be condemned, and the Christian must work to change it.

CHAPTER TWELVE

Economic Intentions of Christianity

IF THE pronouncements of churches on economic issues are to be more than "cheap bluster at an absent foe," as Walter Rauschenbusch once characterized them, they must be supported by a positive intention to act. The purpose of this chapter is to state briefly a few social intentions which are now taking form among men and women who are under the direct influence of social Christianity.

The world conflict has had both a stimulating and a depressing influence on the forming of a social mind. There have been both reactionary and pioneering developments. The former are to be observed in groups emphasizing personal salvation and fundamentalist theology, the long-run influence of which is to draw off energy from social problems. Against this reaction it is not hard to find movements within Christianity which represent a vigorous, realistic and tough-minded attack on social issues both in the national and in the international scene. It is significant that increasingly groups so minded are seeking to utilize the social sciences in the effort to understand the forces at play in modern society and to formulate an effective strategy for dealing with these forces in the interest of Christian ideals. Obviously it is from such groups that the economic intentions to which we have referred are to be sought.

These intentions reveal the directions in which Christian social action is likely to move in the days ahead. In this program, the religious groups expect to ally themslves with specialists in economics, sociology and related fields. Purely as an ethical venture Christian social action does not pretend to be competent or required to describe in detail the means by which its goals are to be achieved. It recognizes a responsibility for finding a method, but will use the resources of social science and experience in developing it. The first task of the Christian ethical thinker is to clarify objectives concerning the kind of society and persons that we want.

"Intentions" are a kind of fusing of objectives and methods, but are by no means a blueprint. They are a statement of direction which social action will take, a clue to probable future policies and programs of Christian groups. In the statement which follows will be found the issues to which the Christian conscience, seeking social expression, is sensitive today and the types of reconstruction of society to which Christian men and women will probably respond and, it is hoped, give leadership.

It is the *Christian intention* to bring the economic system under the control of socialized purposes democratically evolved. Economic life has not been under such control, and consequently has not been instrumental to the achievement of social ends. Obviously the economic system has contributed much to social welfare, but the contribution has tended to be incidental to the making of profits for individuals. Our thesis is that business is an intricate mechanism, but still a *mechanism*, and the ends for which it is used must come from outside business itself; these ends ought to be social goals embracing man's whole personal and social life, not merely his economic life. Can our effort to secure food, clothing, shelter and other necessities and luxuries become an activity which will contribute to the upbuilding of men and enrich the common life? The answer to this question assumes a philosophy of life and of values which makes life dignified and significant. What the Christian view is has been presented. The point here is simply that economic activities are to become instrumental to such ideals.

Business in the past has shown little disposition to accept this interpretation of its function. It has resisted socially imposed ethical controls, whether these controls have come from governmental sources or from the activity of citizens in their private capacity, as, for example, in the organization of co-operatives. Business leaders have even at times opposed the discussion of issues which questioned the system in which they operated, and made use of such epithets as "socialistic" and "communistic" to discredit movements which might result in interference with their autonomy. But now the robber-baron period of economic development is over. The complex, ramified and interrelated system of economic enterprise must be directed and planned. This will come, and the primary question is whether the ends toward which planning is directed are to be socially enlightened. Christian thought asserts that the ends ought to embody the Christian values of freedom, equality of opportunity, collective responsibility and a humanity-wide outlook. Increasingly Christian action will develop and seek alliances which will implement this conviction.

It is the *Christian intention* to work for the elimination of private ownership of property wherever the rights of property conflict with the establishment of social justice or the general social welfare. This position is explicitly stated in the so-called Malvern Manifesto[1] issued by a group of British churchmen. While the line between enterprises ripe for public ownership and operation and others is not easily drawn, few economists today would question that it is the function of the state to issue and regulate money, to conduct postal service, and many would also include water works, electric power and light and similar services essential to the life of a modern society. Businesses which have constantly to be regulated by laws or to be investigated by legislative bodies are probably ready for public ownership and operation, also enterprises which deal with essentials to life, the widest possible distribution of which is crucial to the na-

[1] Malvern Manifesto. The Church League for Industrial Democracy, 155 Washington Street, New York City.

tional welfare. It may be to the interest of the public to conduct such economic enterprises on so small a margin of profit that they will never be an attractive field for private investment, and consequently production will lag behind public need. Without excluding private enterprise totally, education in many phases is clearly an interest of this type; likewise medical care, food, decent living accommodations. Socially minded people are increasingly losing confidence in private enterprise in these fields, and in the future will try some other way.

Without attempting to draw a hard and fast line between what will be publicly owned and operated, what should be left to private activity and what may be left to both, it may be noted that the potentialities of collective enterprise are beginning to be appreciated. Rightly or wrongly people now begin to look to co-operation to accomplish ends which they are unable to achieve through individual enterprise, and the form that this move is taking is political. The state is coming to be judged by its effectiveness in the field of economic co-operation.

It is the *Christian intention* to strengthen the motive of community responsibility and welfare and to weaken the motive of individual gain. The profit motive has been praised as the mainspring of progress and cursed as the root of evil in modern economic society. Doubtless it has been both, but in the future Christian agencies will not be content to see the results of their efforts to develop a religious sense of collective responsibility and community frustrated by an economic system which requires that the individual be primarily interested in private gain. This is only to say that the educational agencies of the churches which are concerned with inculcating motives of love and interest in one's neighbor—neighbor being interpreted to mean all peoples, regardless of race, color, class or condition—are increasingly seeing that the culture, and not merely the individual, must be changed. It does little or no good to try to inculcate these virtues in children only to have them in adulthood go out to make their living in a society which demands primary attention to self-interest.

The motives of mutual aid and community responsibility are as "natural" and basic as self-centeredness and private gain. It is the culture which determines which kind of attitude will develop. The Christian is on the march toward an economic culture which will make essential Christian attitudes possible.

The bigness and anonymity which increasingly characterize urban life are large factors in the frustration of Christian virtues. Christian values emerged historically from the small community. In the small community persons have a better chance of being persons instead of merely names in a telephone book or competitors for standing room in the bus. Anonymous relationships between individuals do not promote responsibility. Every individual needs some type of community living if he is to develop responsible action, relationships in which he is answerable to others and in which his actions are checked by his fellow members. The loss of this kind of relationship is one important factor in the decline of community virtue. It is on the agenda for study and action in social Christianity.

It is the *Christian intention* to support and extend labor organization as a relatively permanent agency through which the rights of workers in all fields are to be conserved. Unions provide one means by which equality of the Christian ethic may be achieved. They provide a basis for negotiation with management concerning matters vitally affecting the welfare of the workers under conditions approaching parity as between management and worker. Christian social action is interested, therefore, in seeing labor organization extended into fields where it does not now exist in any effective way. It is recognized that labor leadership and techniques need improvement, that there is graft and anti-social practice. These are characteristics of growing up, perhaps the "robber-baron" period which labor, like business enterprise, goes through. It is pertinent to note that resistance to the extension of labor organization by business groups inevitably tends to bring out the fighting, vengeful reactions and the kind of leadership which expresses these attitudes. Labor statesmanship of vision and a broad sense of social responsibility is emerging. This Christian social action must encourage and support.

The labor movement at bottom is an educational movement based on essentially Christian ideals. There is common ground between it and the churches which the Christian social actionist intends to cultivate. Promising projects are already under way to bring together organized labor and church groups which are concerned with translating social ideals into social policy and practice. The labor movement has much to teach the churches concerning the realities of our economic society and how to implement their social pronouncements through constructive social action.

It is the *Christian intention* to assist in the development of a type of social and state planning which will eliminate the haphazard character of our economic life with its recurrent depressions, stagnation of activity, unemployment, want amid plenty.

Economic life today is like a business which began as a simple affair in which the owner was at once manager, employer, laborer; growing rapidly, it reached the stage where specialization of functions was required; decisions had to take into account more facts and a longer time-span, and demanded the knowledge of a variety of experts and a comprehensive total plan. This is the stage reached in the economic life of the modern state. Reliance can no longer be placed on the hope that somehow things will work themselves out by trusting the automatic working of the price system. Planning, based on a view of the whole and the needs which the system should serve, becomes necessary.

This is elementary. The real question is how the planning is to be done and who is to do it. Planning is so large an interest, involving the lives and fortunes of so many people, that it clearly cannot be left to individauls but must in some way be brought under the aegis of the central political authority. Of basic and prior importance in planning of this kind are the values—that is, the kind of living and of human relations—which are considered desirable and worthy. From the standpoint of Christian social action, two principles are required. The *goal* of planning is the full development of free, socially responsible individuals. The *way* must be democratic: The main objectives are to be popularly determined, but there must be delegation of power to act. Popular governments have not yet been able to work out a satisfactory method of applying these principles; and the Christian social actionist certainly does not claim to have found the answer. It is, however, an item on his agenda for collaborative study and experimentation with political scientists and statesmen.

The Christian social actionist asserts that planning of the economic life of the nation on a comprehensive scale is essential, that the political agency created by the people must take the lead, that the goals must be the welfare of the people as a whole, rather than the interests of groups, that these interests are to be determined by popular consent and that the methods of achieving them will utilize the specialized knowledge which the complexity of the problems necessarily involves.

It is the *Christian intention* to establish sound economic and cultural bases for rural life. Churches are giving considerable attention to this issue. It is natural that they should, since they draw heavily on rural communities for leadership. Churches have found that the problems of the small community are not to be solved by restricted local action. The farm population makes up approximately one-fourth of the total population but receives only 10 per cent of the total cash income of the nation. Farmers suffered acutely from the depression, but their ills pre-dated the depression. The new technology increased the productivity of the farmer but resulted in displacement of farm labor. It is estimated that half a million families are struggling for a living on land so depleted that a good living is impossible. More than twenty-six out of every thousand farms changed hands through forced sales in 1930. Mortgages on all farm land equaled nearly 42 per cent of its total value.

Economic measures of rehabilitation include a program of soil conservation and retirement of marginal and submarginal land; revision of the credit system to establish direct ownership; extension of farm co-operatives, especially to protect small-sized farms; and extension of electrification. These measures must be accompanied by the improvement of education adjusted to the needs of farm youth, extension of medical services, libraries and churches. It is the Christian intention to support movements, political and otherwise, seeking these ends.

It is the *Christian intention* to work at the reconstruction of political and governmental agencies in order to make them effective bodies for dealing with economic questions. The power behind these agencies must always be the will of the people concerning the kind of society they desire; the political job is to express and implement, not thwart this will. Only the state is today representative enough to perform these functions and to provide directives to guide our economic life. But the breakdown of these agencies when attacking economic problems is all too frequent. While graft is certainly not confined to politics, it is sufficiently prevalent to set the dimensions of a job of reconstruction. The ills of popular government when dealing with economic issues are well known: interference of politicians in technical matters, use of political influence to obtain appointments, appeals to temporary advantage when a long-range view is needed. It should be noted that such ills are accessible to exposure and attack when political agencies are involved while they are often successfully concealed in private industry, particularly when monopolistic tendencies are pronounced.

Our political agencies for dealing with the complex economic tasks of a modern industrialized society are not effective. In many instances they are the product of an earlier period. They must be replaced by mechanisms and procedures adapted to the needs of modern, technological society. It is the Christian intention to support reforms which will give us effective political instruments for dealing with economic issues.

It is the *Christian intention* to secure the most general distribution of the essentials of life for all citizens. These include food, clothing, shelter, education and medical services. The minimum should be guaranteed through collective provisions. This may be accomplished through making some kind of remunerative work available to all who can work, by means of which with judicious management most individuals will be able to secure these essentials for themselves. Some of these services can be provided collectively through taxation and direct aid, and government-sponsored work projects will be required, the extent depending on the economic health of the nation. In the revolutionary days which seem to lie ahead, such minimal provisions for the well-being of people will doubtless be regarded as essential for the defense of the nation. Failure to provide will be shortsighted.

It is the *Christian intention* to support the consumer cooperative movement, not as the solution of all our economic ills but as a means of easing the economic situation for groups within the framework of the capitalistic system. The co-operative movement provides firsthand experience in social planning to meet specific economic needs by those who feel those needs most acutely. Through co-operatives many people have discovered their potential collective economic power even when individually they are economically weak. Co-operatives reveal ways of looking at life and of living which are in sharp contrast with the prevailing individualistic and competitive pattern of our society. Thus are anticipated certain features of a Christian society based on the principle of collective responsibility.

Limitations of the co-operative movement are obvious. It does not abolish poverty. Heavy industry could probably not be financed through co-operatives. The savings entrusted to co-operatives could not be expected to be risked in carrying on large-scale industries through the ups and downs of the trade cycle. Many critics think that co-operatives just manage to head off those more radical changes in the economic structure which they feel to be necessary. Despite these criticisms the co-operative movement has much to contribute to the development of the kind of informed intelligence and social sensitivity which the ideals of Christianity demand if they are ever to be realized. It is the Christian intention to conserve and extend the values which co-operatives have brought into modern life.

It is the *Christian intention* to eliminate the egregious economic injustices which our society now places on Negroes and other minority groups primarily because of color or cultural differences. The economic base of a just society cannot be established as long as Negroes are denied access to education and employment in professions like teaching and medicine and in other skilled and semi-skilled occupations. Educational efforts to change attitudes must be supplemented by political measures to enforce equality of opportunity. The fight for democracy must be carried to our own shores. In this battle the churches may well begin with their own members. Promising work in breaking down racial and cultural barriers has been begun by churches and other religiously motivated groups.

It is the *Christian intention* to lift the nation's techniques for dealing with international business out of the realm of egoistic nationalism, and to place them on the level of a genuine concern for liberty, equality and justice for men everywhere. As in domestic matters, political forms of the pre-technological era are inadequate in the highly complex world in which we live today. It is the Christian intention to make our nation's methods of dealing with other nations an expression of the growing sense of collective responsibility and brotherhood. This issue is sharply focused today: Shall our nation seek Christian and human values, including food for the hungry, for *all* or primarily for itself? When our government is dealing with economically backward nations shall we, in competition with other countries, view these backward nations as a field for exploitation or shall we insist on co-operation in building up the enlightened and democratic forces within these undeveloped nations? The present war will leave a terrifying legacy of distrust and hatred in the minds of our citizens. This must be replaced by a realistic attitude of understanding and willingness to help, as the only possible basis for building an orderly system of international relations.

It is the *Christian intention* to project a collaboration of businessmen, politicians and political scientists, ethicists and others in an attack on those problems of modern society the solution of which requires the technical knowledge of the economist and the knowledge of values and social philosophy of the Christian ethicist—the problems which the economist usually refuses to touch because they are ethical and the ethicist cannot handle because he does not know enough economics. This is a rich field. It needs a type of scientific study which is motivated not only by a desire to understand but by a sense of responsibility for acting on the basis of what is known.

Among the problems requiring study are the following: careful analysis of motives and of stimuli to inventiveness and initiative in competitive and non-competitive business; the effect of security regarding the basic necessities of life on willingness to work; the conflict, if any, between economic principles and the claims of "brotherhood," "neigh-

borliness" and the like; the readjustments in economic concepts and methods that are required when the assumptions
of "economic man" are replaced by the assumptions of "man
made in the image of God"; the effect of limitation or elimination of the prospects of profit on effort of owner-managers
of industry; the content and method of economic education
in preparation for and participation in effective Christian
social action.

The economist apparently prefers to take his ends for
granted, and to work on technical matters unconfused by
values and valuations. There may be sound reasons for this
artificial isolation of his thought from its social and value
context. The development of scientific techniques for getting
at facts requires rigid limitation and definition of the problem to be studied. But after the techniques have been created
and used and the facts gathered, the pieces have to be put
together by someone; the bits of knowledge and wisdom
gained through research have to be related to knowledge
acquired in other fields and to the unsolved problems and
conflicts of the social order. Someone must take responsibility for this job, and if the economist is not willing to do so,
he can hardly criticize those less well-informed on economic matters for making mistakes because of lack of knowledge. The task is a co-operative one. It is the Christian
intention to initiate and support such collaboration.

To be effective, collaboration must be continuous. It does
little good to bring together economist and ethicist for
addresses and discussions at an occasional conference. A new
field requires exploration. Vision and a long-term strategy
are demanded. Appropriate techniques of inquiry, mutual
understanding and definition of problems to be studied are
urgently needed.

The forms of such collaboration will have to be worked
out. Perhaps a university will be found which can sponsor
it. Perhaps special agencies such as the Department of Research and Education of the Federal Council of Churches

can do the pioneering required. It will require a statesman-ship which religious agencies frequently do not have because of preoccupation with self-preservation and institutional in-terests.

This project should not primarily be thought of as a service which churches may render to society, but rather as an inescapable obligation to seek a material embodiment which is implicit in the love ethic of Christianity. The ma-terial basis of community has a spiritual meaning which the Christian is bound to recognize. But handling material affairs intelligently requires knowledge and techniques if business is to contribute to and not dominate social purposes. Hence the Christian must bring together men who are technically qualified by training and experience to help work out the economic social structure which will express the love ethic as fully as may be possible in the particular time and circumstances. The dynamic for doing this and the ends toward which activity is to be directed are given in the Christian ethic.

It is the *Christian intention* to utilize and direct the world-wide aspiration for better living conditions every-where to be seen today, toward an understanding and appre-ciation of the meaning of the Kingdom of God through which this aspiration can be made permanently constructive. The aspiration is an authentic intimation of the moving of an ethical God in the hearts of men who refuse to accept the frustrations and inequities and hopelessness of our present social order, and demand something better. It provides the brute force necessary to break the old forms, but it desper-ately needs a sense of direction, knowledge, techniques. It is blind and needs sight which modern science and a sense of ethical values can give. The Christian sees in this aspiration an opportunity to spread the Gospel, not as a social blue-print to be dogmatically imposed but as a way of living in which the aspirations for a better life may be worked out co-operatively, utilizing all the power and techniques which modern science has made available to man.

This Gospel demands regeneration of the individual as well as reconstruction of society. Such dual demands are not in conflict; they are integrally related aspects of the same movement of personality toward enriched living. Both are necessary if the possibilities of man, as a being made in the image of God, are to be brought out.

Hence the Christian has some optimism as he views the current scene despite the obviously discouraging facts of war, revolution, hate, conflict. He has some optimism because he sees in this aspiration of men for a better way of life the motivation and power needed to build the kind of society which the Christian ethic discloses. Men and women are ready for a revolutionary Gospel of Christianity. The Christian must convince them that his intentions to live it, and not merely to preach it, are sincere and real.

Truly, "the old order changeth." What shall be the contours of the new? The Christian may have something to say about this if he is willing to pay the price of implementing his love ethic with intelligence, knowledge and courageous action.

It is the *Christian intention* to erase from his ideology the misconception that the spiritual and the material are distinct and separate entities, and that religion is primarily concerned with the spiritual. He will consider the material as the only medium through which the spiritual can be known or can express itself. Because man is both spiritual and material, his first problem must always be to find a material basis that expresses and makes possible his spiritual life. But spiritual is a quality of human (i.e., spirit-body) relations. Any attempt to ignore the material and to leave it to chance or charity is certain to result in a materialism of the worst—because the most subtle—kind.

The meaning of this is that all matters which affect the quality of human relationships are of concern to Christianity and are an appropriate subject for religious activity. It is right for ministers to preach about economic themes provided they are informed, are not dogmatic, do not claim special revelation beyond such disclosure of truth as may come through long and patient inquiry, and provided their purpose is to dynamize those whom they teach with the Christian aspiration and sense of responsibility for a better world.

Such are some of the intentions which are forming in the minds of Christians in our times. What do they add up to? They envisage a change of mind in church members concerning the responsibility of churches for the evils of their times. They seek a political order that will be more effective in initiating and carrying through economic changes. They are concerned about the growing power of the state, a development which they consider unavoidable in view of the responsibilities which the state must assume, but one fraught with dangers which always accompany the possession of power. Hence Christians would like to see this centralized political and economic power kept amenable to democratic control and its exercise based on Christian ethical principles. They see that this problem will not be solved merely by the development of good men, in whose hands this power can be placed, important as that is. Of equal urgency is a widely distributed intelligence and ethical sense among people who through the ballot determine the actions of their political representatives in a democracy.

Here is the great opportunity of the churches. They ought to become educational agencies through which Christian social ideals and knowledge of political and economic realities will be inculcated. Naturally this task is shared with other social agencies, the school, the press, the radio. But the churches have a distinctive emphasis. It is the proclamation of an ethic which transcends the contemporary and by which the contemporary is evaluated and judged. In this light, man is viewed as in duty bound to stand for the achievement of a society based on the principles of freedom, equality, collective responsibility and universal brotherhood. This is the view of man and destiny which the churches uniquely may be expected to stress in their educational processes.

CHAPTER THIRTEEN

The Churches and Economic Reconstruction

WHAT should be the role of a Christian church with reference to economic change and the struggle of modern man for a better economic system? Can churches provide a channel for the expression of such intentions?

It is assumed that churches ought to give affirmative and creative leadership in creating an economic system which will implement Christian ideals. This assumption is, however, by no means universally accepted. Many devoted church members find pronouncements by churches on the right of labor to organize, the plight of farmers, war, unemployment, social security and other social issues extremely offensive. Such people would feel worse if they believed there was much likelihood that the churches would attempt to put their pronouncements into effect. Usually little is heard about these resolutions in the local church. The first intimation many members receive that their church "has taken a stand" is when they read about it in the newspapers. The point of immediate concern is to admit that the assumption that the churches have economic responsibility is accepted by only a part, probably a minority, of their membership and clerical leadership.

A church is defined as: "A voluntary association of men and women with the special object of keeping alert and active their sense of kinship with their fellows in God, of cultivating the spirit of comradeship within this divine-human community, of intensifying the consciousness of partnership with God in the larger social enterprise which progressively embodies his ultimate purpose."[1]

[1] *Towards the Christian Revolution*, edited by Scott and Vlastos. Willett, Clark & Co., p. 175.

According to this definition, a church is an institution maintained by persons who find in it the answer to certain needs. It has rootage in a past from which it derives stability, perspective and a corrective to tendencies which might divert it from its mission. From its close relation to human needs and aspirations it is propelled into contemporary life where the needs of persons are at stake.

To speak of "the Church" is misleading unless qualified by some indication of the fact that the term includes an extremely varied collection of institutions. While Christian churches possess certain common loyalties and symbols, they differ in important ways. No one can speak for "the Church."

Recent figures show that there are in the United States approximately two hundred fifty different sects; their membership includes less than half the population. Most of the sects are small; fifty-two of them include 97 per cent of the nation's church members. To discover a significant unifying bond even among members of a particular denomination is often difficult. Variations in belief between different members of the same denomination are often greater than the differences between that sect and another one.

The absence of homogeneity in American church life reflects the democratic origin of the churches and indicates flexibility in expressing the needs and reflecting the interests of members. Such unity as may exist now is the result of the purposeful effort of members. It is a responsibility of members to find common interests and aspirations. This is particularly true with respect to ethical ideals and social needs. "The Church" is a challenge, not a statement of fact when economic questions are the issue.

It is to be hoped that recognition of social action as a legitimate expression of Christianity may increasingly characterize churches and even those groups which conscientiously object to a socially oriented Gospel. That degree of liberalism and toleration may be expected. It is not to be expected that all members will change their views and accept the position here taken. But those members within a church who do attempt to relate their Christian convictions to economic questions should be granted the right to exist and thus welcomed in churches as persons who are expressing an authentic and historically valid form of Christianity. On the other hand, members interested in social action should be ready to grant that others who do not so conceive the churches' function have a right to exist and to work on the kind of program which expresses their convictions and aspirations.

The question may well be asked whether there is no illumination or principle from the life and teachings of Jesus which can settle the question once and for all as to which form of Christianity is authentic. The answer must be: none on which Christian people will agree; and if one turns to the history of the churches, he will find the widest possible variation in thought and in practice. The churches are as nearly true to their history as they can be, when they differ with respect to their responsibility for economic and social action. In a way this is no principle for it almost says that whatever a group of people agrees to call Christian must be regarded as Christian. This is substantially true if one adds: "According to their views and provided they are sincere." Most men would not care to be put in the position of having to pass judgment on the sincerity of a group.

Church members of all kinds ought to maintain fellowship, as far as possible, with churches which attempt to shape the economic system in accord with what they conceive to be Christian values, even when as individual members they do not like that kind of church.

The traditional American policy of separation of church and state presents theoretical difficulties for the Christian social actionist. The man-in-the-pew is both citizen and church member, businessman and church member, C.I.O. member and church member. Personality cannot be divided into segments except at the cost of integrity. Religious activity cannot be separated from "life" and remain religion. Life is a unity. An individual's Christianity is all of his life or it is nothing. By accepting the traditional and allegedly practical division of labor as between these various aspects of life, churches actually encourage an isolation of ideals from practice.

It is also no answer to say that while religion may be carried over into the political and economic area through personal action, the churches as *institutions* should remain aloof. Where, it may be asked, is the businessman who may be convinced that his Christianity ought to be related to economic life and practice to consider the meaning of the Christian ethic in relation to his business? College courses in economics or ethics will not give him that help. Schools of business administration are not on the whole willing to touch these problems. Luncheon clubs and trade associations may help on certain aspects of the question but are not promising sources of illumination. Consideration of the implications of the Christian ethic for business and economic life should take place where the ethic is proclaimed and taught—in the churches or closely related organizations. Many other organizations *might* foster studies and discussions of this kind, but if the churches are interested in seeing their faith secure economic implementation, they would be well advised to have a voice in the deliberations.

It is easy for an institution to side-step a challenge of this kind. The issues requiring discussion are inflammatory. Tensions between people and divisions within the church are likely to accompany frank discussion of the application of Christian ideals to any area of life. The welfare of the institution as a going concern in the community may be threatened. Prophetic religion in the past has taken risks in the name of Christ and blazed new trails. Will the churches today have the courage and faith to do likewise?

There is some evidence that they will. Many churches have initiated significant movements intended to bridge the gap between affirmation of ideals and correlative action in the economic field. Most denominations have today social-action commissions, variously labeled but alike in their effort to stimulate and inform their members concerning the bearing of Christianity on social and economic questions. Excellent work is being done in collecting and disseminating the facts essential to an intelligent understanding of these issues. Many local churches have committees which bring together those members who seek a discussion of social and economic problems in the light of Christian ideals. Such groups often include trained technicians in special fields, which, incidentally, is another encouraging sign of the times.

Another promising development is the fact that theological seminaries include courses in social sciences in their curricula. The courses are regarded as an important part of the professional training of the clergyman. They introduce him to the problems of religious leadership and of the church in rural, urban and industrial communities. Students are also permitted and sometimes encouraged to take work in economics and sociology in near-by universities. It is recognized that, as an administrator of a social agency, the minister needs a rich background in the social sciences. While this healthy development is not new—and may even be less strong now than a decade ago—it is probable that the quality of the instruction is improving, and the place of these studies in the seminary curriculum secure.

Mention should also be made of organizations whose purpose is to bring together representatives of churches and organized labor. The exchange of ideas and problems and the sharing of purposes are valuable to the clergy and labor leaders alike. The National Religion and Labor Foundation has been active in this field for years. It is not officially related to the churches, but is definitely religious in motivation, nonsectarian in personnel and is supported by individual contributions and appropriations from labor organizations.

Churchmen should be encouraged further by the increasing interest among economists in relating their technical and scientific work to political and social philosophy. Their purpose is to re-examine the assumptions of economics and to relate their findings to other disciplines. There is also increasing recognition of the responsibility of the economist, as a scientist and scholar, to interest himself in his political, social and intellectual environment, and in the conditions which obstruct or facilitate his scientific work. These conditions may make it difficult or impossible for science to exist and for the scientist to be honest. He needs to be able to state the kind of freedom which he requires if he is to do a good and honest job. He should, as a scientist, be concerned with the social and political ideals of the people, the state of human freedom, the values to which his fellow citizens give allegiance. As this interest and sense of social responsibility develop, one may expect the traditional attitude of economists, as well as of other scientists, toward ethics and philosophy to change. There will be less tendency to regard these subjects as outside their field or as disturbers of their scholarly peace. In so far as economists develop this interest, there will exist a more promising basis of collaboration with folks interested in ethics and religion.

In many respects, churches are not prepared for this kind of collaboration. They are handicapped in certain ways which will now be examined.

First should be mentioned the fact that in many respects the churches' own house is not in good order; they have not been conspicuously successful in setting an example of good business practice. As an employer, many a church has failed to demonstrate that concern for persons which would be expected from its ethic. The methods by which decisions on program and policy are made in churches are often undemocratic and fail to demonstrate the principle that persons who are to be affected by a decision should have a voice in determining it. Churches do not often demonstrate the Christian ideal of a fellowship which is able to transcend economic, racial and other social barriers. In these matters they have followed custom rather than created new standards of action.

These conditions are an obstacle to the churches' effectiveness in the field of social teaching and action. Men do not take kindly to preachments unsupported by performance.

From the standpoint of effective social education and action, churches are further handicapped by a convention which dictates that they remain aloof from controversies except those arising from theological or creedal considerations. The motive is undoubtedly to avoid creating dissension and divisions among members; but the result is a habit of dealing with relatively innocuous subjects, or of referring to important issues in a highly generalized manner. If the congregation is unified on any particular social or political issue, it is not uncommon for the minister to condemn the opposition, whose advocates are usually not within hearing.

This is not an approach or an atmosphere which lends itself to the clarification of the ethical issues in economic problems. An educational philosophy which believes in recognizing and discussing differences with a view to increasing understanding, in holding conflicting opinions in tension and in achieving fellowship in spite of them is held by some churches, but not practiced by many. Yet it would seem that some such approach is needed if the churches are to play a formative role in economic reconstruction.

Also, most people attending church go in the hope of finding a little peace in a world of strife, and not to engage in controversy. Life is everywhere filled with conflicts and tragedy. There is an almost universal need for experiences which will enable the individual to rise above these pressures and in quiet to gather himself together emotionally and spiritually. Churches meet this need. It is important no less for the social actionist than for others. A certain amount of escapism is probably necessary for any person who is to retain his sanity today. But flight from reality is not the answer. Christianity has a better method which the churches are often in danger of forgetting. Jesus established a clear relationship between conduct and the achievement of inward peace. It is the Christian view that poise is to be achieved not by forgetting the conflicts of life but by seeing them in new perspective, and by facing facts not by running away from them.

A contrary view has become habitual in many churches. It is that peace is to be found in a few minutes of withdrawal from life; the expectancy is created that the church will offer that kind of experience. Thus it becomes difficult in such a church to deal with social conflicts. Minds are more likely to be closed to them than made aware of them.

There are many men and women today who seek inner poise but feel that the price is too great if it requires them to become insensitive to the demands of social action. They stop going to church not because they do not feel the need for inner peace and inspiration but because they fail to find there an active grappling with the problems, social and intellectual, about which they feel most keenly, in relation to the distinctive illumination which Christianity may bring to those problems. These churches develop a function for themselves and gather a personnel that prevent their playing a significant role in social reconstruction. One will not find there any active weighing of the meaning of the Christian ethic for social and economic life.

The "class" character of American churches is an important though not insuperable obstacle to social effectiveness. A local church is often a rather poor example of a fellowship that cuts across the sociological divisions of a community. Thrown together, the churches of a community would be more representative, but the point is that they usually function independently. Each unit tends to represent a particular economic, racial, cultural segment of the population. And on the whole this is the economically "privileged" segment. This does not mean that all members are wealthy. It does mean that financially favored groups are usually in control, and that ideologically the members tend to repre-

sent the views of the controlling group in their community.
When this situation exists, members will not ordinarily think
in terms of fundamental changes in the economic structure.
They, unlike an economically depressed group, feel that they
have more to lose than to gain by basic economic changes.

Local churches are usually conservative in their social and
political thinking. They are hostile to any questioning of
the system of free enterprise, not primarily because they
believe that the subject is inappropriate for consideration
in church, but because they believe it is wrong to question
the system. To attack the pillars of the social structure is
for them as bad as questioning the basic doctrines of the
Christian faith. Perhaps the hostility found in many churches
toward Soviet Russia is due less to its atheism than to its
radical social doctrines which challenge the presuppositions
undergirding the American economic order.

The churches are further handicapped in dealing with
social issues by a symbolism which is historic and esthetic
in its reference rather than contemporary and moral. For
the most part the symbols refer to historic events in the life
of Christianity; the believer's "experience" with them is
church-centered and tradition-oriented. Their effect is to
turn people back to events of the past, and too often to encourage them to remain there. This is not the way to ethical
insight and moral responsibility. The symbolism of Christianity may become rich in associations suggesting the current tragic struggle of humankind for the good life. But this
can only be when experience in that struggle is a vital part
of religious observance.

Churches are burdened by a heavy overhead of routine,
usually placed on the shoulders of their ministers. Many a
pastor is investing the routine with a spirit which gives it
high significance. Communities make heavy demands on
their ministers. They are expected to administer many a
secularized social ritual from which every juice of life has
been drawn. The routines exact a toll. A few years given to

it and the minister is in grave danger of enjoying the routine —at the cost of his intellectual and spiritual growth. The heavy overhead of routine is a handicap because it draws off the energies of clergymen and, to some extent, laymen from the taxing and creative task of relating the Christian ethic to social conflict.

When the churches do take hold of social questions, they are likely to approach them in the crusading spirit. Undoubtedly the dynamism of a crusade is needed to overcome the usual apathy regarding economic matters to be found in the churches. But the crusade as a method of social change has great shortcomings which could easily be fatal in the field of economic behavior. A crusade assumes utter certainty regarding the Cause. Unfortunately this certainty can be vouchsafed concerning few moves in the economic field. Many feel that unless the church can speak dogmatically and with appearance of finality about a subject it ought not to speak. In the area of economic action, patient and co-operative inquiry, flexibility of attitude toward whatever steps are taken, willingness to change and to act, even when one knows that the particular move is not the final solution but is the best that can be done under the circumstances—all these are important. These attitudes seldom characterize crusaders. It is not easy to think of the churches as places where people are "searching" for facts and answers to their questions about religion and social responsibility. The popular belief is that churches proclaim the "truth," and if they do not know the truth they should not proclaim.

This situation tempts a church whose conscience is quickened on social issues to oversimplify and make hasty generalization even when intelligent people know that the issues are too complex to permit finality of judgment. As a result churches which move into the area of economic conflict are sometimes easy prey for "crackpots" whose motives may be beyond reproach but whose information is scant and whose solutions are unworkable. Ministers sometimes demand a solution which they can proclaim as "the Christian answer," and around which they can rally their people. They sometimes embrace alleged solutions about which they can get "steamed up," only to find that they have been sold a whistle instead of an engine.

Is the crusade the only approach which is open to the church? The answer is no. The Christian churches have had from the beginning a far more effective method of producing social change and change in the minds and hearts of men. This approach will be discussed presently.

Another serious handicap of the churches in dealing with economic questions is the casual relationship which many members sustain to their church. Of many members, those carrying responsibility are few. The majority do not find their interests vitally caught up in the life of the church. They may attend, send their children, even contribute, but the attachment is formal. To say, as churches pronouncing on their own importance in the life of man are wont to state, that the church relationship controls and unifies experience is not true for a large proportion of church members.

It is true that many of these "casuals" come to the minister in time of personal tragedy or other crisis. This important fact illustrates the point that for many folks the relationship to the churches is restricted to unusual occasions. Formal religious observances fail to touch their lives as housewives, wage earners, voters, neighbors.

This fact is important in considering the possibility of the churches' exerting an influence on their membership with respect to economic and social questions. It may be doubted whether churches generally sufficiently engage the attention of a large proportion of their members to educate them. If an effective influence is to be exerted, the churches will have to create new attitudes regarding what their rightful function is. Churches which do have a strong hold on their members have it because they succeed in relating religion to the vital concerns and aspirations of their members and the community.

While churches, appraised as potential agencies for social leadership, have handicaps to overcome, they also have exceptional resources. In many respects they hold a position of strategic importance in community and national life. To say that they are handicapped is not to say that, as compared with other institutions, they are not also definitely in a position of advantage.

Among the church's resources first place should be given to its Gospel, the social implications of which can be escaped only by the exercise of great determination and intellectual adroitness. The Christian has only to open his Bible to be confronted with social challenge. "Interpretation" cannot rob him of the prophetic social dynamic and heritage. If he thinks that perhaps Christ said, "Blessed are the poor in spirit" instead of "Blessed are ye poor," he still may read: "Go, give all that thou hast and give to the poor; then come and follow after me." "Lay not up for yourselves treasures on earth where moth and rust doth corrupt and where thieves break through and steal." There is an irreducible minimum of social reference and concern in the Gospels, the Epistle of James, the book of Amos, the herdsman, and elsewhere. Even though the reader find no solution to modern economic issues in the Scriptures, he must still face the fact that they contain material that is extremely embarrassing to one who holds that a Christian church should have nothing to do with social and economic questions. He will have a hard time softening the impact of certain passages.

Besides having Scriptures abounding in references to economic and social life, the churches also have a heritage replete with examples of pioneers in the effort to build a Christian society. Through Christian history there marches a procession of noble men and women who did think, rightly or wrongly, that the church had a message for the organized social, economic and political life of their times. Most of them not only delivered the message but acted on it. They established schools, colleges, hospitals, co-operative communities, factories, settlements, social legislation and many other forms of social action in the name of Christ.

This heritage, containing some of the noblest and most inspiring events in human history, belongs to the churches, as it belongs to mankind. The church member who desires to "carry on" can join hands with this company. He need not travel alone. This tradition means that a church which grapples with social and economic issues is not moving away from its tradition but is identifying itself with an authentic part of it.

The churches furthermore view the human scene from the vantage point of a faith and an ethic which has a supra-mundane point of reference. Their loyalty is to an ethical God. It transcends national, racial, class and social interests. This fact means that the churches are committed to a way of looking at man and human relations which is not limited to a particular culture, and are therefore saved, in theory if not always in practice, from the prejudices, provincialisms, and presuppositions of that culture. This may seem like an extraordinary claim, but the desire to discover values of universal validity is not extraordinary. It is the aim or claim of all religions and most philosophies. The Christian is related to a movement which is drawing and has always drawn on all cultures for insight and knowledge. Its contacts are universal. In this process Christianity meets cultures not merely through books but in the flesh. In its effort to create a world community, the Christian movement relates itself to all humankind. It is world-minded. Often it has unfortunately been imperialistic, and its representatives have suffered from delusions of grandeur and superiority in their contacts with non-Christian peoples. Nevertheless, the orientation of Christianity has been to a supra-national outlook.

The churches are thus in a position to make an important contribution to the development of world-mindedness. The world is being drawn together irresistibly through improved means of travel and communication. Provincial barriers, geographical and cultural, are being broken up. Men must think in world terms. This is precisely what the churches have been doing, and one does not have to maintain that they have done it effectively to assert that the spiritual orientation implicit in the motive is in keeping with the realities of modern life.

The churches are committed to a view of humanity as a whole under God which in the long run tends to prevent their giving their fundamental loyalty to local and national interests and objectives. The accusation of being unpatriotic is a familiar charge against religious people. It is not without basis in fact. They are moved by a necessity to relate present issues and life to a view which transcends time. The total course of man's journey from humanity's beginning to his destiny is encompassed in their aspirations. This is surely an imperial and, I suppose, for some minds a silly and impertinent gesture. It does not mean, as some suppose, that the Christian pretends that he has "all the answers." It does mean that in his practical decisions, his views of the social and economic processes, his attitude toward human relations, the Christian intends to express his belief and faith regarding man's destiny on this planet. He tries to live *sub specie aeternitatis*. His ethic, whether economic or personal, is wrought out in that kind of setting. Christianity is a movement of man's spirit at once and inseparably toward good human relations and good relations to God.

It is an advantage to the churches to have such an orientation in their approach to economic problems, because so few other agencies have it, and in the long run nothing short of such a view or intention can satisfy the human spirit. Perhaps it is only in such a setting that the problems now increasingly confronting mankind can be intelligently understood.

The churches, further, are a promising avenue of approach to social education and action because within their membership are represented many of the outstanding conflicts in contemporary social-economic thought. Hugh Vernon White[2] has pointed out that, whereas in the case of the fight for temperance the churches were largely arrayed against an enemy from without, the immoralities of the social order are rooted in a social and economic system in which church members are implicated quite as much as those outside the church.

On first thought this fact would appear to be a disadvantage. It should be an asset, for it means that to make a beginning in its program of social action a church has only to open the avenues of communication between its own members. As businessmen, farmers, laborers, they have only to talk together about their own problems in order to become a vital human-interest seminar on contemporary social issues. Their views need to be supplemented by other points of view, particularly those of the economically dispossessed group. But such groups are at the door of most churches. Extending the fellowship of the church to them, not for the sake of saving their souls but as a wholly essential means of getting light on a perplexing problem and as a means of saving the church's soul, would be a rewarding experience. An educational-consultative process which unlocked these resources and set people to talking and thinking about the ailments of our economic society in the setting of a common commitment to the Christian faith would be unique.

The churches are exceptional also in the fact that they include a wider range of age groups than most other social institutions. Nursery tots and grandparents are in the churches. Whatever program is undertaken has the possibility of reaching young and old, both those who may be in a position to take immediate action and also children in the

---

[2] "Christian Social Action," p. 25 in *Social Action*, Vol. III, No. 14. Council for Social Action of the Congregational and Christian Churches, 289 Fourth Avenue, New York City.

formative years who will later carry the burden of community activity. The contact of the church with the family as a family is not duplicated in many other social organizations. The churches are in position to reach and influence through their educational processes families as groups and a wide age range of individuals.

Thus we find the churches, viewed as agencies for influencing the social structure and process, handicapped by certain definite limitations but also blessed with exceptional advantages which are offered by few other institutions.

In the light of these considerations, what can a church do when it is committed to a view of the Christian faith which impels it to interest itself in economic issues?

It is important to repeat that the church is here considered as a group of people seeking God through work and worship. The problem is not what a minister can do but what this *group* can do, aided and abetted and inspired by their minister.

Sir Josiah Stamp states that it is the lack of informed opinion in the church that makes it cut such a sorry figure in economic and social controversies. If this statement is true, it is only because the church has failed to utilize its own resources. As attendants—casual or regular—as members and officials, there will be found such persons as: the general manager of a food store, a clerk in the drygoods store, a certified public accountant, a professor of economics, a head of the department store, the chairman of the board of the bank, an expert toolmaker, a building contractor, a high-school teacher of civics, housewives who deal with all these folk and many others. *They* are the church. For representativeness, it will compare favorably with the National Association of Manufacturers, the American Economic Association, or the United Automobile Workers' union.

If the churches use their resources there is no reason why their opinions on economic and social issues should be uninformed. Few other institutions are as well situated for intelligent and representative consideration of public issues.

How can a church make use of these exceptional opportunities for stimulation of constructive thought on economic issues? Primarily by finding a way of encouraging communication between its members. Is such planned communication possible? Unless a way is found, the churches, given their human resources, must be adjudged guilty of a tragic waste of opportunity.

The job of a church is of course not the same as that of an economics department in a university. Its task is, however, in keeping with its historic mission, to help members to sensitize one another to the ethical implications of the economic problems of the society in which they live. Churches also have the responsibility of quickening the conscience of the community and directing the human energies required to change existing evils in an economic system which has too often made well-intentioned people behave badly and ill-intentioned people respected and "successful."

The churches' method is based on a simple and ancient principle. It says that the ethically and spiritually creative situation is the "fellowship" in which people talk about their problems, fears and aspirations. This principle asserts that society may look for the emergence of its creative ideas and ideals from such groups.

The basic conditions governing a group of this kind are: A person, regardless of social status, counts as one human being who is struggling to understand and to be more effective in his activities and relations with people. And he is free to speak whatever is meaningful to him.

When we speak of a church "at work on economic issues," that is basically what is meant. We do not mean primarily that it has a minister who dares to discuss controversial questions in the pulpit; that it conducts public forums and debates or sponsors lectures on economic questions; or that it has a men's club daring enough to have a labor leader address it. All these things may be involved, but that is not the church at work on the economic problem. The church is at work on the economic problem when it has within it people who are seeking reality in small groups where they talk frankly and freely with one another about their concerns for our economic society in relation to Christian commitments and loyalties.

Perhaps this way of stating the method fails to emphasize the intellectual demands which a fellowship process makes on the participants. Thinking should be critical, searching and demanding, but with a difference. The participants *expect to act* on the basis of whatever illumination emerges from the experience together. They will feel an *imperative* to act because their coming together is fundamentally an expression of their devotion to an ethical God who is working through them to achieve a society which approximates the justice, love and beauty discerned, however dimly, in the love ethic of Jesus.

It is doubtful if Christian experience over the centuries has discovered any more effective method of regenerating the individual than the method of fellowship, if by regeneration one means a complete turning of the individual about—morally, intellectually and spiritually—and the setting of his whole personality in a new direction. This regeneration is as much a part of social change as reducing waste in industry. It is reducing the waste of unused or misdirected human capacity. The method is successful because in it the individuals develop a sense of *community* which answers an ineradicable longing in the heart of every human being and also stimulates him to seek a material base for the community. The experience makes heavy demands on the individual. It utilizes his capacities and brings out potentialities that he did not dream he possessed.

The church, then, deals with economic questions by developing groups in which people seek and find religious reality. There they develop a sense of "belonging" and of participating in a common task. They come to an understanding of what is required of them if their society is to be based on the principles of equality, freedom, collective responsibility and universality. Their discernment concerning human possibilities under the influence of religious fellowship is deepened.

The churches have an exceptional opportunity to foster religious groups of this kind within their membership. Their possibilities for stimulating, informing and energizing individuals are unusual. Under what other auspices will one find owner, manager, clerk, consumer, financier, merchandiser, manual worker sitting down together to discuss the meaning of the Christian ethic for the emerging problems of our economic society?

The criticism may be advanced that discussion in such groups would not be rewarding for the better informed. No doubt the quality would vary. Perhaps participants would be found lacking in knowledge of the latest that has been written on the subject under discussion. They might make up for the lack, in insights, experiences and "angles" on issues from which those better trained in academic disciplines might learn. As a matter of fact, the realism of such a group may often be more than thin-skinned academicians and businessmen can take.

Will such groups produce solutions to the nation's economic ills? Probably not, but no one can be sure. At any rate they will produce intelligence of a type that is greatly needed if people are to find the solution to the problems which confront democracy today. Panaceas around which crusades can be started are not needed. Courage and intelligence to apply in daily living and social and political behavior principles already validated in human experience are what the world needs today. Through groups of this kind the church could lift the level of social intelligence of our nation.

The method has a dynamic which might endanger the more conventional pattern of church organization. There would be repercussions. "Fellowship" of the kind to which we have referred would tend to eliminate the casual relationship which characterizes the contact of so many members with the church. To introduce this method in any institution—be it church or university or factory—would be like pouring new wine into old bottles.

One probable result would be the redefinition of the function of the minister. As leader of a church in which fellowship groups were active, he would find the educational demands of his position increased. He would be constantly bringing people together around vital concerns; he would provide them with resources and materials for intellectual and spiritual exploration. He would find himself working within a context of human concerns which would stimulate him to continuous study and inquiry. He would have a more thorough acquaintance with the lives of his people and of the community.

Another result of the use of this method would be seen in the pronouncements of groups of churches on social and economic issues. All too frequently these statements represent little more than the convictions of a few people who have gotten together a short time before a convention, framed a resolution and then discussed ways of getting it before the convention to assure a favorable hearing and adoption. Adoption often means little more than "do not oppose" or "if those fellows want something like that in, let them have it." This is not to minimize the importance of going on record as a means of influencing public opinion. The lack of responsibility which the average local church feels toward resolutions passed by its national bodies results from the fact that the members have had little opportunity to study or express an opinion concerning the question at issue. Local churches in which there were groups of the kind indicated could be expected to demand participation in the process of resolution making; they would usually not be content with mere resolutions, but would demand implementation.

There are of course many other specific ways in which a

church could implement its interest in economic problems. It should set its own house in order financially, economically. It ought to give its minister freedom to proclaim the Gospel as he sees it, while granting members the right to differ and providing opportunity for discussion of differences and for achieving understanding if not agreement. The church will make clear that its proposals for economic action are regarded as means, not as ends; disagreements on means are to be expected and should not be the cause of breaks in the fellowship. Unity in the matter of goals and ends is a necessary and reasonable condition on which a church may insist.

A church should do more than encourage discussion, important as that is. That it will be impelled to do so may be taken for granted. In the course of the examination of economic proposals and alleged "remedies" of various social disorders, a church may encourage and collaborate in experiments designed to test the validity of specific measures, when it has the opportunity and resources. It should encourage its members to act, and assist them in evaluating results of their actions. Its policy concerning the question of how far it, as a religious body, should go in organizing for specific social action must of necessity be a policy of intelligent opportunism. With due regard for the division of functions as between social organizations, the churches must place the needs of people, as envisioned, formulated and determined by the people composing the church, *first*. This means that a particular church may have to go much farther in direct action than others. If it is located in a community which has few social organizations its field of action must be larger than that of a church in a large community. It might be the only agency in position to do the job required in the situation.

A wide variety in policy and practice of churches with respect to social action is normal and should be expected. Local conditions, as well as denominational traditions, determine the extent and nature of a particular church's participation. Increasingly the churches are embracing the principle of community co-operation and avoiding attempts to do what other agencies can do as well or better. Community agencies draw heavily on churches for leadership and support. This indirect contribution to social effectiveness must not be overlooked in considering the churches' program of action.

A church can make an important contribution to social enlightenment by sponsoring groups of members interested in studying certain questions related to their religious development, as they interpret it, which the church officially may not consider within its field. For example, in the case of a strike in a department store or industrial establishment in the community, the members of a church will probably be divided in their loyalties, and because of this fact, in their interpretation of the church's responsibility. Under these circumstances it would doubtless be impossible for the church officially to take action, or in some instances even to consider the issue. It should, nevertheless, encourage a group which did wish to study the situation to do so.

It should be understood that such groups are speaking and acting for themselves and not for the church. This is not an easy distinction for many people to grasp, and criticism will be directed against the church for permitting the group on its premises. The difficulty can in part be avoided by having an understanding with the group that it has a responsibility for protecting the church in matters of publicity. It is a responsibility of the church to develop a new institutional pattern in which it is "normal" to have a variety of groups working within it whose interests and activities are not shared by the church as a whole, and for which the church takes no official responsibility. If this is done, it is equally important that lines of communication and fellowship in the larger objectives which unite all members in the church be vigorously maintained. By doing this a church can exert an influence on individuals and organizations with which otherwise it would have little contact. These groups will also make an important contribution to the social alertness of the church.

Fundamentally the churches' contribution to the alleviation of our society's economic ills is to be made through the establishment of the kind of fellowship which can generate the power and enlightenment required for collective salvation and individual integrity.

With all their strengths and weaknesses, viewed as an instrument of social education and action Christian churches have a creditable past and even greater potentialities for the future. Basically their responsibility involves no distortion of the essential genius of Christianity. By fostering and enriching communication between members in the spirit of that "fellowship" which churches are dedicated to maintain, they can make a distinctive, urgent and needed contribution to individual integrity and social enlightenment in a world torn with strife. Power, insight and knowledge necessary for shaping a Christian society are potential within the Christian churches today. Release and direction of these resources, now largely untapped, are the major responsibilities of Christian leadership of the future. In this opportunity the churches may rest assured that they will "be the Church" in the most authentic meaning of that term. For in "the Church" modern man, gripped with fear and hopelessness, will then be able to find inspiration and divine comradeship requisite for achieving manhood and community as conceived in Christian thought.

PART III

DISCUSSION AND CRITICAL COMMENTS

By the Authors

CHAPTER FOURTEEN

Discussion of Merriam's Essay by Knight

IN DISCUSSING Mr. Merriam's essay I shall follow the two main heads suggested in our joint introduction. The first issue has to do with the harmony or reconcilability of Christian and liberal ideals. Brief notice of this will be followed by a fuller comparison, from my point of view, of our respective conceptions of the content of liberal ideals of individual and social life, and of the social procedure appropriate for realizing them. In order to be useful and brief my discussion will relate chiefly to differences and will appear critical in tone; but let me say once and for all at the outset that I have found my colleague's essay genuinely educative as well as stimulating, and even inspiring. The main problem of criticism arises from uncertainty as to how far we are really in disagreement. It is difficult to be sure of the precise meaning of any abstract formulation of general ideals, and of course essays of the character and length of these cannot deal with detailed programs of action.

My discussion of the first issue will be summary for the further reason that I have doubts as to its practical importance. Mr. Merriam gives much less explicit discussion even than I have done to the meaning of Christianity, not to mention religion in general; and what he does give is more of the nature of a statement of his own ethical position than of argument for the view that his position is to be identified with that of Christianity, or of religion. In a way characteristic of Christians, he practically assumes the identity of religion with Christianity. I do not think this is intellectually admissible, or perhaps entirely becoming; but this question has little practical import for a discussion of the problems of our own culture. Merriam's treatment would hardly differentiate Christianity from Judaism, as to present-day ethical content, and the two practically cover the meaning of religion in our culture situation.

In Merriam's essay the statements about Christianity which call for notice in a brief review are to be found primarily in Chapters Eight and Nine. In Chapter Eight we are expressly told that Christianity is not to be limited to the clergy, and it is also made clear that it is not to be limited to members of churches. It is stated further that we must go outside the Scriptures for its content, since "the Christian must be granted a sense of the meaning of history." Passing over the question of fact here we find that the essential principle seems to be contained in the statement that "men glimpse the eternal; they live in the present; they seek to incarnate the eternal in the present; they fail, but they do not give up, for the attempting is the meaning of life as the Christian sees it."

In Chapter Nine the four fundamental values (to be discussed later) are said to be based on a theory of the universe which views man's economic and other activity in a suprahuman dimension, as the fulfillment of the meaning of existence, and that "so to act is to do God's will." Again, the meaning of religion is found in the task of binding together our fragmentary knowledge and aspirations in a coherent and dynamic world view. With reference to the genius of Christianity, it is an error to define its content in terms of the world view of a previous age, for Jesus commanded his followers to expect new disclosures of truth, from the Spirit of Truth. Such a definition is said to be the basis of attack on Christianity by external enemies, while its internal enemies attack it by seeking a haven of refuge from the realities of the life about them. Although this discussion runs in terms asserted to be Christian, I suggest that it is better taken in a general idealistic sense, apart from any religion. And the contention that the churches should be the leading agents in promoting such ideals and reforms rather raises without answering the question whether such churches should be called Christian, or even called churches.

The issue here is admittedly culture-historical, and in part verbal. My own essay, contrasting Christianity with liberalism, is not necessarily antagonistic to Merriam's position. There is no opposition if my references to Christianity are taken merely in the historical sense, i.e., in terms of any of the meanings Christianity has ever had or now has for the great bulk of professed adherents, or for any major organized Christian body. I have emphasized that the meaning of Christianity has changed in the course of history, and naturally it may change again, perhaps along the line indicated by Merriam. Indeed, it undoubtedly is changing along that general line, and the change has made substantial progress. Moreover, I am in full agreement with my colleague in regarding this as a consummation devoutly to be wished. For the triumph of the Christian-liberal reinterpretation would make it possible to use the vast moral and material resources of the churches for social good as well as for fellowship valuable in itself. I merely raise the practical question whether such a "conversion" of the churches is a more promising line of endeavor than the cultivation of moral idealism through other channels, and the intellectual issue whether the change proposed is to be viewed as a change of (or in) Christianity or as a movement away from it. Merriam himself does not seem to be entirely consistent; for he qualifies his abstract statement by saying explicitly that Christian ideals are based on a theistic world view and he frequently refers to Christian theological doctrines and cites documents of historical Christianity.

I do not believe this question to be merely verbal or academic, and will restate some of my reasons for holding that the second view must be taken, that the movement is not merely away from Christianity but away from religion, in any admissible meaning of the term. In so far as there is now any organized movement of the sort in question, it is that which goes under the name of Humanism. Its proponents do not generally, I believe, call themselves Christians, but do generally call their position a religion. I cannot view it even in this light, particularly because of its close tie-up with the philosophies of scientism and pragmatism, which I cannot regard as religious or even as affording a sound intellectual basis for ethical idealism. Nor am I able to visualize the continuance and development of strong "churches," under such a credo—or of strong societies, whatever they might be called. The substance of the movement seems to consist of propaganda by a few exceptional individuals who have found themselves in the position of pastors and have managed to commit (actively or passively) to their own enlightened outlook congregations usually built up under different auspices. I must doubt whether such groups can be long maintained apart from the influence of exceptional personalities and the confidence and loyalty which they inspire.

It would of course be futile to argue as to what change the concept of religion may ultimately undergo. Nearly any belief or attitude held with fervor can now be called religious without too much violence to usage. I can only suggest that in serious discussion the use of terms should recognize important distinctions, and that it is surely advisable to separate religion from philosophy and ethics, and from science. Two distinctive features of religion seem to me fundamental. The first is that religious belief rests on faith, in some real contrast with observation and reasoning, and with objective criticism. For religious ethics this means some appeal to supernatural authority. In the second place, the obligation in religious ethics is an emotion, directed toward personal objects, earthly or divine or both—the Jewish-Christian "love" of God and man—in contrast with general values. Merriam's ethic is religious or semi-religious, in the Jewish-Christian sense— and by my liberal standard defective—in considering only personal goods, omitting all reference to truth and beauty and progress in cultural life as value imperatives.

I do not think Christianity can reverse itself on religious essentials common to all phases of its nineteen centuries of history, diverse as these have been. (Merriam's Jewish-Christian theism will be more explicitly considered later.) Let us briefly recall the main historical phases. Christianity grew out of the preaching of a Jewish prophet, under peculiar conditions. The Jews were a small political folk, intensely group-conscious in religious-historical terms, caught in a position of hopelessness by the expansion of imperial Rome. The position of Jesus must be regarded as an expression of defeat and despair with respect to this world, but as an appeal, in the joyous confidence of absolute faith, to divine miracle on a world scale for "salvation" from an intolerable social situation. His ethic of love and righteousness was primarily a condition for bringing about the miracle and was specifically a condition for individual participation in its glorious consummation, the Kingdom of God on earth. This ethic could never be regarded as a rule of life, or of social order, in a continuing earthly society.

Historical Christianity was founded by followers of Jesus after His death. To begin with, it was a mystery religion with Jesus, now the resurrected Saviour, as its cult hero. Its essential tenet was salvation by faith in the Saviour and His redemptive sacrifice ("washed in the blood of the lamb") manifested in a confession and a few ritualistic sacramental acts. An austere moral life was also required, though not as an explicit condition of salvation; the connection was explained by a reinterpretation of the ancient Covenant of Yahweh with the ancestors of the Hebrews. In its later adjustment to the necessities of life under mundane conditions, on its ethical-religious side (in contrast with the magical-sacramental side, which was greatly elaborated) Christianity came to embody a combination of several versions of voluntarism, i.e., it has attributed the evils of the world to sins of will and preached repentance and righteousness as their cure. Apart from explicitly treating spiritual love and fellowship as intrinsic values infinitely more important in themselves than anything else, even life (a position alien to Christianity), the most extreme form of this view is that it is a sin to expect or in any way strive for well-being in the earthly life. One should gratefully accept whatever comes, devote oneself wholly to the love of God and man and look forward to boundless compensation in a life after death. Another form of the voluntaristic position, one more closely related to the life of this world, and in a way optimistic, is the idea that earthly evil is sent by God as a punishment for sin, and will disappear if men repent and embrace righteousness. This view is similar to that of original Christianity, but without the romantic "eschatology" of a miraculous transformation of the world. It rests on a personification of the universe in a deity whose essence is power and will, ambiguously both loving and wrathful, and a retributive theory of morality, in contrast with a social view in terms of action, motive and result. In practice, the hierarchically organized church came to be a despotism based on the claim to represent God on earth, with plenary authority in this world and the next.

There is still another form of voluntarism, an authoritarian version which is not explicit in the Christian revelation but at least seems to be natural to men living under the conditions of civilized society, and which has found a large place in Christian belief. From the accusing and denouncing prophets (such as Amos) onward, it has regularly been a first step in thinking about social reform, in contrast with accepting everything as it is, but it proceeds by methods of this world without appeal to miracle. I refer to the view that men in positions of authority or power, political rulers and "the rich," could if they would (if they were righteous) take care of everyone in need, and so order things that all men could be happy and friendly. Accordingly, the way to make an ideal moral utopia is to coerce or punish, or to liquidate such rascals. This is the view typically held today by radical agitators toward employers, and largely by the romantic masses toward "the government." It is the view of things commonly encouraged by spokesmen for religion when they take a reformist line. Although it is not the main theme of my collaborator in his essay as a whole, it is amply illustrated in his repeated castigation of American businessmen for acting irresponsibly and for selfishly opposing restrictions and reforms. Of course, I am not saying that there is no truth in this accusation, for there clearly is a substantial amount. But it is quite as certain that a large part of the "reforms" opposed by businessmen are really vicious, while most of them are debatable; and even the reformers' objectives can be condemned in terms of a moral and social philosophy as plausible as that by which they are defended. The assumption that opposition to proposed changes is entirely or mainly due to the selfishness of a few individuals is indefensible—and, one may also suggest, specifically out of place when advanced on "Christian" grounds.

In Christian history as a whole, religious spokesmen have usually adopted some version or versions of the "sin theory" of social evil. They have used their religion to sanctify existing government, however oppressive, as long as it was friendly to the church or, better still, under its dominance, and also to sanctify property ownership and economic privilege, subject to the same conditions. But they have taught both that all inequality, authority and law are rendered necessary by the sinfulness of man, and are essentially a punishment for sin, and that they would be wholly beneficent in the hands of righteous men. The freedom and equality for which religion has stood have been purely spiritual, never material. For such reasons, the history of Christianity does not seem to me to point in the direction of rational ethical and social idealism, and that is the substance of what I tried to say on this subject in my essay. The type of idealism now advocated under the auspices of the most advanced liberal

Christianity, including Merriam's Christian liberalism, is still blemished by the old shortcomings.

However, there is something to be said on the other side, and its general character may well be indicated at this point, with a view at least to clarifying my own position. It is rather trivial to admit formally that there is some truth in the sin theory, that much of the evil and suffering in the world is due to selfish and immoral behavior, that the need for law and authority is partly due to this fact, or that men in power are subject to special temptations, to which they often succumb. Hence, the idea of organizations such as churches standing for and teaching righteousness has real merit as well as romantic appeal. But it involves several dangers. The greatest is that people may not recognize the limitations and may both expect too much and neglect more fundamental lines of attack on social problems. It is a strain on credulity, in the light of virtually all religious history, to think either of churches not advocating concrete programs beyond their competence to judge the consequences, or of their being disinterested and uninfluenced by the desire for power and its material perquisites. As history shows, they are not likely to stop with urging people to do as well as they know, and to study problems earnestly and impartially. Merriam himself goes much further, proposing lines of action which any student of economics and politics must see would be pernicious. The religious attitude seems inimical to objectivity, even when it is above suspicion of self-interest (as far as this is possible) and when it is also "liberalized" as far as it can be and remain religious, in some distinction from ethics and philosophy.

From the liberal point of view there is no serious objection to men believing in eternal and unchangeable values, i.e., believing that they exist, under the condition that they do not pretend to know or to teach others what these values are in the concrete. And the same may be said of belief in an eternal and unchanging spiritual or divine reality, as the "ground" of values, and even of interpreting goodness as doing the will of God. But such beliefs become mischievous if the believer claims any knowledge of what God wills on any particular question, or what absolute values mean in the concrete case, beyond what is learned by use of human intellectual and critical faculties in free co-operative discussion with other inquirers. It should be ethically useful to find the hand of God or the working of an ethical will in history provided, again, that this is not allowed to encourage haste and dogmatism in drawing lessons from history. Under proper safeguards, belief in God may be valuable as a sanction for a belief in the validity of moral values in the abstract. But its actual consequences have usually been of quite another kind, namely, dogmatism, intolerance and the worst form of lust for power; and it is hard to expect the future to be radically different from the past.

There are special dangers in a theism, or in a belief in absolute values, which is based upon historical Christianity with its included background of Judaism. Merriam points out that the modern Christian must not hesitate to go outside the Scriptures. From my point of view, this is to the good, but two facts should be noted. First, going outside the Scriptures will inevitably mean revising these writings in a sense more or less contrary to their verbal import; and this cannot be carried far without destroying their special authority. Again, I have already questioned whether a religion or a church can claim to be Christian if it rejects the authority of the Bible and commits itself to appraising all its teachings on their merits, on a parity with ideas from any other source.

On the other hand, if any special significance is attached to the teachings of either the Old or the New Testament, these will surely imply conclusions which are false and wrong, by the standards of liberal social ethics accepted in our culture. The nature of the society which is presupposed and enjoined in the Old Testament is monarchial theocracy, with a law contained in an ancient revelation. The history of this cannot now be known, and it is not subject to revision, though it contains such barbarous anachronisms as the command to execute witches. A serious religious regard for the Old Testament could hardly be anything but a source of confusion and conflict in the mind of a citizen of a democracy such as Great Britain or the United States, or even a modern totalitarian state. Obedience to God necessarily means obedience to some human representative, king or high priest, with prescriptive authority to declare or interpret the law, and this does not accord with the conception of popular sovereignty. Modern Christians and Jews are apparently saved from mental conflict by refusing to take their professed religious beliefs seriously in the conduct of political life.

With respect to the New Testament, the statement to be made would be even stronger. The only concrete political doctrine found in the recorded teachings of Jesus and Paul is the injunction of obedience to established authority. Even law is referred to only implicitly and in very general terms, or even disparagingly. There is little or no recognition that there may be conflict between law and authority, or between different authorities or laws, and that the citizen may have a problem of deciding whom or what he ought to obey. There is not the least intimation that he has any responsibility for the content of the law, or any rightful authority of his own, or rights to be supported against authority. The whole of social duty appears to be summed up in a will to obedience and non-resistance, and to love, regardless of the merits of the object.

Of course historical Christianity took a very different position. It organized itself as rapidly as possible under the form, and with the trappings and perquisites, of a theocratic empire, somewhat on Old Testament lines. But the church, organized on a strictly authoritarian pattern, claimed that its law, or arbitrary fiat, was the law of God; disobedience was sacrilege, and it claimed the right and the power to dispense forgiveness and unlimited reward or punishment in this world or the next. I cannot see much point in saying that all this was a perversion of "true" Christianity, unless some definite, intelligible and defensible definition is given for the latter.

We turn from the question of the meaning of Christianity, or historical Christianity, and of "Christian liberalism," as presented in Merriam's essay, to the different question of the relation between this Christian liberalism and liberalism as I conceive it and have presented it summarily in my own essay. I may mention again the difficulty of comparing two formulations of ethical ideals, where neither purports to state an explicit program or rules of policy, and where the two authors speak for the same general school of ethical thought. At the same time, I think that in this field also there are differences between Merriam's position and my own which are important for an understanding of the social problems confronted by our democratic society, and for intelligent action with respect to them.

In relation to the ethics of historical Christianity, I find Merriam's actual position and my own far more "on the same side," in opposition to the traditional religious view, than opposed to one another. We both stand for facing the problem of an intelligent organization of social and economic life with a view to realizing critically defined values, in terms of the improvement of continuing social life on earth. His essay does not mention salvation or immortality; and I believe we are in agreement in assuming that whatever men or society can do about these problems is to be done by earnestly and intelligently attacking the problems of this life. The ideal moral life cannot be merely a way to save one's own soul, to say nothing of salvation through any sacramental ritual or by arbitrary belief or faith. Nor is either salvation or human betterment to be achieved by negative conduct, indiscriminate giving, or renouncing the world. Of course both of us hold to the intrinsic as well as the instrumental value of rational sympathy and love for one's neighbor, for all humanity and even for all creatures who are capable of enjoyment and suffering. However, I think Merriam will agree that ethical universality must be qualified. It seems both absurd and morally wrong to think of love or any form of regard as being "equal" toward all human beings, either as a feeling or as implying equal obligations. As Merriam's anti-pacifism implies, it must on occasion be one's duty to thwart and even to destroy individuals for the sake of more general values.

The reader will find a striking similarity in the terms in which our two essays formulate the general ideals which are to motivate and guide social action. The four fundamental values, stated and developed in Merriam's Chapter Nine and interpreted in economic terms in his Chapters Ten and Eleven, will form the basis for my discussion of the issues. The proposals for action outlined in his twelfth chapter need not be criticized in detail, as this would repeat the substance of my fifth chapter, or make obvious applications, and would unduly extend this review. The role of churches in social action, the subject of Merriam's final and longest chapter, must be passed over here, apart from obvious implications of what I have said in the preceding section.

In spite of the similarity between our general positions, including Merriam's rejection of the traditional religious ethic of submission in favor of a "philosophy of force," my criticism will run along the same line as what I have said about historical Christian ethics. In fundamentals, I still find his position more Christian than liberal. This applies to two main weaknesses in his argument. The first is a tendency to oversimplify the problems, to overlook many essential factors in moral life and social action. The second weakness, a particularization of the first, is assigning too large a role to the will, to "good intentions," in contrast with intellectual analysis and the rational use and development of means or power. To bring out certain relationships which seem to me important among Merriam's ideals of liberalism, I shall take them up in an order slightly different from his. I must put freedom at the head of the list and couple equality with freedom and also consider together the other two, universality and collective responsibility.

A major concrete difference is that Merriam hardly refers to efficiency or progress. But I find another fundamental contrast in principle between our two conceptions of freedom and equality. The difference, again, is one of omission on the religious side. Both religious and liberal ethics are theoretically individualistic; but the former differs from the latter in ignoring the intellectual and constructive aspect of conduct, including both the fact that it is always a matter of rationally using means to realize ends—and of conserving and increasing resources—and the fact that the ends must be rationally chosen. Ends, as I have stressed, are never really final but are merged or integrated in the general purpose of achieving the "good life," individual and social, the conception of which grows and changes with cultural progress. And this redefinition is a primary social-ethical task for a society which has reached the stage of consciously confronting the quality of life as a social problem, i.e., for a true democracy. The means, again, are "what they are" at any moment, but in the long run are almost wholly the product of action. Religious ethics refuses to recognize clearly that the achievement of the good life, in practically every aspect, is directly or indirectly limited by the means available. Hence it ignores the progressive aspect on both sides—increasing the stock of means and the efficiency with which they are used, and the constant redefinition of ends and ideals. Merriam's position seems to have these characteristics.

It is the requirement of effective organization, in relation to formal freedom, and the conflict between the two, which gives its concrete form to the problem of economic ethics in modern society. In common with religious, voluntaristic or

—as I think it fair to say—"sentimental" reformers generally, Merriam treats the social-economic problem as essentially one of redistribution. He shows little regard for the problems of efficient production and of accumulation, or for the close connection between distribution and these other essentials. A student of economics—hence a student of the social problem from the standpoint of concrete objectives and concrete measures which are meaningful in terms of the facts—must find my colleague representative of naive reformist public opinion in tacitly assuming that both the "distribuend" and the "distribuees" are "given." He passes over the problem of incentive to production and to effective organization with bare if not deprecating mention. In the same connection, he refers freely to "exploitation," which "every one knows" occurs, and to the need for laws limiting freedom so as to prevent exploitation, but gives no definition or test. He fails to consider that limitation of freedom to exploit must be achieved by giving *power* to one or a few individuals, directly reducing the freedom of the masses. Bad in itself, on both sides, this prevents the controlled from doing good as well as evil and places the controllers in a position to do more damage than results from individual freedom, limited by the principle of free-association. It also saps the incentive to action, especially to innovation and improvement, with the hazards (risk) which such activities involve. He also objects strongly to competition and acquisitiveness in the economic order, though at one point (in the tenth chapter) he recognizes that political activity is also competitive. It is in fact far more directly a struggle for power, and there is good reason to think that in so far as the motives differ at all, both these and the consequences will be worse in politics than in market competition. The alternative to competitive politics is political monopoly or dictatorship, and this would be the natural result of giving the state a paternalistic role. The evils of concentration of power in the state are but cursorily mentioned.

The discussion is typical for religious reformism in advocating ideal ends to the virtual neglect of means and procedure, on the assumption that such concrete problems will solve themselves if men's hearts are right in relation to ultimate values. But these also conflict, and this fact is ignored. Such a position is rational only in terms of a faith in God which Jesus and his earliest followers had but which is impossible to the modern mind. Or, it might rest on such an idealization of human nature as would keep the problems from arising. On the other side, we find the now fashionable disregard for the large amount of validity in the original liberal theory of the "invisible hand." Effective market competition does eliminate arbitrary power, promote freedom and efficiency, put consumers as a body in control of production and distribute burdens and benefits in a way which conforms to one form of individualistic justice. (The New Testament—the Apostle Paul speaking—asserts that a man should reap what he sows.) The first concrete economic problem for society must be to achieve such competition as far as possible. The religious argument also ignores the real weakness of competitive organization, the divergence of actual economic relations from the pattern of effective competition, the reasons for it and the appropriate action. And it fails to confront the vital issue in individualistic economic justice itself, which brings it into conflict with other valid ideals. The fact which sets the main problem is that the individual is largely a social creation, together with the fact of social-cultural differentiation. Merriam's treatment further ignores the value or ideal of interesting activity in economic life, which must form the bulk of conduct, and the main opportunity for self-expression and self-development, and "useful play." One of the main sources of human interest in action is competition (here in the psychological meaning of emulation, not market competition); and another is "taking chances," in the pursuit of an uncertain reward—the correct meaning of the much maligned profit motive. The evils of intricate organization and extreme mechanization seem to me at least as great in this regard as the inequitable distribution which results; but such organization is the price of efficiency and a high standard of living.

From the standpoint of liberal ideals, freedom must be considered in close connection with equality—my reason for changing the order of Merriam's four items. The greatest weakness of liberal ethics is that, viewing freedom as freedom of action, it defines equality in terms of this freedom for *given* individuals. This conception conflicts with substantive economic equality, in terms of income, standard of living or power. Both ideals, both forms of equality, demand consideration, and liberal thought tended to neglect the latter. Equal freedom to use unequal power or resources (regardless of kind) may mean any degree of substantive inequality. It may even negate effective freedom of action for those who have inadequate resources, and may place such persons at the mercy of others who happen to control the means necessary to life—without implying any arbitrary power in the hands of the latter. Merriam's position represents an important advance over historical Christianity in clearly recognizing that the individual must have means as a condition of participation in the culture of his age, and of enjoying full human status, as well as for life and comfort, and that he ought not to be satisfied either with mere "spiritual" equality or with charity. But another long step is necessary to bring his position into line with true liberalism, where the ideal is that the indivdual should do things for himself, stand on his own feet and not have either the fruits of action or needful resources handed to him by anyone else or by society. On the other side, liberal thought naively and falsely assumed that productive resources are innately given to the individual or are the fruit of his own activity, and that in either case their possession and use are natural rights. Even superior natural powers ideally create an obligation at least as much as they confer a privilege. Finally, the factor of uncertainty, or luck, is necessarily large and operates to distort the comparative standing of in-, dividuals; the ethics of the incentive and reward for risk-taking is a knotty problem which most students and practically all preachers of reform either fail to see or do not care to face.

At the bottom of the whole problem of economic ethics lie divergent conceptions of merit or desert, or of ethical individualism. In the view of traditional liberalism, as in that of common sense in large measure, desert is defined by performance, and performance (with given capacity) is measured by market price under free exchange. According to the brotherhood, or "love" ideal, desert is defined ambiguously by human need and a right attitude of will—"good intentions." The standard of need suggests approximate equality; but equality has no definite meaning and to be defensible as a norm must be endlessly qualified. All these conflicting criteria —equality, need and performance (capacity and effort)—possess ideal validity. The last must be given large recognition in organized life because it is indispensable for productive efficiency under modern conditions which require large-scale organization. Thus the problem is one of compromise and balance. In any case, it seems virtually self-evident that organized social relations must be governed by impersonal rules, and that distribution on the basis of performance is the only possible rule, and also the only one reconcilable with freedom. "Love" can play only an indirect and limited role. Distribution can then be modified in favor of other principles by the free action of individuals (charity) or by compulsory social action, wherever the gain to be had is reasonably sure to outweigh the loss. But any other primary system of organization implies either chaos or a dictatorship.

The other two of Merriam's four values—collective responsibility and universality, which I find also to be closely interrelated—must be considered briefly. No one, or at least no liberal who is to be taken seriously, has ever questioned

collective responsibility as an ideal, or even as humanly necessary. As usual in connection with abstract values, an issue
arises only in the interpretation and application. The de-
sideratum is the best distribution of responsibility for the
individual life between the individual himself and various
institutions and groups—the family, divers voluntary associations and numerous political entities, up to the sovereign
state and some world organization. As usual with religious
and other reformers, Merriam hardly refers to the real and
tangible issues. In liberal thought, the primary responsibility rests first upon the family, to give each person his start
in life. It later passes to the person himself, acting on his
own or in voluntary groups, as he reaches maturity, while at
every stage the neighborhood and the state are under obligation to help in meeting emergencies or by relieving acute
distress, however caused. Further, the liberal state has rapidly
assumed responsibility for equipping the youth for life, in
the way of education, both cultural and vocational, and for
various public services, all at the cost of the relatively
well-to-do.

On the theory and practice of Christianity in this connection, I can only recall briefly what was said in my essay.
Christianity has resembled liberalism in being theoretically
individualistic, hence cosmopolitan. But thoroughgoing individualism is an absurdity in view of the biological and
social-historical facts of life. Naturally, the real position
of both movements has been different from this ideal. Both
have accepted the family, substantially as found in the
European tradition, as the elementary and "sacred" social
unit. Organized Christianity has accepted and sanctified any
social structure and political and economic order which
happened to exist, in so far as these served its own varied ends.
Liberalism abolished formal classes and transformed the
state from a despotic to a democratic basis; it greatly reduced
social control over everyday life while giving the state increasing responsibility, as mentioned above—some of which

had been halfheartedly borne by the church. The main change wrought by historical Christianity is to superpose insistence on religious homogeneity, with unitary ecclesiastical organization and ecclesiastical control, upon allegiance to a particular state, implying a minimum of cultural homogeneity required for harmonious political life. Religious universality means that some one church—that of the particular spokesman—must absorb all others, of all religions, and impose its requirements of belief and practice upon their members. However, any candid discussion must recognize that the incorporation of the individual in any real and effective organization involves loss of freedom, going with transfer of responsibility. The state in particular, with its territorial sovereignty and uniform law, violates the liberal ideal of free association. And the family has an organic unity based on biological differentiation (sex and age) and is formed under law, with theoretically indissoluble obligations.

Merriam's discussion of collective responsibility makes it clear that the state is the collectivity he has in mind. He hardly refers to the problem of the rightful limits of state control over the citizen, or of majority rule over a minority, though the seriousness of this problem has been recognized in political discussion throughout the era of liberalism. Nor does he raise the question of who is the state—what particular political unit should assume any given responsibility—much as that question also has been discussed and debated, in America in particular. We also find little recognition of the serious problems involved in taking a national state as it now exists as the collectivity which is to implement collective responsibility and within which universality is to prevail. That the boundaries of states are not fixed and accepted but are actually the subject of disputes (and the occasion of wars) is less important for general analysis than the fact that complete universality is not desirable within the boundaries of any large state, while this would still fall far short of real universality. We are told that the Christian community must be open to all men because a God of love has created man in his image. Even this commits Christian liberalism to a particular theistic basis, and the statement of fact as to "openness" has never been true without sweeping qualifications for prescribed conditions. Economic inequality, poverty in resources and in wants, and injustice are just as real in the relations between communities of all sorts, including both states and churches, as in relations between individuals.

It is primarily with reference to families that Merriam himself stresses the evils of inequality and insufficiency. He specifies these evils in concrete terms of the handicapping of many children in their start in life, through bad food, homes and medical care, while others have superior conditions. It is the case of the children which undoubtedly furnishes the strongest argument, practical as well as sentimental, against excessive inequality, since the children are the future members of any society. And children certainly may be "corrupted" by poverty or by wealth. But these abstract truths are neither in question nor helpful. It is all very well to say that society should make the same effort at full provision for its children as does the family, and that the obvious method is collective action; but it does not contribute to the formulation and execution of a plan for achieving universality unless we are shown that society can be universal in scope and are given some feasible program of collective action on this scale. Surely, moreover, a fair discussion of the problem should take notice of the enormous amount of action already taken by liberal states through such agencies and organizations, political and voluntary, as already exist or could practicably be created, and also of the difficulties and problems which have prevented such measures from being carried much farther than they have—other than the alleged selfishness, irresponsibility and lack of vision of "business."

The problem of relations between states is barely mentioned by Merriam, in connection with the idea of universality, and not at all in connection with his other ideals. We find a reference to the difficulty of carrying over the ideal of fellowship from the small Christian group to the world outside, but we are told that the desire for universality is expressed in the missionary movement, and in other interests. The desire of Christians to convert adherents of other religions is doubtfully in point in connection with collective economic responsibility, in view of their religious intolerance and the historical fact that churches have sanctioned both concentration of wealth and a status organization of society, including slavery and serfdom. Merriam's brief reference to world conditions seems to be motivated by the desire to bring in some discussion of the problem arising out of a world at war, to mention the need for a world state (without any discussion of the problems involved) and in particular to denounce pacifism. It is noteworthy that the statement calling for a Christian philosophy of force does not distinguish between international war, civil war and ordinary police activity; nor does it face the issues raised by recognizing the right of self-defense on the part of a nation as the bearer of a particular type of culture or civilization.

I cordially agree with the view that a people with a higher or better civilization has a moral obligation to resist, by force if necessary, degradation to a lower level. I would merely like to see it recognized that superiority is a matter of judgment on which impartiality is out of the question, and that such a country as the United States, in fighting for its institutions and ideals, is also necessarily fighting to maintain its unequal position in wealth and technical efficiency, standard of living, education and other advantages (particularly for its children), all of which violate the abstract principles of equality and universal collective responsibility. They even nullify freedom in the substantive meaning of effective freedom, of which power is a necessary component.

More generally, I should like to see it recognized that the ethical problem for the individual, or any group which acts as a unit in any way, is an intellectual and practical problem of compromise and balance between numerous valid ideals, and that the means necessary to a good life for all are woefully inadequate. These facts raise the issue of population in relation to resources and many forbidding questions involving the family and the whole institutional structure of world society. Adequate consideration would make it evident that human betterment is far more a problem of science than it is one of good will.

CHAPTER FIFTEEN

Discussion of Knight's Essay by Merriam

MR. KNIGHT has made a searching analysis of Christianity and of the ethical problem of Western culture. His essay bristles with provocative observations which invite discussion. The spirit of honest inquiry animates his analysis. This quality is important because the issues with which he deals are inflammatory. Too commonly they are discussed with a display of prejudice and partisanship which only befog the subject.

Because Mr. Knight has succeeded in isolating and clarifying basic issues, I have been able to see more distinctly our differences in viewpoint. It will be the purpose of this chapter to locate these points of disagreement and to comment briefly on them. As I now see it, there are certain weaknesses in Knight's proposals. The alternatives which I shall present are doubtless also vulnerable, but they endeavor to take into account facts which I think Knight leaves out of consideration. The end which both of us seek is a few principles on which we may act with intelligent regard for the facts of life. Therein is the unity of this undertaking.

Even if space permitted, there would be little point in considering Knight's argument item by item as it develops under his skillful handling. The details would confuse the issue. Instead, I shall state and restrict my comments to major issues. These are two.

First, I find difficulty in Knight's interpretation of the meaning and role of religion, specifically Christianity, in relation to liberal values. He seems to overlook certain facts which, if considered, would necessitate a revision of his conclusions. I think it would be fair to summarize his position by stating that the Christian ethic has no important contribution to make, either to clarifying or solving current socio-ethical issues. I disagree.

A second major question which I shall discuss concerns the relation between the achievement of liberal values in our society—including freedoms of various kinds for individuals and groups—and our economic system. If I understand Knight correctly, he is saying that the liberal or democratic way of life is possible only under the system of free economic enterprise. If the free market goes, along with it goes the whole complex of values which we associate with modern liberalism. Again, I disagree.

There are several other questions which I should like to talk over with Knight, but these two are central. I shall consider first his interpretation of the Christian ethic to which he devotes all of Chapter Two, and part of Chapter One, and which reappears in various parts of the entire essay.

The Meaning of the Christian Ethic: Knight approaches the question historically. He does not concern himself much with contemporary religion. His historical survey is condensed and brilliant. From it he derives certain broad generalizations regarding the nature of religion, the content of the Christian ethic and the interests which Christianity through the years has upheld. Within the limits set by his facts, his generalizations seem valid. There are other facts which he ignores.

For example, one of his conclusions is that throughout history religion in general and Christianity in particular have sanctioned the *established* and *accepted* modes of thought and action. Christianity's adherents have tended to accept passively whatever material, social and political conditions happen to exist. If Knight is correct, then obviously little force or light for changing or meeting creatively new social conditions may be expected from Christian groups.

Two questions may be raised: What meaning is given to such terms as "established" and "accepted"? And considering the highly differentiated character of religious group life, can Mr. Knight's generalization be sustained?

Concerning the meaning of *established* and *accepted*, it is clear that these are relative terms, relative to particular groups. Consider American society. What is the accepted view in ethics, economics or politics? Is there an established view regarding the New Deal, or divorce, or free enterprise, or anti-Semitism, or how Negroes should be treated, or the validity of the sacraments? It seems obvious that the answer depends on what group or what part of the country is being considered. Even if an American religious group tried its best to conform to Knight's thesis and to sanction the established, it could not do so.

The fact is that in a dynamic society like ours, social forces, precipitated in part by the mingling of cultures and in part by new ideas released by modern science and technology, have so changed ideas and customs as to produce a fluid condition which makes such terms as *established* and *accepted* almost meaningless. To tell the man from Mars that in going to Chicago he would find religion supporting established customs would be to mislead him. He would find that, but he would also find religions undermining established customs, from any viewpoint which he might have as to what is established.

If it is maintained that within any particular group one finds religion sanctioning the established, then one runs athwart the fact of individualism and dissent in religion. In Protestantism, particularly, dissent is an ancient and honorable tradition. When applied to this phenomenon of religious history, the argument would be that, within the individual, religion sanctions those tendencies and beliefs which are traditional. Knight gives no evidence that this is the case. He is dealing with religion as a sociological matter. Even if his proposition were true of individuals, their differences in modern society, even within a single Protestant group, are such that the terms "established" and "accepted" have little specific meaning.

Thus I find his terms unilluminating for this type of study. He, further, ignores the resisting, protesting element in religious group life. Did any religion ever get started except as a protest against some type of established thought and behavior? Quite commonly Christianity has felt itself "against the world" and responsible for maintaining what it believed to be right and true against majority opinion. It is not easy for me to think of the blood of the martyrs as having been shed, or the punishment taken by religiously motivated anti-slavery groups, the peace churches and contemporary workers for racial and economic justice within religious circles as having been meted out, because these individuals or groups were following the accepted social line. The tradition of resistance to established customs for the sake of the Kingdom of God is a fact of religion, a fact to which, as I read Knight, he has failed to do justice. The result is that he fails to understand Christianity and is misled as he assays the potentialities of religious movements in the ethical and economic sphere.

I do not wish to overemphasize the resisting, dissenting element in religion except in so far as it is necessary in order to get a fair balance in view of Knight's emphasis on the conservative factors. I agree with him that there is a powerful non-prophetic, obscurantist force in Christianity which will typically resist change. While a pull of this kind is a fact, there is always a counter-force emphasizing the radical application of Christian principles of human relations. The latter is as much a part of the body of fact which the religious historian must consider as the former. Historic Christianity has both sanctioned and undermined established ways of thinking and acting. Its distinctive concerns lie elsewhere. Sometimes its interests lead it to sanction the customary; at other times and in other groups, to repudiate *it.* A more illuminating category of analysis is required if we are to understand its nature.

This leads to another of Knight's generalizations. He states that it is characteristic of Christianity to propose vague goals, and while cultivating an inner attitude of acceptance of these goals, to ignore the means by which they may be achieved. The religious mind is not concerned with and typically sees no problem in questions of method. "Faith" in the goals is all that is required. God will do the rest in his own good time and way.

Let us admit that there is truth in what Knight says. But how explain certain facts which must be considered alongside these well-known tendencies? There is today an absorbing interest in churches in discovering ways of implementing Christian ideals in community life, international relations, economic and political life. Many churches have active commissions engaged in research, education and, in certain fields, in experimentation in the effort to find ways of achieving Christian values in the tension spots of contemporary life. They are enlisting some of the best minds of our day, not only in theology but in the social sciences. I do not think that these activities can be lightly passed over as atypical or as unnatural growths out of keeping with the genius of Christianity. They suggest a vital interest in methods of implementing Christianity's ethical goals. It is not necessary to prove that these efforts are wisely directed; this may be debatable. It is not debatable that there exists today, and probably has always existed, a significant group that is not content merely with proclaiming Christian ideals but is attempting to relate all the wisdom afforded by modern culture to the task of building a social order on the Christian pattern, and to discover in detail what that pattern is which can have some claim to be called Christian.

Further light on this issue may be derived from considering the psychological and educational issues of Knight's proposition. To ignore means of implementing ideals to which lip service is given is to encourage sentimentalism and hypocrisy. A sense of reality is essential for character and social effectiveness. How may ideals get incorporated into action? Can verbal commitments change conduct? Modern religious education is at work trying to find an answer. It is influenced by recent studies in psychology and sociology. Modern religious education accepts the proposition that producing enlightened goodness is more than a matter of inculcating good sentiments. It does not accept Knight's proposition that religion is mainly concerned with "conditioning" the young to traditional ways of thinking and behaving. There is wide acceptance of the view that, if ideals are to be effective, there must be activity of a particular kind. The individual must be led to analyze his own social situation, to reflect on and discuss critically with his group historic Christian teachings which bear on this situation, to consider the possible actions and then to act; following action, to evaluate on the basis of the events which follow. In some such way, it is believed, intelligence, aspiration, social experience and behavior may be blended.

This type of religious education does not seem to me to follow the line suggested by Knight in his conclusion that religion ignores means. It does help to explain the interest in creative social exploration and analysis to be found in the churches today.

In his discussion of sentimental "moralism" perhaps Knight is in danger of underestimating the importance of the inner attitudes of individuals. It is not enough to know what is right; the desire to *do* is equally important. A truism, to be sure, but not to be dismissed. It is the Christian teaching that the "heart" must be considered. Men's purposes and motivations are important, as well as their social conditions. The perpetual struggle within the individual against self-centeredness, narrowness of loyalties, insensitivity to the needs of others and the yearning that individual life should have meaning have always been a concern of Christianity. Such matters are of great importance in connection with the economic and political problems discussed in Knight's essay. Perhaps the chief difference between modern and historic Christianity at this point lies in the former's use of social sciences, particularly psychology, in its effort to understand and deal with the problem of helping men achieve mastery over self. There is no conflict between a concern for the inner life and a concern for social realities. The way the daily bread is earned, the kind of experiences one has with one's fellowmen influence this inner life.

"For the record," I shall mention without discussion other generalizations of Knight from which I dissent: that Christianity typically takes an attitude of irresponsibility toward social relationships; that Christian belief excludes a rational or intellectual approach to ethical problems; that the Christian mind is a closed mind, and is therefore opposed to the liberal or scientific approach; that (already mentioned) it is the Christian ideal to condition children to unquestioning acceptance of dogma and myth and to inculcate a belief in the sinfulness of criticism and questioning.

In fairness to Knight it should be said that he does not say these views are held by all Christians at all times. He observes that Christians are great compromisers. Churches bow to the inevitable and eventually accept views after they have been generally accepted. In his opinion, this only illustrates the churches' inherent incapacity for social leadership and the futility of looking to them for initiative and light on social and economic problems.

I propose to Knight that he think of Christianity as a quest for righteousness in which righteousness is conceived as two-dimensional. In one dimension is man's relation to his fellow-man; in the other dimension is man's relation to God as the ultimate source of righteousness. In this age-long quest, the concepts of righteousness change as culture changes and as new social settings propose new problems for righteousness, with, however, the values or broad concepts of them remaining recognizably constant. The unity of Christianity is thus to be found in the quality of the quest and in the sense of kinship which, transcending historic periods, Christians feel toward one another.

One of the most serious weaknesses of the Christian ethic, in Knight's opinion, is what for want of a better term may be called its mystical base. A mushy foundation, he regards it. The Christian typically, he alleges, claims that he receives divine guidance in matters of conduct, as well as in interpreting the meaning of the passing scene. Such a view can be of value, he says, only if there is found to be some agreement among Christians concerning what God wills. The fact is that there is little agreement. Further, Christianity encourages the belief that such disclosures of God's will have greater validity and authority than the more painful processes of rational thinking, including scientific discipline.

I would agree with Knight that the Christian usually thinks of his effort to know and to do the right as somehow divinely guided. At least he regards such aspirations as the best part of his nature. It is also true that one of the results of this way of looking at life has been to disparage the intellect; also to let loose many a crank idea, all in the name of God. Christianity has recognized the difficulty and has been realistic about it. It has established the principle, however neglected in practice, that the critical and social judgment is an inseparable part of the ideology of guidance or revelation. Alleged revelations of God's will must be subjected to drastic and critical analysis precisely like other ideas. There is not that passive acceptance which is often thought to be the psychological accompaniment of revelation. As a matter of history, the alleged revelation is usually unacceptable because it so often challenges and shocks conventional views.

Many illustrations of this fact might be cited. I shall mention two cases.

Jeremiah is represented as the recipient of a revelation.

The disclosures were contrary to popular opinion concerning the desirable strategy with respect to Babylonia. Likewise they required Jeremiah to play a part contrary to his own conception of himself. He did not accept the disclosures readily. He subjected them to prolonged criticism. He argued with God; he even accused God of misleading him. Out of his anguish came picturesque prophecies which recommended a kind of appeasement policy with respect to Babylonia. They were not accepted by his contemporaries, although they subsequently proved more realistic than the proposals of the powers that governed the nation. Perhaps by reason of the thinking process which his experience with God induced, Jeremiah was enabled to see events more clearly than his contemporaries. Certainly because of this experience he was enabled to stand up to the persecution which was visited upon him because of his unpopular pronouncements. In any case, his attitude toward divine guidance was neither passive and uncritical nor did it involve suspension of intellectual activity. There were introduced into his mind, and into the social process, ideas which were startlingly different from what was congenial to him and his fellows.

The Apostle Paul shows a similar critical process, but with an added element. Claimants to divine revelations were rampant in his time, as in ours. In accord with the psychology of the times, speaking "with tongues" was a common form. Paul insisted that such people be required to make sense out of their alleged visions, and translate them into terms which would make possible understanding and evaluation. He further insisted that the ultimate test was conduct. If the claimant to divine revelation lived a better life, judged by Christian standards, Paul thought the revelation had value. If he were dishonest, lazy, a cheat in human relations, then fraud or self-deception might be suspected.

The requirement that alleged revelations be subjected to rational and social scrutiny by competent judges is an essential part of Christian thought. It is not foolproof. Those who judge may be so enmeshed in the accepted cultural patterns as to be incapable of imagining any view which goes against their conceptions of what can possibly be true. Thus the prophet may prophesy in vain as far as his own generation is concerned. I think that a fair view would be that one may well leave open the question as to whether significant ideas and imperatives for social action come from divine guidance. However one may be inclined to suspect the interpretation of the source of these ideas, they ought not to be ruled out because one does not agree with the theological orientation of the prophet.

In any social situation the number of people who are able at once to secure a firm grasp of essential facts, and at the same time dissociate themselves and their judgments from the prevailing ways of thinking sufficiently to achieve objectivity, are few. But these few are important. We know that again and again such persons appear and are disowned by their contemporaries. Little is understood of the inner dynamics involved. One cannot even say they are learned men, that is, that they have stored up more facts than others. But they see farther and more clearly. It is the Christian experience that they would better not be written off as dupes or frauds, even though there will be plenty such. They will not be employed to govern the nation, perhaps not to teach our children. They may, nevertheless, be the source of our most penetrating ethical insights.

It is the Christian view, moreover, that God, concerned with human relations, speaks to each generation, not alone through such exceptional individuals. He speaks also through the minds of men who patiently and with every resource that their culture provides seek to discover facts about the world, society and the individual. He speaks also through the aspirations of men for better living conditions. Christianity leaves the way open for certain discontinuities in human mental and spiritual growth, but it also holds that honest and courageous search for truth and more humane ways of living together is God-at-work in the soul of man. This is the view of divine guidance which seems to me more characteristically Christian than the interpretation which Knight presents.

There are two more of Knight's criticisms of the Christian ethic on which I should like to comment briefly. One concerns the Christian principle of love; the other, the alleged "moralism" of the Christian ethic.

According to Knight the universal love which Christianity teaches is an undiscriminating love. The Gospels urge men to love everybody, even as God in His love sends rain on the just and unjust. This means, to Knight, a God without moral sense, without capacity or will to distinguish between levels of goodness.

The passage concerning rain suggests to me the existence of forces influencing human life which operate independently of man's control, to which he must adjust himself. Knight's main point, however, is that if everyone is to be loved, then love cannot provide the basis for discriminating between good and evil.

In reading this section of his essay, I wondered if Knight had forgotten the great emphasis which Christianity places on sin. Jesus clearly teaches that there are certain types of action which are to be expected of people who have love in their hearts and other actions which, whatever be man's verbal affirmations, grow out of an absence of love. In his thinking, at least, love has a cutting edge and a power of discrimination which makes it an important ethical concept. Similarly, Paul, contrary to Knight's interpretation, focused his attention on right living. Love-in-action, according to him, is justice, sobriety, rationality as opposed to injustice, intemperance, sentimentalism. He specifically presents Christian love as a quality of attitude which hates injustice and is "happy" only when linked with truth. Whole sections of his letters are discussions of what love means in the life situations of his fellow Christians. While Knight correctly notes similarities between Paul's religion and the mystery cults, he fails to mention this strong conduct-emphasis throughout Paul's teaching which differentiates his religious message from the mystery religions of this time. Christianity, deeply influenced by Paul, survived while these competitors declined.

Both Paul and Jesus forged a link between the attitude of love and conduct. Those who claimed to accept their teaching were told what the test of their faith was in such simple but radical criteria as: Have you given help to your neighbor in need? Have you resolved your conflicts with other persons? Have you conquered your lust for self-glorification and power over others?

The universality of love in the Christian ethic means responsibility for maintaining attitudes of good will which extend to all men and transcend the barriers of race, nation, formal religious connection and class. Differences in belief, custom, tradition do not call for suspension of this attitude or for sentimental blindness to these differences. There should be a fundamental respect and interest in the person as a human being, as the essential basis for communication which may lead to understanding and co-operation. Without this attitude of love there can be no healing of the sores of human conflict. It is an attitude which says: This person whom I do not like has as much right to exist as I have; it is my duty to begin relations with him which may lead to understanding; this is impossible if I feel superior to him, desire to have power over him or wish to make him like myself. Regardless of his views, I see in him possibilities greater than he has yet achieved; it is my duty to sustain a relationship which will help him achieve them.

I regard as valid Knight's point that it is not easy to translate such an ethic into terms applicable to the relations between corporate bodies and nations, or to the kind of impersonal relations which characterize men's contacts in the modern world. Admittedly the Christian ethic is derived from the relationship of small, intimate, face-to-face groups. It is doubtless true that it was such relationships that Jesus primarily had in mind. From its Old Testament traditions, however, Christian ethics derives insights and values which comprehend national and group righteousness. All ethical concepts derive from intimate group relations. Experience in the family and community provide meanings for such concepts as love, justice, respect for others, freedom. Our modern problem is to enlarge the scope of these values to include larger constellations of individuals, persons whom we shall never see but whose welfare must be embraced in our thinking. This problem is common to all ethics, Christian or otherwise.

One may well entertain a doubt whether character and ethical attitudes can be achieved in the impersonal relations which characterize modern urban, industrialized society. In these anonymous relationships persons easily become *things* touched by segments of ourselves. It is easy to be callous in such relationships, and hard to feel that responsibility which is the essence of socialized character, because the controls characteristic of the small group and neighborhood are absent. Christianity has no simple answer to this problem. Its search for an answer moves in the direction of seeking a form of organization which, based on sympathy, seeks justice for others.

In concluding this section of the chapter, I offer in Knight's words what seems to me to be an excellent statement of the modern ethical task as conceived in Christianity today. This task is to *integrate* "the new insights with ideals which have survived in our tradition from earlier times." Knight will find hearty response from Christian churches if he extends an invitation to share with him in this task. It is an excellent statement of what increasing numbers of Christians are trying to do.

Liberal Values and the Free-Enterprise System: Perhaps the most important thesis which Mr. Knight presents is that the preservation of freedom and liberal values depends on the preservation or, as he may prefer to say, the restoration of the free, competitive market. In Chapter Five he seems to me to say that if the free-enterprise organization of economic life disappears, along with it will go individual liberty and the other democratic values which we prize so highly. "Co-operation" as a method of production having demonstrated its ineffectiveness, the only alternative to the free-enterprise economy is dictatorship, which means the destruction of liberal values.

Knight summons all who care about individual liberty—political, economic, intellectual, spiritual—to save this fast-disappearing economic mechanism known as the free market.

I believe that Knight is wrong. When he states the ethical problem of our times in these terms, it is impossible of solution. If liberal values depend on the restoration of the free market as the dominant mechanism for performing the productive and distributive tasks of our society, then, in my opinion, we may as well bid farewell to these values. The problem must be set in other terms if we are to make any progress, namely: Assuming that the basic economic procedures are to be controlled by citizen action through political agencies, how can maximum efficiency and maximum freedom be secured? To state the problem is far from solving it but does determine our approach and make all the difference in the world regarding the direction and nature of the search. Since I believe that Knight has failed to state the problem of liberal (or Christian) ethics in realistic terms, I cannot find in his essay help to modern man as he grapples with the forces which sweep around him, in the interest of his ethical aspirations.

In assaying the validity of Knight's thesis, it is not necessary to consider the definition of terms. His definitions may be found in Chapter Six. It is, however, important to note the three ways in which he qualifies his position.

First, he states that the operation of the free market must be constantly improved through scientific studies. The results will mitigate some of the weaknesses which have characterized it in the past, specifically its tendency to oscillations and periodic "depressions" and "inflations." Knight assumes that such reforms as are found to be desirable through research will be accepted by participants in the free market, whatever personal sacrifice may be required, presumably because they will see that it is to their interest to do so.

This is an important but dubious assumption. Enterprisers in the past have often seemed more interested in immediate gain than in the long-run and healthy condition of the national economy. Perhaps things will be different in the future. Knight is entitled to hope so. It would seem reasonable to suppose, however, that some imposition of reform measures, scientifically validated, would be necessary and that this would take the form of legal enactments and regulations of one kind or another. If true, this would call for a form of government action of a somewhat more vigorous type than Knight in general is inclined to favor. There are important political implications which he does not explore. How shall reforms of the free market recommended by economists get translated into action? The voices of scholars in this field have often seemed faint, divided and frequently not highly regarded by the powerful interests which operate in the free market. A broad perspective embracing the welfare of the nation is not to be expected of them since, in Knight's thinking, "charity" must be excluded from the free market. A man must be presumed to be in it for what he can get out of it, which, if it means anything, must mean that his interpretation of his own interests must be accepted as valid for him, however mistaken he may prove to be.

Knight's second qualification brings politics into the

operation of the free market in a positive way. He asserts that legislation is to be enacted from time to time to eliminate "predatory monopolies." Taking the dictionary definition of the word, "living by plunder or spoils," it occurs to me that there is a sense in which a large part of free-market activity would at one time or another present predatory aspects. Freedom of the market means opportunity to gobble up one's competitors, or where that is impossible to effect an alliance which monopolizes the market to the exclusion of others. So persistently does this tendency exist in modern life that one wonders whether it may not be an inescapable characteristic of the free market operating under modern social conditions. If so, Knight's qualification would inevitably result in the elimination of a free market.

In some respects this is the situation to which we have come today. There is a mass of laws and regulations aimed at eliminating predatory monopolies. They restrict the free market. We find that somehow the enterprisers get together. That their alliances are predatory they will never admit. When the public accuses them of predatory tendencies, the cry of socialism is raised, and it is claimed that free enterprise is being destroyed, as, indeed, it is. I doubt if the economists can define predatory in a way that will make it acceptable to the monopolists; and I do not see how the enterprisers who are squeezed out can be prevented from trying to get back into the market through legislation favoring them but in the name of the public's interest. The effect of Knight's proposal would be precisely what we now have, something that fails to work, that has constantly to be suspended in order to meet the demands which an increasingly complex society is placing on the economic system.

A third limitation of the free market on which Knight insists is that utilities in which competition has proved wasteful be *conducted*, not *regulated*, by public authority. Apparently Knight prefers some authority less than federal. He is shy of giving such responsibility to Washington.

This qualification raises the question as to when competition is wasteful, and which essential economic needs are best met by the operation of the free market, which by public authority. Knight does not give us a principle by which he would exclude from operation by public authority such enterprises as housing, transportation, medical services and foods essential to life. I infer that he would exclude them. But are waste and inefficiency in meeting the needs of people less conspicuous in these latter fields than in such matters as light, power, water, which, I believe, he would include?

How wasteful must a particular enterprise become before Knight would recommend that it be withdrawn from the operation of the free market? There are many candidates for adoption by public authority. As the span of wartime conditions lengthens into what is sometimes called peace, their number seems likely to increase. If this happens, is there any way of maintaining a free, vigorous, self-reliant citizenry? This is the issue which I do not feel Knight really faces beyond indicating his distaste for the mixture of statecraft and economic enterprise.

Many people share Knight's belief in free enterprise but recognize that it is not suited to the exigencies of war. They are willing to accept the suspension of the free market as a temporary measure but insist that it be restored when peace is declared. Leaders of both the Republican and Democratic parties, or aspirants for leadership, are saying something like that. This seems to me an artificial simplification of the problem, and to overlook the fact that modern life, even without open international warfare, presents situations which free enterprise, as Knight describes it, is unable to solve. These conditions antedated and will survive the present war. They will still have to be met. I cannot see that the free market, even chastened and qualified as Knight would have it, has any possibility of meeting them. His dismissal of possible alternatives with the statement that state planning and control have always failed and always led to destruction of individual liberty is not helpful and is inconsistent with his willingness to turn over many important economic enterprises to public operation.

In brief, I do not believe that the restoration of the free market, as Knight presents it, is an option open to us. It may be that the free market might be retained in certain economic areas. I do not pretend to say which these might be, but that they could include the larger and more basic industries which set the pace for our economic life I do not think possible. One of the most important problems confronting the postwar world will be unemployment. Failure to meet it will be fatal to democracy and the liberal values in which Knight is interested. "Restoration of free enterprise" may be a good political slogan, but it is unrealistic. Does anyone today seriously doubt that the government must play a leading role in postwar economic reconstruction, not as a relief agency but as a body from which must come the primary directives for national economic activity?

This kind of development seems to me indubitably "in the cards." I should like to see all economists and political parties accept it, and having accepted it propose for public choice clear alternatives concerning the kind of governmental directives which will help us achieve a stable, productive economy. It will require the invention and improvement of governmental policies and agencies operating in economic life. It will also require an intelligent citizenry informed on matters of economics. It is misleading to turn attention to the *restoration* of a form of economic life which is gone beyond recall.

An attempt to resuscitate the free market under the name of liberty is the surest way to defeat democracy. It will bring on a type of regimentation far worse than anything which Knight seems to regard as typical of state control. The market will be "managed" by powerful groups which will also control the government and deprive the citizen of freedom.

These groups will effect alliances with similar groups in other nations. They will be obliged to do so by competition. We shall find ourselves shackled with a type of internationalism which can only set the stage for future wars.

The defects of the free market are, however, more than mechanical. The essentially individualistic and competitive character of the free-enterprise system frustrates a subtle but powerful impulse moving men today. This is a demand for a form of *social relatedness* adapted to our economic life. Modern man wants to do the work of the world in ways that do not require that he put his neighbor out of business as the price of his own success. With all its gilded façade of freedom that is what the free market really means ethically. *Social enterprise* rather than individual enterprise is what will today unlock the potentialities of men. Perhaps that has always been true, but today we have the possibility of achieving it, thanks to modern industry and science. This is a subtle but real reason why we shall not go back to the free market.

Knight believes that individuals should be free to make wrong choices. Under free enterprise, most men have no choices today. They have to take what they can get in a social order which holds little for man as an individual but only as he relates himself to his fellows in an organization. Hence men see more hope in creating a state which they can control and through which they can exercise choice than they do in attempts to restore a free market which increasingly for the masses is not free and never a real market.

That modern man tries hard to get something for nothing and to secure benefits without taking risks I do not believe is generally true. Knight states that market operations actually show little gain when losses are taken into account. What shall we say of the free-market skill in dodging risks and saddling the losses on the gullible investing public? The modern economic system has found ways of distributing losses which enable the apparent risk-takers to escape the consequences of their decisions. This is bad for their characters, from both Knight's ethical viewpoint and mine.

A concept of freedom does not require that all activities of the individual be uncoerced. If this were not so, then obviously there could be no freedom. The issue is: In what areas will restrictions be least destructive to the human spirit? Or positively, what of man's activities, subjected to organization and to principles of order, will make possible the largest amount of freedom in other activities? While inefficiency may be tolerated in many aspects of life, it is no longer possible in the modern world to tolerate as much inefficiency as has characterized our economic life. "Tolerate" is the correct word, not in the sense of any particular individual wishing or not wishing it, but in the sense that society cannot maintain itself; it will disintegrate. The economic area, despite all the strictures against the "social planners," must be brought under some principle of order. The free enterprise system is in reality the opposite of order. It contains no principle of social good. The belief that it expressed some kind of autonomous and "natural" inevitability was an illusion; the plea that it be maintained as a kind of "playground" for the undisciplined impulses of men is untenable in view of the stakes involved. Inevitably it gives way to order introduced by men of sufficient power to dominate it in behalf of their own interests, or it is displaced by a principle of order in which the welfare of men, democratically conceived, is accepted. Today this principle of order expresses itself through or under political organization, that is, through citizens organized in the most inclusive social category. It is the Christian hope and belief that the values underlying this order will conceive man as a being with certain inalienable rights to develop his highest capacities as a human being and as a child of God.

INDEX